From the Holocaust to Maine

Maine

Testimonies of the Survivors

Jack Montgomery

Holocaust and Human Rights Center of Maine

ISBN: 979-8-9998107-1-7

Contents

For Rosemary, Isla, Byrd, Lola and Henry. And for Marika

No class or group or party in Germany could escape its share of responsibility for the abandonment of the democratic Republic and the advent of Adolf Hitler. The cardinal error of the Germans who opposed Nazism was their failure to unite against it. –William L. Shirer, *The Rise and Fall of the Third Reich: A History of Nazi Germany*

CHAPTER 1

Foreword

Jack Montgomery

W hen I have described this project to both friends and strangers, the first question many ask is, "Are you Jewish?" The quizzical look that usually accompanies the question is loaded with unspoken meanings. "You don't look Jewish," "Your name doesn't sound Jewish," and most significantly, "I don't get it, why is a non-Jew so interested in the Holocaust?" Sometimes that last question is asked outright by both Jews and non-Jews.

One part of the answer to it lies in two events that occurred when I was about nine years old. I was born exactly at mid-century, in January 1950. I grew up in and around Montclair, New Jersey, in a uniformly white, Christian bubble. I was oblivious to all things Jewish, or Muslim, or black, or anything else not like me. Church meant Episcopal.

The first event occurred when I was spending the night at my grandparents' home, which I did from time to time. I felt very grown up and independent on these occasions. On this particular evening, as I climbed into bed, I noticed an old *Life* magazine on the side table with a photograph of a young girl on the cover. She appeared to be just a few years older than me. It was Anne Frank. The article was about her last days of life in the Bergen-Belsen concentration camp, only a few weeks before the end of World War II and the camp's liberation. As I read the article, I was dumbstruck. In that instant, my young and until then very insulated mind understood for the first time the meaning of true evil – and that children were at risk from horrible people. That image, that story, and my shock have never left me. It did not occur to me at the time that Anne Frank was Jewish – I didn't know what "Jewish" meant. What I did know was that she was a child, like me.

ANNE FRANK ON PAGE FROM HER DIARY

The second event came a few months later. My family had moved into another new uniformly white and Christian neighborhood in North Caldwell, New Jersey. The families on our street had arranged a welcoming cocktail party for my parents. As the evening progressed, one of the women made an antisemitic joke. My mother didn't laugh. "What's the matter, Gloria? Didn't you think it was funny?" asked one of our new neighbors, to which my mother replied, "Actually, I'm Jewish." Actually, she wasn't Jewish. She was raised a Christian Scientist, but I think she was agnostic by that time. Her response had nothing to do with her religion. It was sparked by her deep dislike of any sort of prejudice or cruelty. In any event, that was the last neighborhood party for my parents. She told me the story a short time later – she was anxious that I heard it and understood it.

The lessons from those two events were planted firmly in my mind. There is evil in the world, and it is often directed at Jews, among others. You don't laugh at "those" jokes. You don't play along. You say something or do something, however small, to let your disapproval be known. Ignoring it or playing along is cowardly and ultimately hurtful.

It wasn't until much later in life that I appreciated the courage it must have taken my mother to say what she did at that party, because she was a very isolated person and needed all the friends she could get. But she would not go along with the crowd. That was something I never forgot.

I have spent the last 60-plus years absorbed in the history of the 20th century, and particularly of the rise of totalitarian governments in all their repressive manifestations. This leads me to the answers to why this non-Jew cares so much about the Holocaust. First, I quickly learned that the vast majority of the victims of the Third Reich were Jews, but the frighteningly efficient Nazi machinery was also turned against leftists and moderates, writers, artists, Roma, teachers, journalists, professors, librarians, booksellers, people who harbored Jews, Protestant ministers and Catholic priests and nuns, gay people, anyone who made a derogatory joke or remark about the regime, and many others. German death squads, the *Einsatzgruppen*[1] entering captured territory during their invasion murdered Jews, as well as intellectuals, members of the Catholic clergy, Roma people, and many others. Second, the Nazis were hardly the only mass murderers of the 20th century. The Soviets under Stalin, the Italians under Mussolini, and scores of other nations perpetrated their own vast repressions,

---

1. See **Einsatzgruppen** in Appendix.

though only the Stalinist Soviet Union competed with the Nazis in terms of scale.

In short, it came to me early on that it would be a grave mistake to conclude that the accounts of repression, sadism, and annihilation that follow in this book represent an anomaly of human nature, something unique to the people of Germany under Hitler. It is the scale, the efficiency, the depravity, and the audacity that render it such a critical aspect of modern history.

Additionally, we need to understand the perpetrators as well as the victims of these crimes. How did Germany transition from an enlightened republic with centuries of high culture into a monster state in just a few years? What combination of fear, insecurity, and cowardice explains the rise of Hitler's sadistic regime?

It is for those reasons that the Holocaust still matters today. Yes, it is about the Jews in Europe, but it is about much more as well. It is a case study that deserves careful examination, particularly among young people, who, sadly, might have little understanding of the events of 1933 to 1945.

I believe that the germ of totalitarianism and repression is present in all nations and, perhaps, in most people. Hopefully, it remains dormant in the absence of stress. But it may flourish in an environment of fear, anger, social dislocation, and economic uncertainty. Its principal catalyst is the rise of leaders who can galvanize those forces into a political movement. The stronger those environmental factors, and the more charismatic and ruthless the leader, the greater the risk of totalitarianism and its inevitable cataclysmic repression. Cowardly silence in the face of evil by those who know better is a critical element in this toxic process.

On the other hand, the antidote begins with education and an understanding of the natural progress of the disease among a motivated citizenry courageous enough to address the existential threat it poses. It comes back to the lessons my mother imparted to me at age nine: You don't play along. You speak up and do something, however small, to let your disapproval be known. Ignoring it or playing along with that behavior is cowardly and ultimately harmful to us all.

***

As I write these words, I believe we are entering into very dark times. Antisemitism, racial hatred, and authoritarianism are closely related viruses that are deeply embedded in the human body politic. They have been there for an incalculable amount of time. They are never cured. At best, we can for a time experience a partial remission. But the resistance of our species to those infections is fading at the moment, and the wave of illness is growing. The disease will run its course until the next partial abatement. This is not a happy thought, but it is what drives me forward to write this book.

It is in that context that I have two related hopes for this book. The first is that it might serve as some sort of inoculation against the disease – not preventing it, but mitigating its effects. Every person, young or old, who reads and understands these accounts of these Holocaust survivors will be armed with the truth about what happened during the Nazi years. If that person has the courage to speak that truth, it will help to protect us against the ravages of hate and fear. But much courage will be necessary in the years ahead.

Secondly, I firmly believe there will come a time when the illness will abate, although I have no idea what circumstances will bring that about. This brings to mind the account of Jutka Isaacson. In June 1944, Jutka and her family were forced by the Nazis into a Jewish ghetto in her town of Kaposvár, Hungary. They knew they were about to be transported to a concentration camp. Shortly before leaving, Jutka risked her life to bury some important objects behind bricks in an old basement. These items included some family heirlooms and her graduation certificate from her *Gymnasium* [high school]. She hid those items in the belief that someday the darkness would pass, and she would return to recover them. That day did come, and she did return. In the photographic portrait that I made of her 30 years ago, she wears the necklace that she had buried. More importantly, the graduation certificate she recovered allowed her to gain advanced admission to Bates College. She went on to become a Bates College dean, a Bowdoin College trustee, a writer, and an educator.

I see that as a metaphor for what I hope this book may become: the things we save can become the means for our recovery. Likewise, learning and remembering the stories of the people in this book can give us the basis for hope. Their survival through the Nazi era and their ability to rebuild their lives was the result of varying factors, including the indomitable will to persevere, the instinct to navigate the evil system in spite of their powerlessness, the unbreakable bonds between family members, and a lot of luck. In the end, they were survivors. Thus, I offer their stories here as testaments to their ultimate hope, optimism, and inspiration.

CHAPTER 2

A brief note on sources

I completed photographic portraits of these survivors from 1993 through 1995 with the support of my former law partner, Sumner Bernstein, and the Holocaust and Human Rights Center of Maine (HHRC). The images became the subject of a traveling exhibition in my home state of Maine and were then put on permanent display at the Maine Jewish Museum in Portland and at the HHRC facility in Augusta. They were accompanied by text written by Professor Stephen Hochstadt, the son of Holocaust survivors and a highly respected scholar of the period. The portraits have been seen by thousands of people over the years, and the museums have repeatedly been asked if a catalogue could be made available. After some false starts, this project moved forward over the past year.

I quickly concluded that I wanted to give the survivors (only three of whom remain alive at the time of this writing) the opportunity to tell their stories in their own words. Thus, the principal authors of this book are the 20 Holocaust survivors who wound up living in Maine at some point in their lives. Most of these accounts were given in numerous interviews conducted by the Holocaust and Human Rights Center of Maine, the USC Shoah Foundation, and others. Others are taken from books written by the survivors themselves, and, in one instance, from the testimony of a survivor who escaped in utero, was born in a displaced persons camp in Italy, and went on to become a highly esteemed federal judge. In editing these accounts, I have tried to remain true to the originals, making occasional word changes to clarify meaning, to clarify the chronology of important events, and to shorten some very lengthy text. I have sought to include a three-dimensional account, including the survivors' lives before, during, and after the Holocaust. I have also added an extensive appendix to give context to various terms, individuals, places, and events. Many of the original testimonies are in the public record and are available online to anyone who wishes to read the full accounts. I urge you to take the time to listen as the survivors give their accounts. A full table of sources is found at the end of the book.

In addition to their connections to Maine, there is one other critical factor that binds these survivors: they were all very young at the time that Nazism came to dominate Germany and then the rest of Europe. In many instances, they had very full and happy childhoods until Germany's racial laws came into effect, when the overt antisemitism of their teachers, former playmates, and others led to several years of oppression before the "Final Solution"[1] began to be implemented. They are also bound by the fact that they survived, while millions – including their families and friends – did not. I am moved by every aspect of these stories, not least by the survivors' determination to rebuild their lives here in the United States. I am forever grateful to the survivors for giving us this record, which no amount of denial or historical revisionism can ever erase. We owe them a lot.

The cover photograph is taken from the identity card of Malka Muz Singal, mother of United States District Court Judge George Singal. It was taken after she and her young daughter had arrived in a displaced persons camp in Italy in the fall of 1945. The story of their survival is one of the remarkable accounts provided in this book. I remain deeply moved by the well earned look of triumph on her face. My thanks to Judge Singal for providing that photograph and others that appear in the chapter about his family.

Jack Montgomery
Freeport, Maine
August 2025

CHAPTER 3

Julius Ciembroniewicz

Julius Ciembroniewicz

August 2, 1929–March 18, 2018
Silesia, Poland

My name is Julius Ciembroniewicz. I was born in 1929 in the western part of Poland, which is called Silesia. My father was a Doctor of Philosophy and a professor in a college where he taught languages. He originally wanted to become a physician, but he was a Jew, and in prewar Poland there was a fair amount of discrimination against Jews. If a Jewish person in Poland wanted to study medicine, he had to go abroad.

It was probably 1937 or 1938 (so I was eight or nine years old) when the Germans started more aggressively to persecute Jews and other nationalities inside Germany. I was a child, but I distinctly remember extreme uneasiness in my father and our friends about what was going to happen. We had serious problems, but we couldn't do much about it. We did not expect war to break out so quickly, but after it started, of course, we lost everything. We left our house, our friends, our clothes. Everything was left behind. We could never go back again.

The Germans exterminated not only because of one's racial background. In the countries they occupied, they exterminated as quickly as they could the intelligentsia – professors at universities, people who could provide guidance in the future for occupied countries. Because of this, my father knew he had to disappear. He had no other choice. We had no way to escape to Western countries. You have two choices: to be exterminated or to try to survive.

So my father changed his name and obtained a totally different identity. He opened a small food store. In fact, it was a cubicle with virtually nothing in it, but it did not exist long because we had to move. We were moving continuously from place to place, no more than five or six months in one place.

At one point we were in a Jewish ghetto in Cracow. At this time, the ghetto was only partially surrounded by barbed wire and fence – it was partially open. It was in the old part of the city of Cracow, with many old buildings, narrow streets, and many synagogues. It was not a very affluent part of the city. Before the war, in an area of three or four blocks, there were maybe 5-8,000 people. At the time we went through, there were at least 40 or 50,000 who were forcibly moved into the area, so it was extremely overcrowded. We had to get passes to go in and out. It was a time when we knew that Auschwitz and other concentration camps were being formed, and we knew there were others somewhere. We also knew that people who were taken to them did not come back, but at this stage we had not yet comprehended the immensity of this catastrophe – that millions of people would go and never come back again. We didn't know it yet. At this stage, we thought that perhaps they would keep us in concentration camps but not kill us. We were not aware of this plan of extermination.

It was about 12 months after the war started that my Jewish grandmother was killed. She came to visit us. It was at night, and Grandmother was in bed. It was in winter. The Gestapo came in. Her husband was taken to a ghetto, and she was shot in our apartment, in the place where we stayed. I escaped with my brother – we jumped from a window. My mother ran away. My father was able to escape too.

From now on, we were completely separated. My father found me a place of hiding in a Salvatorian monastery. I was 12 years old. My brother was placed with a family in one of the villages. I didn't see him for four years. We were separated completely. I was separated from my father. Most of the family died. I spent close to three and a half or four years in the monastery, until the end of the war.

It was an interesting experience to be in a monastery. It was a Catholic seminary and monastery where they had young men who studied to become priests. They were very good to me, exceptionally good – they did not put any pressure on me to do anything. None whatsoever. But it was interesting; not being inside a monastery, one probably has a much higher opinion about people who decide to combine their studies with the monastic life, but I discovered they were normal people with many problems.

It was difficult; I was alone and I was the only one of my age. As mentioned before, Germans exterminated professors in universities. Many Jesuits in Europe were very well educated and were professors in universities, so a few of them were hiding in this monastery. They took care of me, which really helped me to survive those few years. One was a professor of biology, a second one of mathematics, and the third one was a linguist. They really guided me. In retrospect I found it exceedingly helpful. I studied biology, mathematics, languages, and I spoke Latin fluently. I already spoke German and learned French and English. I have eternal gratitude to them because they risked maybe not their lives, but they could probably have gone to concentration camps by helping me.

When the war ended in 1945, I was 16 years old. I had no place to go and just wandered around. I stayed with some people I knew before. Eventually I found my mother and joined her and my brother. We searched for a friend of mine, Henry Laker, a Jewish boy who went to my primary school. His whole family died – he was the only one who survived. He had been taken in by a peasant family who kept him during the war. We found him and, of course, we renewed our friendship.

We were very angry – extremely angry. We had lost our childhood, our families. We had no friends, no education. Anger was probably the strongest feeling we had, apart from elation at being liberated. In our fury, we felt that someone had to pay for it. Someone did it to us and we didn't deserve it. Why? We couldn't understand it. We were only 16.. Why had it happened to us?

Henry and I wanted to go see Germany occupied by the Russians. It was probably ten days or two weeks after the armistice agreement was signed. We traveled to Germany. There were no buses and no trains, so we hitchhiked with Russian troops. We just stood by the side of the road. There were trucks going and they would pick you up. They'd give you food and take you a few miles. It was about 150 miles to Breslau, which was a big German city that was totally destroyed by Allied bombing. We were, of course, elated to see it destroyed because we were angry. For the first time in our lives we saw Germans working, supervised by Russian soldiers, which was again a sight which pleased us immensely. They were picking up rubbish and cleaning the streets for cars to pass through, et cetera.

At one of these places there was a group of Germans working. We became very angry at them. With a sudden outburst of fury, we started to beat them. We beat them with whatever we had in our hands. We picked up rocks and were beating them and screaming at them. Of course, the Russian soldiers permitted us to indulge ourselves. We did it for quite a few minutes and they really could not defend themselves because probably the Russians would join us. I remember one of the Russian officers came by and took some photographs of us, then he talked to us. We had a hard time communicating, but he spoke a bit of Polish. He did not encourage us, but he did not discourage us from doing what we were doing. We resumed it after he left for a few more minutes, but suddenly we stopped. Later we were profoundly embarrassed, of course, by the things we did. It was an extremely embarrassing episode. We did it only once; we were totally nonviolent, but we were extremely angry. I think at this place it ended. Our anger escaped – not completely, but a significant part of it. We would not be violent again. We knew it. It was gone. However, anger in some way persisted.

We didn't know what to do with ourselves. There was no school. We joined a gang in black marketeering. It was not a violent gang and did not commit any violent crimes. We did it for about nine months. It was in many ways a very pleasant experience. First, we had someone to relate to. We were a group of people who understood each other. We belonged to something.

But after nine months we left it and went back to school. We knew what we wanted to be – we were both intending to become physicians, and both of us did. It was very difficult. We had no education, so within a few years, we had to condense the knowledge others acquire over a period of many years. It was possible with special coaches for people like us. We worked extremely hard. I became a doctor in 1955. I finished college in Poland, but I could not get into medical school with my background. For three years I tried, but without success. First, I did not join any communist organization, which was a very important requirement to get into a university. Secondly, my background with a father who was a Jewish professor was a problem. I had a hard time, but ultimately got into medical school and finished it.

I became a neurosurgeon. I went to England first. Despite significant travel restrictions from communist Poland, if you were granted a stipend by the English school or government (which I was), that permitted you to leave. So I left Poland and defected, and I did not go back. I was interested in traumatic neurosurgery, and I was in Liverpool a year and a half. After that, in 1959, I came to the United States. The Rockefeller Foundation designated stipends in medicine for each medical specialty – two stipends for the "most promising" people in the specialty. I was privileged to be chosen in neurosurgery, and I was offered the opportunity to go to any place I wanted.

I was originally in Boston. I was really interested in academic neurosurgery. However, I liked to fish. I liked nature. Each time we had free time, my wife and I would come to northern Maine. I called up friends and said, "Listen, I'd like to go to Maine. Would you please make some inquiries?" They called the secretary of the Board of Registration in Maine and said, "We have a neurosurgeon who may want to go to Maine. Would you be interested?" He said, "Sure." I met with him, and we moved to Maine.

During his medical career in the United States, Dr. Ciembronwicz practiced surgical medicine at Boston University, taught at the Harvard School of Medicine, and was a resident at Boston City Hospital's Lahey Clinic. After he and his wife moved to Maine, he prac-

ticed medicine at Kennebec Valley Medical Center and later at Maine General Medical Center, serving as Chief of Staff and Chief of Surgery for many years. He was a founding member of the Holocaust and Human Rights Center of Maine.

CHAPTER 4

Tama Fineberg

Tama Fineberg

Born May 1, 1937
Mlyniv, Poland

M y name is Tama Fineberg. I was born in Mlyniv, Poland
on May 1, 1937. I am the youngest of six. My father was
a very skilled carpenter. My mother always said he had hands of
gold. He could make very intricate, wonderful things. He used to
do apprentice work – young people would learn from him, which
is how he made his living. He also built the house we lived in, and
he made all the furniture that we had.

The Germans were going to get after the Jewish people. To annihilate us, I guess, was their goal. Next thing you knew, they were
putting barbed wire around our little *shtetl* [village] in Mlyniv. I
remember them rolling these huge barrels, pushing them along the
streets. It was barbed wire. They surrounded the whole little *shtetl*
with that wire.

My father knew that no good was going to come out of this. So
he made this beautiful hutch that we had in our house. He took
that hutch and opened up the bottom part of the floor and made
it look so that when you closed it, you'd never know it was able to
open. He dug a hole underneath, a small area, and he always said
to my mother, "Something is going to happen. And when it does,
I don't know if I will be here. I want you to take the children and
go down." He knew something was going to happen.

They came in the middle of the night. The Germans knew that
he wanted to get some people together to fight against them –
they considered him an instigator. So they took him. They broke
the door open, came in and they grabbed him, and I believe that's
when he was shot because they weren't about to tolerate anybody
who was going to try and do something. I remember everybody
screaming. My mother was crying. My father said, "Remember
what I told you," in Yiddish.[1] She said, "I will," and that was it.
I never saw him again. I just remember a lot of screaming, a lot of
crying, and my mother, when she heard that, took my sister and

---

1. See **Yiddish** in Appendix.

me and we went down where my father told us to go. We sat there and closed the lid. I was 5 years old.

My father had made it so that you'd never know, if you opened the cabinet, that that bottom lid opened up. We sat there, and I guess time went on, it must have been nighttime, or daytime, whatever, because we heard Germans coming into our house and kept saying over and over "No Jews here."

Then continued looking and searching and then a lot of them started taking things – we heard them taking our belongings. They would take whatever they wanted at that time. I heard the footsteps, and then, after a while, it got very quiet, and we just sat there while my mother pleaded with me not to say anything because I was so young.

Then she thought, maybe she'll take a chance and take a look and see what's happening. She opened the lid from the cabinet and peeked through; she didn't see anybody in the house, just rubble, just things that were thrown down. The three of us came up and I remember going through and she said to me all the time, "Please don't make a noise, don't make a noise," because in the windows we could see those terrible helmets that the Germans were wearing and I remembered the tips of their rifles, walking back and forth, back and forth. And she says, "Now, please, be very quiet," and took my hand and my sister's very tightly. We went through the back door and through alleyways and we were running and running until we got to the barbed wire. My sister tried bending it apart so that we could crawl through, and as we did, my hat got caught on the barbed wire. She said, "Don't go back for it, we have to leave it," and that's when our running started again. We just ran and ran and ran until we got away from that barbed wire. We ran into the woods.

And then I don't know what happened. My sister got separated from us. I don't know how it happened. But my mother kept looking for my sister and she kept looking for us. We went to all the little farms where my mother knew the people – they used to come to us, you know. When she asked, "Did you see my daughter?" they'd say, "She was just here, and she was looking for you." Each time we just missed each other. The last person that we finally went to said to us that, yes, she had seen her, but by this time she had given up all hope of us being alive. My sister apparently told her: "If they were killed, then I don't want to live." She had given herself up, and they killed her. That was the end of my sister. So that just left my mother and me.

Now it was constant running – running and hiding, hiding and running. We came to a cemetery where we hid. My mother prayed for rain so we could have something to drink. At night, she would go searching the farms for something to eat. When farmers fed the pigs they would dump a bunch of slop. My mother knew when this would happen, and would hide around the corner to grab that slop, whatever she could, and to feed me and herself.

Hunger is like a knot in your stomach that's craving for something. I remember walking in the night and seeing a farmhouse. I looked through the window and saw a family sitting at a table and I said, "Mama, someday, can I be doing this? Will I sit at a table again, like we used to – like those people – instead of all this running and hiding all the time?" And she said, "Yes, yes, yes, my child, you'll see, we're going to make it." She was a very positive and courageous woman.

Once, we were in the woods where a lot of people were hiding like us. A lot of them dug holes to make an area to sit in. I remember there was another woman and her child sitting in a hole like we were. If you see another kid, you sort of try to play – even in these horrendous times, you try to play whichever way you could. I went over to play with this little girl, and my mother said, "Tama, come here!" As I did, a bullet went through the girl's shoulder. And then a lot of bullets, like machine guns going off. One of them grazed my left thigh and blood was all over the place. My mother did the best she could. She tore off a piece of her dress and tried wrapping it up, but blood kept coming through. She tried healing it, getting whatever she could to put on the wound. That was another time that I was spared. And then we were running again.

That's all I remember of my life as a youngster. It's just the dark and the fear and the continued running. Once we suddenly ran into this German fellow with a gun. He said, "Halt," while his gun was pointing at us. I don't know where he came from, but there he was. My mother looked at him and pleaded for our lives. In Yiddish she told me to cry. Being a child, I didn't want to cry at that moment, not realizing the terrible situation we were in. I remember my mother pinching me so hard that, well, I started to cry. She said to the soldier, "Please, you must have a family. Look at this child, she is crying. How can you possibly kill this child and me? I did nothing to you. What have you got to gain by killing us?" And I cried and cried. He looked at me and she repeated: "Surely you must have children!" He said, "I do. Take your child and run." And we ran again.

Sometimes farmers helped us. But they had signs up on their houses that said if you harbor a Jew, not only are we going to kill the Jew, but you as well. They were petrified, but some of them wanted to help so they would give you a little bit of food and tell us to go away. They were afraid for their families. They were afraid for themselves. The word was out that if anybody was caught hiding a Jew, not only would they be shot, but their whole family as well.[2] When something like this goes on around you, you can't really blame the people that much. However, some people, no matter what, will try and help you. This is how we tried to survive – this is how we carried on.

One time we got to a big barn and the door was open. My mother crawled in with me and it was dry – it was like heaven, you know – and we climbed up into a loft where they kept a lot of straw for the animals. She made a bed for me and we were slept

---

2. See **Third Ordinance on Restrictions on Residence** in Appendix.

there. All of a sudden she smelled something and woke me up. There was smoke – the barn was on fire. I remember that night. I didn't want to get up – it was the first time I had something that was a little bit better than that terrible hole. She said, that the place was on fire, so we had to get out. We couldn't go down because everything was burning down there. But there was a little doorway or a little window up on the top. She opened it up and told me to hold her hand, because we were going to jump. When I said I was afraid to jump, she replied, "We have to, we have to jump or get burned alive in this place!" So we jumped and, you know, it's amazing that we didn't break a leg, we didn't break an arm. It's like somebody was looking over us. Yet again, we continued to run. My whole childhood, that's all I knew: constant fear, constant hunger, constant thirst and constant running.

One day went into another day and on this particular day there were about ten of us in this unoccupied house. I remember being there with my mother and we heard soldiers. So naturally, we assumed the Germans had tracked us down and found this group of people who were Jewish. We thought, that they were going to put us on the trucks. *They're going to get rid of us.* There were wooden floors in that house, and we heard the sound of boots, walking. We were thinking they had found us and that would be the end of us. Everybody started huddling to say their goodbyes.

But then we heard voices from above in Russian who said, "Don't be afraid, we're not going to kill you." Somebody said, "It's a trick, they only say that to get us out and then they'll get rid of us." The voices kept pleading, "Please come up, we're not going to kill you." Little by little, somebody went up, and when he was upstairs he yelled back, "They're not going to kill us, they're not the Germans, they're the Russians!" Everybody fell to their feet and kissed their feet and hands, because we thought they finally had come to help us. Somebody came to help us! They had big trucks. They said, "We're going to get you out of here and bring you back to your own places." The trucks, I remember, had benches on each and a canvas top, with an open back. We got in and I sat across from my mother. But they still had rifles, and for some reason one of the rifles discharged – just discharged, nobody aimed at anything – and it landed right near my hair. Once again, somebody up there seemed to have kept me safe.

They took us back to our hometown. When we got there, my mother ran to try and find our house, but it was impossible because the bombs had completely destroyed it – the house was nothing but bricks and wood. She knew the area, but there was no house there at all. Everything was gone – completely gone. At some point, my mother says, "This was our home." But to a child, this couldn't be a home. I mean, nothing was there – it was all gone.

She went over to a Russian officer, and said to him, "I'm a very good cook. I will cook for you if you give me lodging, a place to stay with my child." He agreed and took us to a place with a lot of Russians. The Russian officer gave us a little corner and said that we could stay there. In return, she did exactly what she said – she cooked. The officers were so thrilled with her cooking, they loved it so much, that they wanted to do something for her.

I guess a few weeks or months went by when the officers said they had a big surprise for her. "You come with us." She went with them, and they took her to this place in a basement. She walked down and there was a German officer sitting in the chair with his hands tied on his back. They said to her, "Here is a gun – you can shoot him because he is one of the people that killed your people." My mother took the gun in her hand, looked at him but said, "I can't do that. I cannot take a life like that. Even though they did such terrible things, I can't do it." She turned around crying and walked out. As she went upstairs, she heard the gun go off. They killed him for her. She simply couldn't do it.

We were liberated. Now the whole hope was to push on – we had to get away from here, we had to get to Palestine. That was the whole idea – to get to Israel. You must make plans. You must get out there. You have to fill out forms, which we did. Then they put

us on a cattle car, I remember, and we were driving and driving.
The next thing I knew, is that we ended up in Germany. We were
heading to Israel, but first we had to get to the German side – that's
where they had DP or Displaced Persons'[3] camps.

The Jewish land – which was hopefully the land of freedom
where nobody would kill you, and where nobody would call you
"you dirty Jew." It was for a new start, a new beginning, that was
the hope of all the people going there. 'Next year, Jerusalem' was
the big hope and the big dream. Whenever you prayed, you always
prayed: *Next year, Jerusalem, we should be in Israel.* We got to these
DP camps that were run by the Americans. That was already like
going into heaven because they had barracks for us, long army
barracks, and they gave us food and drink. Each family was assigned
a little room of our own. We could sleep on a cot, with green army
blankets. I remember those green army blankets.

But my mother, in the back of her mind, always knew that she
had brothers and sisters in America. She was the youngest of 13
children. So, she went to the newspaper place, in Munich (Germany), and placed an ad for the American papers. She described
all her brothers and sisters that she could remember and provided
them with information about where she was staying. She said,
"Please, if anybody is out there, get in touch with me and let
me know." Well, time went on, and we didn't hear anything. By
now we had gotten our notice that we were getting ready to go
to Israel. So, everybody started packing whatever little belongings
we had, and we marked "Israel" on whatever we had, when my
mother received a telegram. A cousin in Evansville, Indiana, had
been reading the newspaper, came across these names and immediately started making phone calls. My mother had a brother in
New Jersey, a sister in California, and another brother in Maine.
The phone calls were just going from one to another, like a relay

---

3. See **displaced persons camps** in Appendix.

thing, you know, and things started working immediately. They started saying, "We have to get her out of there." And we received a telegram saying, "We have your name, we are getting papers. Don't do anything and don't go anywhere; we are going to take you to America." That was like an unbelievable thing that could have possibly happened, but it did. That was when she said, "My child will not be going to Israel, we are going to America, the golden country, the land of opportunity."

We sailed to America on a ship called the *General Black*. The journey took 11 days. You know, they talk about the Statue of Liberty. Coming in on that boat and seeing that Lady standing there, it was like she was holding out her hands and saying, "Welcome, Welcome." I will never forget that feeling. Look – I get goosebumps just thinking back to that! I didn't know about the Statue of Liberty, but her standing out there gave you the most wonderful feeling. It's like we were coming home. For some reason, it was a wonderful feeling. I was 12 years old when we arrived on October 19, 1949. I'll never forget that date – the beginning of a new life.

We came off the boat and I think they gave notices of boats arriving, so there were a lot of Jewish people who came to the boats to check to see if there were any relatives or anybody that they might know. They would come, and of course they all spoke Yiddish, and they talked to us. They asked my mother and stepfather where our destination was. And just as proud as can be, I stood up and I said, "Portland, Maine." A guy looked at me and said, "Portland, Maine? You're going to schlepp this kid all the way to Portland, Maine?" I was so insulted – to think that! What does he mean saying such a thing? "You don't want to go to Portland, Maine," he said. But this is our home, this is where we're going, and this is how it was. My uncle, my cousins, they all greeted us at the station.

There was a problem: I was 12 years old, and I didn't know how to read, write, or speak English, and they had to start me in school. Where do you put a 12-year-old who doesn't speak it, read it, write it, or anything, you know? I was just like a dummy. So they took me into grade school, I think it was the sixth grade, and the teacher, Mrs. Ferguson, was wonderful. I had Mrs. Ferguson and Mrs. Murphy, both of whom I'll never forget. They took to me, and they took the brightest child out of each class and had that kid sit with me in the back. They would bring up little books with the ABCs, you know, the alphabet. Little by little. It took a long time before I said anything, because I was so afraid I would say it wrong. Now, coming to this country, I spoke fluent Russian and Polish, and I understood German of course, and Yiddish was my native tongue. But coming here, I was so tired of being the odd person, everything being wrong, and I wanted to fit in. I didn't want to speak Russian or anything else, I just wanted to concentrate on English. My mother spoke long before me because she spoke broken English, and that was okay. But being a child, if you said something that wasn't correct, they would laugh at you. I couldn't take having them laugh at me, so I didn't speak. The teacher was wonderful, she tried to get me to speak, but I couldn't say anything. I couldn't get it out until I knew in my mind that what I'm saying is right. We were coming from recess, going up the stairs, and one of the kids accidentally caught the back of the heel of my shoe. I turned quickly and said, "Excuse me." That was the first American word I said.

That whole time, it was an awful lot of sleepless nights because images of the past came back. The horror and the terror of the dead bodies lying in the woods, lying in the field, lying in the streets. Just people dead, lying there. I had a very difficult time – I often couldn't get these images out of my head. As time went on, I tried pushing them away. As a matter of fact, they wanted me to speak in schools and stuff like that about my experiences, but I couldn't do it, it was very difficult for me. I couldn't seem to go back because of so many years of trying to get it out of my head. I had a lot of nightmares. I was always being chased, and I would wake up screaming. I really didn't want to relive it. I just thought if I stopped thinking about it, I wouldn't have it in my head anymore. I couldn't go see movies that had Germans in them. To this day, when I see that German helmet, I get goosebumps up and down – my skin just crawls. That horrible siren sound was always in my head, and it scared me. Horrible, horrible pictures kept coming through my head.

Tama and Abe were married on October 23, 1955 in Portland, Maine, where they raised their family. They had two children, four grandchildren, and five great-grandchildren. Tama has spoken repeatedly to school groups in an effort to educate them about the Holocaust. Abe died in in 2021.

CHAPTER 5

Gerda Schild Haas

Gerda Schild Haas

November 23, 1922–June 23, 2021
Ansbach, Germany

M y name is Gerda Haas. I have lived in Lewiston, Maine for 40 years. I was born in Germany, in a small town called Ansbach. I was one of two daughters of the Jewish butcher in town, and I had a very nice childhood. My sister was a year older and we were very close. It was a small, medieval town where the Jews had been since the 13th century, so my family had been there for at least three or four generations. We lived in a nice house, and we thought we would be there forever.

I was born in 1922. I was 10 years old when Hitler came to power – my first 10 years were really a lot of fun. But then slowly things changed. My parents worried about the future, about the business, about the old grandmother that lived with us, and about us two girls who were just growing up. We saw billboards that urged everyone to vote for Hitler in the next election, and we heard on the streets remarks against the Jews, and soon we saw slogans against the Jews hanging over the streets. Little by little the happiness of our youth faded away.

At first, I didn't take it all that seriously. It was more important to go to school, to have friends and to play and jump around. But then school turned against me, too; I had to sit in the back of the class, and I wasn't allowed to answer the teacher's questions. I had poor marks at all times, no matter how hard I tried to work. My girlfriends didn't talk to me anymore and people would throw stones. Little by little I became the enemy, and that wasn't much fun at the age of 10, 11, 12. Things had slowly changed.

The system in Europe is a little different than it is here. From grade school you go right into Lyceum, and the boys go into Gymnasium, which is always a little confusing for Americans – it's not a sports school, it's a real academic institution. We girls went to the Lyceum at age 10. We had just started when Hitler came to power. As a matter of fact, I had to bring proof that my father was a World War I veteran, or I wouldn't have even been accepted. I stayed in the Lyceum for only four years instead of the customary six. When I was 15, in 1938, a law came about that no longer permitted

Aryan schoolchildren to sit in the same room with Jewish school children. So naturally it wasn't the Aryans that had to leave, it was the Jews that were kicked out. From one day to the next we were told that we no longer had the privilege to go to school.

My sister went to a Jewish agricultural school. She was a year older, so that was okay for her. But I still had to go to school, so I was sent to Berlin to a Jewish school which would exist only for another year. Then it, too, was closed. At least I was old enough to go to nurse's training, so that's where I went. I left my family to go to school in Berlin.

I was called back in 1939, when life changed for the whole family and for all the Jews in Germany. A little bit into the historical background: on November, 9, 1938, a German diplomat was killed in Paris by a young Jew. Hitler took that event as an excuse to take revenge on all the Jews in Germany. He collected all the Jews in the little towns, the villages, and in the big cities, and interned them for a night or two. In the middle of the night we were sent to a collection center – all of us. The women were let go in the morning, but the men were kept. The women were told they would not see their men again unless they sold their houses to the party member that was already waiting there, and we would have to move out of our hometown.

At the time we thought it was just plain chicanery but looking back it's easy to see that it was the first step toward the extermination of the Jews, because it was much easier to collect all the Jews from the big cities rather than go into the small towns where we had lived so many hundreds of years. So we went home. We sold the house to the party member for a ridiculously low sum, which we didn't even get, and then we were told which bigger cities we had to go to. We went to relatives in Munich, and they kept their promise – my father and all the other men were soon released and joined us.

I didn't carry the whole burden of this. It were still my mother, my grandmother and my aunt who did all the packing. Father was still away. I can remember how hurriedly they packed. Everything had to be left behind. We could only take what we could carry. It was frightening, but I'm glad I wasn't the one to carry the responsibility. My mother was just crushed. She had never made real decisions in all her life. Now, suddenly, she was without her husband, and she had to make these crucial decisions to sell the house that the family had owned for I don't know how many hundreds of years, and then go into the unknown. We weren't allowed to just buy a house or rent an apartment – we had to find a Jewish family to take us in. Fortunately, we found a very distant relative who gave us one room and the sharing of her kitchen, which was wonderful. So all this was already in preparation towards much worse things, though we didn't think so. We thought, as soon as Father comes, we'll try to get out of Germany and start a new life. But it just wasn't that simple.

In Munich I wasn't the one to worry all the time. I was so young, barely 16, going on 17. We weren't allowed to do anything. We couldn't go to the movies or shopping or anything, so we found our own joys. We went out in the evening and looked at the stars. I got my love for the stars from those times, because there was nothing else to do. The cousin that we lived with was knowledgeable in astronomy. It's a wonderful thing of human nature, that you still find little pockets of enjoyment. And we did. We took long walks, one of the things we were allowed to do. We rowed on the pond, that was also something we were allowed to do. My mother did the heavy worrying – how to get food, how to get clothing, what to do with her two young girls, not to let them sit around. We had no schooling to go to, you have to understand, so we were really just wasting our time.

Father had to leave. We were afraid that the men might be victims. We didn't really think that the women and children would be in danger. It was never done that women and children were harassed or even killed or sent away, but men, yes – we feared the men would be. So we went through every avenue possible to get my father out. Finally, he joined a transport that went to England which British Jews had arranged. I think it was 5,000 men between the ages of 18 and 45 that went to the Kitchener camp that they had made available for Jews. Father was just 44 and asked to go as the butcher of the camp, and – lo and behold – they needed a butcher. He got in together with his brother and the two went off. I remember very vividly how we took him to the train and how he said goodbye to us. My mother gave him her ring that she had on her finger. He took it along with him and he gave it back to me years later. I still have it – the one and only thing I have of my mother's, and I treasure it very much.

At the time, my sister and I were 17 and 18, and mother was 44. We lived very, very badly. We lived in that one crowded room. We had no money; all the money that mother and father had and the money that was from the house was confiscated right away. Once every month Mother had to go to the bank and practically beg for a little bit of money for the month to support her two girls and herself. My grandmother went with another aunt. The aunt that I mentioned before that lived with us had died, so it was just the three of us together now.

We had hoped that Father would be able to get us out into England, and he almost did, but he left in July 1939, and, as you know, on September 3, 1939, England declared war on Germany, so the borders were closed immediately. Then we knew we were stuck. Now I too began to worry. I didn't look at the stars so much anymore and I thought about my future.

Mother had the good idea to send us to nursing school, to nursing places. My sister who was 18, got into a Jewish hospital in Frankfurt as a student nurse. I was only 17, so I was taken as a baby nurse in Berlin. That was the time that we were separated.

Hitler was now, of course, solidly entrenched. He was in the middle of a war and at the top of his power. In spite of the war and the other worries he must have had, his main concern was always how to deal with the Jews. He made hundreds, if not thousands, of laws against us. One of the laws was that we couldn't travel. We were by then already marked with the star. This was an ordinance to separate us and isolate us to point us out to everyone else. We couldn't travel, and upon danger of death, we couldn't take the star off, because we were constantly asked for our identification on every corner. Any SS man could shoot or arrest us.

One of the laws that Hitler made – one of the most crucial laws for the 12 years of his reign – was that anyone who was in a German uniform was outside the law, outside the jury, outside the legal system. Anyone in uniform was encouraged to harass and even kill the Jews, without fear of punishment. You see, it was a very far-reaching law, and these guys took advantage of it. They could do anything to us that they wished, and they knew very well they couldn't be punished for it.

I was never beaten, but I was always careful. We were slowly conditioned into the role of the victim. We were the ones that were hunted, and we looked it and we acted it. We had no new clothes to wear, and we had no coupons to have our shoes repaired, so we looked the part that Hitler wanted us to look. The SS were in their shiny, beautiful, leather clothes with the buttons and the hats and everything, and they looked the part of the victor. I think you must remember how important appearance was, how important looks were. They were the supermen, and we were the Jewish rats and swine that they made us out to be. And of course, I stayed in the Jewish hospital as much as I could so as not to get in touch with them.

Things got pretty bad from 1941 on. The first transports left, and unhappily my mother was in one of the very first. She wrote to us that she had her notification to come into the transport. We managed to call her. We no longer had telephones, so we had to make elaborate arrangements to go to a neighbor where I could call her. I still could use the phone in the hospital.

She was fairly hopeful that she would survive this. She says, "I'm packing," and she wrote a letter to my father the day she was supposed to appear at the SS collection point. "Dear Siegfried, don't worry, I'm packing, I'm with all my friends, everybody else is called up as well. And the children know, and the children wanted to come with me, but I told them not to. It's better they stay here. And soon I will come back." She was full of her religiosity. She was a very religious woman: "It's God's will and I know he's going to let me survive and reunite me with you."

The official story of the Nazis was, right to the end, that the Jews were being resettled in the East, and that they had set aside large camps for them to be resettled and to do work for the German war effort. And we believed that. First of all, we wanted to believe it. Secondly, it sounded logical. We knew he hated us. We knew he wanted to get rid of us.

We could no longer go into any other country. So we figured he made arrangements to have us all resettled somewhere where we could all be together in kind of a ghetto-like large place, which seemed all right, and that we should do work for the war effort. We were very willing to do that. In fact, we had hoped that we would be useful enough to the Germans so that they would indeed use us. On the other side, we were praying and hoping with all our might that the Germans would be defeated, that Hitler would be killed, and that everything would be all right again, and that because we could do some work in the meantime, we would survive. We believed it on the one hand, and on the other hand, we never heard anything to the contrary. The people that were sent away never wrote.

I knew my mother was being sent to Riga – that was told to her – and she told us that on the phone and said so in the letters. She says, "I'm being sent to Riga together with all the other Jews in Munich, and we'll do war labor," or whatever it was called. She

said, "If I can, I'll write you from there, but if not, don't worry."
I never heard from my mother again.[1]

Soon enough both my sister and I were also shipped away. The
Jewish home in Frankfurt where my sister worked was liquidated
and all the nurses were first sent to do work for the Siemens
factory in Berlin, the same city where I was working as a nurse
for infants. I saw my sister a few times when she and I both had
time off. But of course, we couldn't get together on the city's
transportation system, so we walked for hours and hours just
to meet for a few minutes – with our stars on, of course. We
knew then that we too would be deported at one time or another.
Deportations were going on all around us, at all times. We nurses
even had to help in the collection centers. So we made some plans.

We were no longer the innocent kids that we used to be in
1938 and 1939. You grew up in a year very quickly. It was going
into 1942, and we knew that we were going to be deported. We
agreed that we should not try to join each other's transports.
We thought we had a better chance if we were alone. Indeed,
for me that turned out to be the case, but my sister was transported with the Siemens factory workers, and I think they went
to the Auschwitz-Birkenau extermination camp. I'm not sure,
and I don't want to do the research. It would be very easy for
me to find out, but I just don't want to. Very soon, I too was
deported. But miraculously, I was deported to Theresienstadt,
not to Auschwitz, not to Riga. Again, I didn't question it – I
thought that was luck. Much later I found out that the Germans
needed one place that they could show the world how nicely they
had settled the Jews. They still talked about the ghettos that they
were sending Jews to. Indeed, they needed one place that looked
like a ghetto, and that was a ghetto that could be shown to the
world, and it was.

---

1. See Rumbula Massacre in Appendix

In 1944, while I was there, an international commission came, and as far as I know the international commission was totally fooled. They really thought that the Jews lived fairly well. I mean, we didn't live in great comfort, but this was the middle of the war and we lived rather normally. I worked as a nurse. At first, we slept on the barracks floors without anything, just with straw and the few belongings that we could take along. The first few weeks we did just the most menial work, cleaning the toilets and sweeping the streets. That was 12 hours a day, from seven in the morning till seven at night, with a short break when we went to one of the places with our little cup to get soup and a piece of bread. We weren't terribly hungry. But of course, we weren't very well nourished either. Interestingly enough, we all got very, very heavy on that diet. We all looked very puffy and heavy; it was a rather unnatural kind of thing. For instance, before we left Berlin, we young nurses all worried, what are we going to do when we have a period? How can we take enough protection with us for this? But we needn't have worried – because of the poor food and the hard labor, we never had a period there, and as far as I know nobody did in the camp. So it was an unnatural existence. But soon enough I became a nurse, and then it was a little bit better. I got extra rations, and I didn't have to sleep on the barracks floors anymore.

We got up at seven in the morning and worked straight through till seven in the evening. When we had the night shifts, we started at seven in the evening and worked straight through till the day shift came at seven in the morning. We got our food brought to us; we no longer had to go stand in line with our little dish and get our food. We ate our food very quickly – there was just so much work, we couldn't take time out. I was a children's nurse. There were a lot of children in the camp who were then sent away again. Hardly any of the kids were allowed to stay. It turned out that for most of the people, Theresienstadt was just another collection center.

I was at Theresienstadt for a little short of two years. I got there in March 1943, and I left in February 1945. I'd like to talk a little about the liberation for me. It wasn't liberation for the camp yet. In February 1945, it went from mouth to mouth through the ghetto that we should volunteer for a transport that would go within a couple of days to Switzerland.

Of course, we all snickered. That was unheard of. At first nobody volunteered, but within hours the rumors intensified. People who we thought would know, who worked for the Jewish government within the camp, said, "Try to get into that transport, it really is going to Switzerland."

So my best friend Eva and I finally decided we would volunteer. It was Eva who was the optimistic one. She said, "Come on, let's volunteer." So we did, and a few days later we got our notices. It said that within the next few hours we should be at a certain collection point. Contrary to all the other slips that people got when they were deported, when they were called up for a transport, this one delineated what we could bring or what we could not bring. It said that we could not bring things that looked like bedrolls or stuff that looked bad. We should only bring one neat-looking suitcase. I don't know where we got it from; honestly, I guess it was provided to us. First, we had to go through interrogations with the commandant. Not everybody that finally registered was taken – they took only people that looked fairly good.

It all came about because in the fall of 1944 Hitler was being defeated and the war was coming to an end. Hitler still thought that he would win, but Heinrich Himmler, who was his second-in-command and his designated heir, no longer thought that Germany would win. He tried to make a separate peace with the Allies. He would let all the surviving Jews in Germany go to Switzerland. In the meantime, a Swiss man named Jean-Marie Musy arranged with Switzerland to take them in, but only temporarily. Then they had to go out again. After several months, the negotiations came to a point where the first transport of Jews left Germany. It was arranged that a transport of 1,200 could go, for the exchange of money. Now, logically enough, they picked people who looked rather decent. They didn't pick the skeletal Jews that were in Auschwitz and Majdanek. It went by number, and 1,200 of us were allowed to go. My number was 1174, and Eva was 1175. So we just about snuck in.

What was it like? First of all, we trembled that it wouldn't go to Switzerland. It wasn't in a cattle car; it was in a regular train car. We sat in a compartment, Eva and I together. We still had our stars on. We had to stop many times for bombing, so it was a slow process. But the Germans weren't so ugly to us anymore; they were a little nicer. All of a sudden, as we came to the border of Germany and Switzerland, we were told to take our stars off, and so I ripped it off.

Then the Germans walked through the train and were very sweet to us and encouraged us to look nice and to smile and to fix our hair a little bit. They encouraged the men to shave and to look nice so that we would look decent for the Swiss authorities. Then they left and when the Swiss authorities came in that was just a different world. We were railroaded into Zurich. I have a picture in my mind of the train station in Zurich. Eva and I finally dared to let the window down and we leaned out of it, an act we could never do before, a simple thing like looking out a window. I remember very well the thing that struck me the most was that the women wore stockings. I hadn't seen a pair of stockings in years. The next thing that Eva and I found so astounding was that they turned all their lights on in the night and that there was no blackout. We were indeed in a country of freedom. They purposely had all the lights on because they wanted the overhead fliers to know it was Switzerland – they didn't want to be bombed. Suddenly there was this immense difference between war and peace, and it took a while to get used to it, believe me. The people smiled. I hadn't seen people smile in years. The Germans didn't smile at us, and we Jews had no reason to smile.

I think we bore that stamp for the rest of our lives. We were just heavy inside of us. We weren't light-hearted. We weren't like other people our age. I was now 24 years old.

After the end of World War II and liberation, Gerda was reunited with her father who had survived and was then living in New York. Once in the United States, she met and married Dr. Rudolph Haas and later moved to Maine. She graduated from Bates College in 1971, followed by a Master's in Library Sciences (MLS) from the University of Maine a few years later. She worked as a librarian at Bates College for many years. It was during a summer seminar held on the Bates campus in 1984 that she and others established a task force that would later lead to the founding of the Holocaust and Human Rights Center of Maine, in 1985. Gerda worked tirelessly to educate others about the Holocaust. She authored two books which recounted her experiences and those of others under Nazi rule. Gerda died on June 23, 2021, leaving four children, 11 grandchildren and five great-grandchildren.

CHAPTER 6

Judith ("Jutka") Magyar Isaacson and Rose Magyar

Judith ('Jutka') Magyar Isaacson

July 23, 1925–November 10, 2015
Kaposvár, Hungary

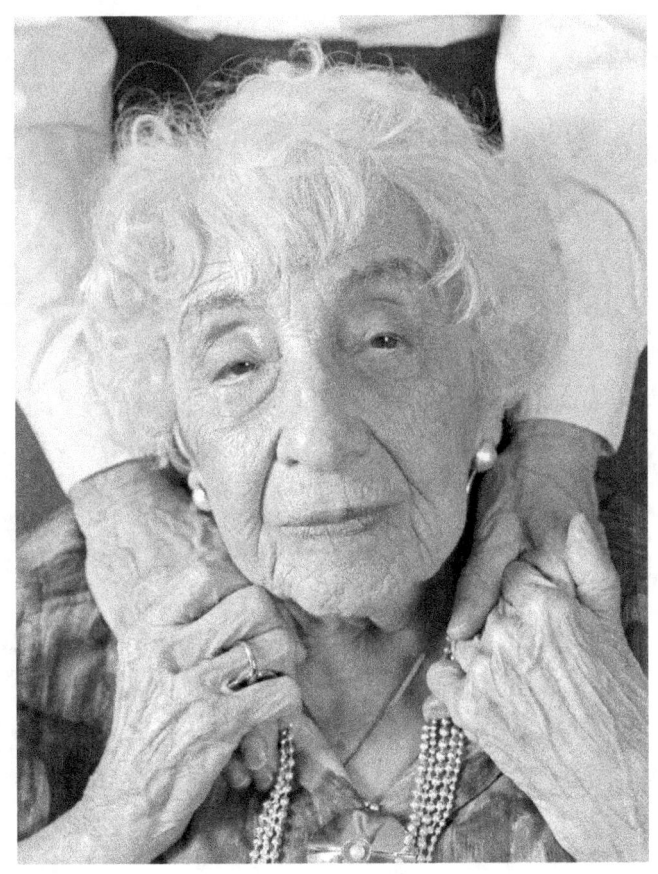

Rose Magyar

September 22, 1901–March 6, 1999
Kaposvár, Hungary

Rose Vago Magyar was born in 1901 in Kaposvár, Hungary. In 1925, she married Jena Magyar. Their one child, Judith Magyar, called "Jutka" by her family and friends, was born in 1925, following World War I and the Hungarian Revolution of 1918. Remarkably, Rose, her sister Magda Rosenberger, and Jutka remained together throughout the Holocaust – including confinement at the Auschwitz, Hessisch Lichtenau, and Lager Tekla camps – and they survived to tell their stories.

ROSE: I was born in Kaposvár, Hungary – the place of my birth and my family's, my school years, my love, my wedding, my child! In spring it was bathed in the scent of the acacia forest. Acacia honey, the best in the world.

Thirty-six thousand people. Very small by American standards, but not at all the same in Hungary. True, the whole industry consisted only of one beet sugar factory and two steam-driven flour mills. Otherwise, there were single-owned workshops and skilled tradesmen. One did not wear ready-made clothes or eat store-bought preserves.

There was an elegant white jewel of a permanent theater in a flowery park; a summer theater snuggled in another park; a third park, with a bandstand, where you could sit on a bench or on the terrace of a lovely restaurant, to listen to the music while eating wonderful pastry. You could dine there under the stars in the evening, while listening to Gypsy music. The two hotels have restaurants too, with outdoor tables in the summer, concert halls in the winter, where the balls gave occasion to the Hungarian spirited cheers.

Poetry was an important part of culture. When a new poem by a beloved poet, appeared in the *Budapest Journal* on a Sunday it was a big event.

The professors of the *Gymnasium* lived on the same level as any doctor or lawyer. A university professor got more respect than anybody.

JUTKA: We were not well-to-do people, but we lived very comfortably in a small but elegant little home in the town of Kaposvár. My grandfather owned a bakery that was next door to their house. My family was Jewish, and I was close to my mother's sister, Magda.

On March 13, 1938, I was 13 years old. Just a few weeks before, I had been asked by my teacher, Professor Biczó, to come to his office. As I entered, he leaned back in his chair, crossing his short arms over his stout chest. "Well, Magyar," he said, "I understand you recite poetry." He had heard! I nodded, feeling my face grow warm. Dr. Biczó closed the book ponderously as he added, "I understand that you won first prize in the lower-form competitions."

That gave me back my courage: "I did. With a poem by Ady."

"Ady, no less! Well, I've got something far less sophisticated for you." His thin lips dipped at the corners, then slowly eased into a smile. "How would you like to be the sole representative of the lower forms at our March Fifteenth Festival?"

March 15th was the anniversary of the 1848 Hungarian revolution, and the yearly festival was the only public performance offered by our *Gymnasium*. Everybody of importance came, from the mayor to the shopkeepers. Within the world of the lower forms, a solo performance at the festival was like winning the Nobel Prize. There was nothing higher to strive for.

"At the March15th Festival?" I gasped, hardly believing.

"Yes, at the festival," he smiled, and handed me a book opened to a lengthy poem.

I blushed deeply, and Dr. Biczó chuckled. "Recess is nearly over," he said. "You'd better get back downstairs."

I learned my poem by heart and rehearsed it for hours each night. During the evening of March 13, I had supper, poem rehearsal, and homework. By parental edict, bedtime came punctually. I slept on the studio couch in the family room, and had already crept under my *dunyha* [down comforter] when father turned on the forbidden voice of the BBC from London, broadcasting in German. Our radio set was a novel gadget, its unnatural voice a shocking intrusion. But I knew how to block it out. Father knelt in front of the radio. His fingers turned the dials – the BBC was difficult to get.

I was drifting off to sleep when a male voice announced: "This is the BBC. Hitler's armies occupied Austria today... At this very moment, Jewish women are on their hands and knees mopping up Vienna's major promenades..." I sat up, terrified. Hungary would be next on Hitler's route. And we were so near.

ROSE: I became aware of all the things against the Jews as soon as anybody in 1938. I saw newspaper photographs of Jewish women cleaning the pavement in Austria after the Germans took over in the *Anschluss*. I heard rumors about concentration camps, but I couldn't believe it. I was so optimistic all the way through and partly survived since I just didn't believe anything so terrible.

JUTKA: Would my mother be mopping up the main street in our town? I already saw her in my mind, slumped on her hands and knees, her lovely hands blue from the icy rags and her black wool coat dragging in horse dung.

As soon as Father shut off the radio, I asked him: "Will Hitler try to take over Hungary too, Papa?"

Father bit his lower lip. "I hope not."

"What if he decides to gobble us up?" I anguished. "Would our army repel him?"

My father was a reserve army officer, and I expected total reassurance. But he only muttered as if to himself, "They would, if they could."

Seeing my fright, he embraced me. "Don't fret, Jutka. We'll stop them before they cross that border! Go to sleep now, there is school tomorrow."

"What about Jutka's recital?" Mother burst out at breakfast the next day. "A Jewish girl can't very well appear as a symbol of Hungarian womanhood now."

Father's blue-gray eyes grew dim behind the glasses, and he said, "I guess you'd better resign, my little heart, before they tell you to. Go and see Dr. Biczó about it first thing this morning."

At quarter to eight that morning, I was in Dr. Biczó's study. He did not seem at all surprised to see me. Did he know I was Jewish? Yes, he did, but it did not matter. This was Hungary, not Austria.

"Shouldn't I resign, just the same?"

"Absolutely not," he said. "This is a private institution of classical learning, not some public school."

"Yes," I murmured, "but will the principal allow it?"

Biczó jumped from his chair to pace the room. "He'd better allow it, if he wants his festival." Dr. Biczó waved me off, kindly but firmly.

If Easter was for Christians and Passover for Jews, March 15th was a holiday for all Hungarians. We children always wore spring coats and white knee socks for the first time, no matter how icy the weather. It was the only way to display the ribboned corsages – red, white, and green, like a bouquet of spring flowers. As I stepped onto Kontrássy Street, breathing the sunlit, purified air, I hummed one patriotic song after another. The scare from two days before had vanished. Vienna, and Austria seemed far away, and Hitler's armies safely beyond the borders.

Today, our classes were celebrations, and the whole day was spent with history, poetry, and song. In the evening, I arrived at school in a splendid costume, jumping with excitement. Among the participants, I was the only child. Our art instructor made up my face with the concentration of a true artist. She held me at arm's length. "You look lovely, Magyar – the picture of a little Hungarian girl."

She thinks I don't look Jewish, I figured, and I skipped off, foolishly taking it for a compliment.

My poem was second in the program. I trembled behind the heavy, plush curtains, waiting for Dr. Biczó's cue. At the stroke of his plump finger, I parted the crimson drapes and stepped on stage. Mother had warned me of this terrifying moment: "Just pretend that all those heads are cabbages." But unfortunately, there were no heads for me to see. Only darkness, threatening darkness. Under the dazzling light, I stood isolated, vulnerable. I curtsied, lifting the embroidered silk skirt with two fingers, and heard my voice choke up as I announced the title and author. Breathlessly, childishly, I began:

"Hungarian girls, say,
What day is today?
Magyar people's glory
Stems from this day."

"Shut up, Jewess!" a belligerent voice thundered from the void.

Coarse shouts startled me from terribly near: "Dirty Jew! Away with the kike!" Shrill, mocking whistles sprang up from all directions, hissing their hatred and spite.

I shivered, terrified.

Our friendly auditorium, where I had so often played and exercised, was transformed into an enemy den. Unseeing, I faced a nightmare. My knees shook above the white knee socks and my teeth chattered audibly. All my instincts propelled me backstage. But I would not give in. I took a deep breath and dug my nails deep into my palms. My eyes had become accustomed to the spotlights, and I forced them to stare into the void. I gave another curtsy, this time low, unhurried, formal, just as I had learned in folk dance. Proud of my newfound courage, I smiled involuntarily.

Applause sprang from the dark hall, first sporadically, then solidly from all directions. Here and there, a mocking whistle soared above the clapping, but no one shouted anymore.

I decided to recite my poem from the start:

"Hungarian girls, say
What day is today..."

My voice surprised me. It was fuller, stronger than before, almost adult. The large hall echoed it encouragingly, and there were no interruptions until the final din of applause. One more curtsy, and I backed offstage, exhausted but exhilarated.

"Well done," said a smiling Dr. Biczó, and I ran to change into my navy dress uniform with the tricolor corsage.

It was with some trepidation that I went to Dr. Biczó's study the next morning to return the book containing my poem. What would he say about the Nazi interference? Could he possibly understand how terrifying it had been?

He received me kindly. "Excellent performance! Your voice is well suited to a large auditorium." Not a word about the demonstrators.

"The whistles..." I mumbled.

"Oh, yes!" he interrupted. "Some lunatic fringe, no doubt. Do you know, Jutka, how many Fascists there are in all our city? No more than 100, surely, in a population of 35,000." He rapped his pencil against the desk for emphasis. "They pose no danger. I hope they did not frighten you."

"Oh no."

But things changed quickly after that night.

After the German occupation of Austria on March 13, 1938, the condition of Hungarian Jews deteriorated daily. In May, discrimination was sanctioned by the First Jewish Law, causing economic hardships.[1] In September, Jewish students lost their scholarships, and new Nazi textbooks changed history overnight. From Roman times to the present, the Jews emerged as villains. Most of our professors ignored the new politics – Aladár Kóváry, my history teacher, being the only exception.

Mr. Kóváry suddenly emerged as an avowed antisemite, and he seemed to get a perverse enjoyment out of spouting obscenities at

---

1. See **Hungarian anti-Jewish laws** in Appendix.

the Jewish girls. He towered on his podium, a bony giant with a small head, wiry eyebrows, and piercing eyes. He flapped his arms like a bird of prey and stretched his long neck as far as it would go. Behind his back we called him *Csutka* [Adam's Apple]. In class, we snickered at the oversized protrusion, which bobbed up and down like a yo-yo.

Mr. Kováry neither assigned papers nor gave any written exams. Our grades depended solely on oral presentation. Even the best students worried about grades. With a single B, the chances of acceptance at university would become precarious. Wickedly, he chose Jewish girls to recite the most antisemitic passages. But soon we each found our defensive tactics. I, for instance, would introduce each paragraph with: "According to the latest historical hypotheses..."

My classmate, Évi Kárpáti, was far more creative. She rose with a defiant shake of her head to declaim, "In the Middle Ages, all the usurers were Germans!" Then she quickly corrected herself, "Sorry, I meant Jews." At other times, she recited like a little dramatic actress: "The holy heroes of the holy wars staged holy pogroms." She got away with it because she was so popular and so comic.

Soon Kóváry ignored the rest of us, having found an easy victim in Böde Winternitz, a gawky girl who sat in the back row. "Come on, Winternitz," Adam's Apple thundered. "Don't omit anything! Surely, those Jews deserved what they got! Now, give us the reasons, you red-faced monkey!"

I turned back in my seat. So did 38 other navy-clad girls. What would Böde say? Her face turned crimson, and her dark eyes pleaded. "The Middle Ages..." she stuttered. "The Jews... The moneylenders..."

"Cow's udder between bull's horns!" Kováry bellowed. Thirty-nine uniformed young ladies dipped pens into inkwells and copied "cow's udder between bull's horns" into their notebooks. (We loved to spread Kováry's novel vulgarities during recess.) Böde clutched her desk and closed her eyes. Two tears slid down her inflamed cheeks. But her tormentor hadn't finished.

"Tell me, you offspring of blushing idiots, where did those worthless Jews come from? Stay mum another minute and I'll flunk you out of here without another chance. One less Jewish intellectual to worry about! Go, hide yourself in your father's grocery shop!"

On May 24, 1944, Jutka and her family were forced to move into a ghetto in her hometown, just as Jews had been forced into ghettos in the Middle Ages. The area was enclosed with barbed wire and guarded. Fortunately, her grandparents' house was within the ghetto, so for a short time she was in familiar surroundings. However, four families were now crammed into the house, waiting with great apprehension for the Nazis' next move. As part of the oppressive measures, all Jews were required to relinquish important items including many food and household goods, heirlooms, valuables, radios, and typewriters. For Jutka, the typewriter was particularly difficult to part with. The families, now crowded into the ghetto and forbidden to leave, feared they would starve.

ROSE: Late at night Jutka took the typewriter to one of her gentile classmates. The father, a prominent physician, opened the door, and accepted it, asking only one thing: Jutka should not greet or talk to his daughter on the street. The posters screamed all over: "Anybody who accepts articles for keeping from Jews will be treated as Jews." In the village, the public crier announced it with drums.

Soon after these orders were announced, Jutka asked the family, "If I can hide things so that it is impossible to find them, will you then say okay?"

"If you find such a place, then yes."

Jutka disappeared. Next evening, the big job was finished. Everybody had to agree. There was an old cellar from the old house, before the newer one was built. They used to put carrots, all kinds of vegetables there in a big pile of sand for winter. The cellar was never used anymore. The steps were crumbled, broken down. There were window-shaped indentations in the thick brick cellar wall. How did Jutka know that if she would take out the outside bricks of these blind windows, she would find only soft loam inside? That is her secret. It is a fact that, operating with a kitchen knife and a small shovel, she and Magda made such a nook, that in the lower part they put a ten-quart container of lard. Later, Jutka added in airtight boxes, documents, my mother's watch, rings, letters, photos, a small amount of currency, and other things.

> *Jutka had risked harsh treatment by burying family heirlooms in the basement in the days before deportation. Those items included her father's gold watch case, her diploma from the* Gymnasium, *and some family jewelry.*

ROSE: Meanwhile, the ghetto bustled. The vans had already finished the looting of the houses. They took away all furniture, beddings, carpets, clothing. Our own furniture slept undisturbed in our warehouse, where hundreds of tons of flour used to be before, completely forgotten by all of us. It really seems now unbelievable. Anyway, it did not make any difference. Some people found it and took it anyway, after we were gone.

Now they brought in the Jews from the surrounding towns and villages. They arrived in long rows of carts, horse-drawn and piled up with the pitiful articles left in the already looted households. Wash basins, chicken cages, bedding, cribs. Families, mostly without a man. The short, thin clerk, with the close-set small eyes and the Hitler mustache, who was now the "Lord of the Ghetto", bicycled there all day or strolled with his court of gangsters and shrieked, whether he found some reason to do so or not.

He kept turning into the houses and hollered with a blood curdling voice, "House Kommandant," until a clumsy old man, or some crying woman, appeared. We were not allowed to step out of the ghetto, but the gentiles walked through it, as it was on a main road to the city. Of course, it was forbidden to talk to the Jews.

JUTKA: Soon after our move to my grandparents' house, we had our last gentile visitor – the wiry Urich, a baker's helper from another part of town, who once worked for Grandfather as an apprentice.

"Is the old man at home?" he asked me crisply, striding through the cluttered shop.

"Grandfather is out in the courtyard," I said, and trailed him there.

Grandfather was reading his newspaper under his favorite tree, its wide branches laden with apricots, round and small, green with promise.

"*Jó napot* – good day," Ulrich mumbled, without tipping his hat.

"*Jó napot*," gasped grandfather, taken by surprise. "How come you visit a Jew?"

"I have permission," Ulrich announced, his foxy chin held high. "I came to measure the premises. The house and the bakery will soon be mine. Let's start with the rooms."

"Józsa!" yelled grandfather. Grandmother's worn face soon appeared at the kitchen window. "Ulrich wants to say something to you."

"What is it?" she wanted to know.

"Tell her," Grandfather beckoned to the baker. "You used to eat her cooking. Remember?" Grandmother always fed the help with the same excellent food she cooked for her family, which was unusual.

"*Jó napot*, Mrs. Vágó," bowed an abashed Ulrich, politely enough. "Do you mind if I look at your rooms?"

"My rooms?" complained Grandmother. "A different family is now in every one. Some haven't even made their beds yet. Can you believe it?"

"Never mind, Mrs. Vágó," Ulrich soothed. "Let's not bother."

Grandmother's head disappeared into the kitchen. Ulrich turned back to Grandfather, "Will you show me the bakery, old man?"

"The bakery?" Grandfather grunted. "I padlocked it. Damn Nazis! They took all my machinery."

"I know," said Ulrich, suppressing a grin. "Don't you curse them."

"Aha!" thundered Grandfather, eyeing him over his spectacles. "I get it. You joined the Nazis yourself! Did they give you my machinery, too?"

"It's none of your business," retorted Ulrich. "Anyways, you should have retired by now. Eighty, aren't you?"

"Eighty-three," bragged Grandfather, getting up from his bent-wood chair. "And not a sick day in my life. You try and match that."

"Why not?" said Ulrich. "I'm halfway there."

He measured the rambling buildings, peeked in at the windows, counted the fruit trees, and paced out the large vegetable garden with his spindly legs. "It's a fine place," he grinned, returning.

Grandfather eyed him and said, "I built it from scratch 50 years ago. And by God, I'm still the master here."

"Not for long," said Ulrich. "A train is on its way, old man. You people will be on a transport to the concentration camp before these apricots ripen."

Grandfather touched a baby apricot with a trembling finger. "I won't leave this house alive," he murmured. "Never."

"Sorry, Uncle Vágó." Ulrich shrugged his shoulders. "It's out of my hands. You Jews will soon leave, and you won't come back, either. No use hiding your valuables."

"I'll never leave this house alive," Grandfather repeated. "Want to bet?"

"It's a bet," Ulrich said.

Jutka's grandfather won the bet. He died a few days later, in his own bed.

ROSE: I don't talk about fate, I just record it here: Soon after the war, lightning struck Ulrich and he died...

It was around the time of Ulrich's visit that a couple of boys came home on furlough from the Ukraine, and now they were trapped in the ghetto. They talked of brothels behind the front, filled with Jewish girls. Whoever got pregnant was shot. After that, they spread the rumor – who started it, nobody knew – that the Germans would not take married women. So, in great haste fake marriages multiplied. Anybody who wanted to marry got two days furlough from the close-by labor camps where some local men were held. This was an inducement too, to come home and see the families.

After the war, Rose wrote a poem recalling those last days in the ghetto:

MOVE TO THE GHETTO

MIDSUMMER. ENDING AFTERNOON.
SUNSOAKED SWEET ROOM. FALSE COMFORT.
CURTAINS SIGH IN THE BALMY BREEZE.
END OF THE CLING TO PHANTOM PEACE.
TEARFOGGED EYES STARE, CONFRONT, AMAZED
IN THE BLURRED MIRROR: WHY?...NO REPLY.
THAT SHADOW ON THE SUNLIT BEDSPREAD
NEVER WILL BRUSH HER HAIR AGAIN.
THAT FAMILIAR SHADOW ON THAT
LACY FRILLED BEDSPREAD.
NOT TOMORROW, NOR ANY OTHER
TOMORROWS. EVER.
OH...BYE...
KIND NEIGHBOR WANTS TO BUY

OUR FIREWOOD, OUR WINTER COAL.
"DON'T SELL? YOU WILL NOT NEED IT ANYMORE!"
FOR OUR CHILD, FOR US, SO FULL OF TACT.
A DEATH SENTENCE. AS A MATTER OF FACT.

ROSE: When we were deported, we were first to be taken to the temple in the ghetto and then by trucks to a stable near the train yard. So, we went to the temple in the ghetto. The yard of the temple was full of news of suicides. Old men hung themselves, widows and sick people took poison. The people listened without criticism or approval. They just simply could not feel anything.

When we were carried on trucks to the stables for deportation, the city played dead. Every door closed, every window shuttered, not a soul anywhere. I had one thought: They close their eyes and wash their hands. Then, the first time, I was thinking, nobody was on the street either to show any spiteful glee, to shout, "Good riddance!" I try to imagine, what did our neighbors do, feel, in their closed homes? Thinking we were being taken to be killed...

As the time of our departure from the stable approached, we were ordered to leave most of our belongings before boarding. The order went out, "One coat to each!" So, I put on my relative's short beige trench coat.

"With your short hair, now you look like a young girl," flattered Jutka.

We did not know yet the lifesaving importance of that sentence.

> *Although she had no inkling at the time, Rose's relatively youthful appearance would soon save her from the gas chamber.*

We stayed at the stables for three days. My daughter Jutka had a very good, wonderful professor who came out to the ghetto before we got deported, looking for her and saying goodbye, and he gave her a little book by the Greek philosopher Aristotle.

JUTKA: We Jews were left to wait for the trains in a stable. Soon, we listened to shrieks coming from curtained torture chambers. The Nazis wanted to know where the rich hid their treasures. My friend Ilona's mild-mannered father shrieked the longest. When the Nazis finally parted the curtains, Mr. Pogany stumbled out, hardly recognizable. His blond hair was disheveled, blue eyes blinded, spectacles shattered, fingers bleeding. The Nazis had shredded his back, his hands, and his feet. But Mr. Pogany had not told them that he had hidden his whole coin collection, the labor of decades, in an unused well.

ROSE: As we stood on the last day, ready to board the train to leave, the sky got overcast. Deep thundering sounded from far. All at once, such a whirlwind sprung up, the like of it nobody remembered. Among the thunder and lightning, the dry, sandy ground flew up with all its molecules. The dust raged, whirled around us. We felt that it will pick us up too and throw us around. In one minute, everybody got dark grey. I looked up at the sky angrily. Then came a huge, furious shower, as if now the clouds would want to give back the flying-up earth. In one moment, we all got wet. The dust, which covered us from the whirlwind, became at once a sticking, thick mud. With the drenched hair, there was no middle class there anymore, just a filthy mob.

On July 5, 1944, the Jews of the town – including Rose, Rose's mother, Jutka, and Rose's sister Magda – were packed into cattle cars that were then sealed. Over three and a half days they were transported to Auschwitz with barely room to stand, only a bucket for a toilet, and tiny amounts of water. Few of them would survive until the defeat of Germany ten months later, in May 1945. Many did not live to the end of the train journey.

ROSE: At last, the wagons were full, the door closed. The train started. The stables slowly disappeared. The wheels accelerated, we passed the sugar factory, the last of Kaposvár. So, it is really true. We are being deported.

JUTKA: Dr. Gero and his young family were huddled near us. He was a dentist, his wife a piano teacher. They had two children, Tori, age 8, and Marika, age 6, who was known in Kaposvár as an exceptionally talented young pianist. During the journey, I often sat with Marika on my lap, her blond curls sticky, her childish mouth gasping for air. By the second day, she wanted no more stories or games. "Lack of oxygen and water," her father explained. Marika dozed on my lap, panting and sweating, until the mug came around. One gulp per person per day was our ration for those three and a half days. We had dry food in our rucksacks, but we couldn't move to reach it, and besides, we were too thirsty to eat.

Marika took her gulp of water and sighed with relief. "Take one more, Marika," I urged her in a whisper, "It's all right." Surely, I reasoned, there must be one extra gulp for our youngest.

Marika's blue eyes were filled with reproach. "But Jutka," she said, as if we were playing some game, "It wouldn't be fair." She passed the mug.

ROSE: The children dropped their heads on the shoulders of their mothers and slept sweating. Marika, who came with white gloves on the wagon, was a piano prodigy. Seven years old, she had been promised a great future. She slept already only in a little shirt. The sweat in black drops stuck to her little face. There were also four other children with us and gorgeous, red-headed 15-year-old twins.

ROSE: It was the third night. The train ran faster than ever. A few old ones stopped breathing. Lots of others muttered incoherently. The Rabbi's daughter was in convulsions, when suddenly the train stopped with a jolt. The door opened. The fresh night air poured in and a never-ever-heard name was on the big station: AUSCHWITZ.

When we finally got to Auschwitz and I got off the train, I thought a lot of people were dead already on the train, or mad. And then they came, those guys, all kinds of prisoners with shaved heads, and helped out the older ones. They told us that the old ones and the children will go together and the old ones can take care of the children. I believed them. I recall the prisoner in striped pajamas who stayed on the ground and helped people down, or lifted the old ones and the children. He wanted to lift my mother too, but she said in a fresh, kind tone, as to a son, "I will just hold your hands and I can get down by myself!"

The man gently gave her both his hands, almost with love, and she said sweetly, "*Danke schön* [Thank you]."

These were her last words I ever heard.

Across, behind the station, an unimaginable large red fire, its red flames covering half of the starless, black sky.

JUTKA: Beyond the railroad tracks, once more the line branched in two. Why? What was going on? I slipped ahead to investigate. Under a bright light, an SS officer was conducting a selection. I did not see any of my friends, but I did recognize several women from our wagon. From a distance I watched the selection. Children and older women went to the left, the rest right. Perhaps we girls will be safe, I thought. But the next moment, I saw youthful Mrs. Gerd being shoved to the right, away from her children. Selections at Auschwitz.

I was scared for them, especially for Marika, and I went ahead to listen as a stocky SS woman tried to calm everyone. To each frantic question, she gave a curt but reassuring reply, "Yes, mothers may visit their children. Please understand, women over 40 and children under 16 won't have to work, so they must be separated from the rest. Don't worry, they'll have comfortable quarters. Yes, you may visit each other tomorrow." It all sounded reasonable. I returned to my place in line and naively relayed all that false information word for word.

ROSE: Then it was my turn at the head of the line. The German's stiff, indifferent face showed little change. He asked, "How old are you?"

I answered before he finished his question, with lightning speed, "Thirty-eight."

That computer part of my mind even decided that 38 would look less a lie than 39. This all happened really in the subconscious – I hardly had anything to do with it. And the man showed both Jutka and me to the left, to be spared for the moment, and he went on to pronounce his sentence on the next couple.

I thought, "And I am almost 43. I made it!" I trembled.

That was the last that the survivors saw of anybody under 16 or over 40. It is unlikely that Marika and the other children survived even a few hours before being sent to the gas chamber.

ROSE: We were made to take a bath. We were very thirsty, all naked because they had taken our clothes. We came out all naked and were dying from thirst and no water. Then they completely shaved all of our body hair. We were then given rags to wear and a drink of water. Later we were moved to the Birkenau subcamp. There was a smell in the camp. It was burning bodies, but I didn't know that at the time. I thought it was a chemical factory. But my sister Magda knew. She learned from a Polish nurse but she didn't tell me.

JUTKA: Later there was another selection going on. We had gone through selections, but this time they made us all undress, thousands of women undressed naked. We were all shaved. No pubic hair, no hair, bald and naked. Thousands going in single file with your heads up and holding whatever rags you had. So, I looked around and I thought, my God! It can't be real! It was just really like a nightmare, but worse than *Brave New World*, which I had read the summer before I was taken. I thought, if I ever survive, I've got to go to Hollywood and try to help someone make a picture to recreate this scene, because nobody would be able to imagine it. Auschwitz was not like now, with grass. Then, it was just mud or dry mud, depending on the weather. Nothing living. Just those crowds and crowds of people. All you could see was these naked women marching and curving around, spiraling, in single file. Very threatening, very unreal.

Of course, we had to be silent, absolutely silent. So, it went on, for hours, it seemed. Finally, our turn came. We were separated from anybody we knew except my mother, my aunt, and I. We always held onto each other. The three of us got in line and got closer and closer to where the selection was going on, with an SS officer with a pistol in his hand. And next to him a woman SS guard. Then the dogs they always used to catch people, should they be running. The three of them were standing there and this single file coming by. He sent people, going either straight, or right, or left.

Ahead of them, I watched, and I could see that the majority went straight ahead. The very weak and sick or old, the oldest were about 40 because, by then, everyone over 40 or under 16 had been gassed. But those who seemed old and weak and sick were sent left. I could tell there wasn't much hope for them. The tall, strong, and often good-looking young girls were sent to the right. When you see a line of handsome young girls, all naked, going to the right, and you've been warned not to go on a girls' transport, of course you try to avoid it because they were being forced to go to the front to become prostitutes for the soldiers. My mother went first, I was after her, and my Aunt Magda came after me.

We worried that my mother would be sent with the sick because she was among the oldest there and she was in bad shape by then. But maybe I caught his eye. Whatever, he just sent my mother straight ahead. And I was next. He sent me right with the young girls. I had two instinctive feelings. First of all, I just wanted to stay with my mother because that's all we tried to do for three weeks

– just stay together all the time. It seemed like it didn't matter whether we died or not – just stay together. The other was not to go on a transport for girls. So I just went after my mother. The SS woman called out. They always talked as if they meant well, like a teacher. "Oh, don't go there, he'll shoot you!" And I said, "I don't care." And I really didn't at that point. My grandfather taught me German, so I was able to talk German to her. I didn't care. I just thought it was better to be shot now than be separated, to go with a girls' transport, get raped, and get buried alive. That was much more of a nightmare. So, I just walked after her, naked. And I expected him to shoot me in the back. I still remember that feeling, expecting that bullet to come. And it didn't.

ROSE: My memories of those days: It could be about 5 a.m. The camp is very busy. We see huge iron kettles, carried by two panting girls on each side. Far away, thousands of men in striped pajamas march in lines of five. At the distant edge of the fantastically far horizon a colossus of shaved men wrapped in those coarse dark grey horse blankets proceed, as monks, on an ancient, horrid funeral. At the right, about 50 women in white kerchiefs sit on the ground, sorting rags. Now, scores of young boys appear, each carrying in his hands some peculiar grey bricks, highly piled, as slaves in Egypt.

Rose, Jutka, and Magda remained in the extermination camp for one month and were then sent to work as slave laborers in an underground munitions factory in Hessisch Lichtenau, Germany. Just as the war was ending in Europe, in April 1945, they escaped transport to a death camp. The Nazis were working overtime at the end of the war to hide the evidence of their crimes and murder as many Jews and other prisoners as possible. Luckily, Jutka, Rose, and Magda were in an American zone at the time they achieved freedom. A month later, Jutka met a Lewiston, Maine, native

named Irving 'Ike' Isaacson, who was serving as a cap-
tain in the U.S. Army and Office of Strategic Services
(OSS), the predecessor of the CIA.

ROSE: I think back to the time we first arrived at Auschwitz.
I did not even know about the gas chamber and the incinerator.
They lied to us: 'The old ones are taking care of the children.' The
rest of the nine months, we were in German concentration camps.

When the Americans occupied Leipzig, in April 1945, we were
finally liberated. The best shining morning in my life was when,
after the cannons stopped, I have seen that marvel: an American
soldier climbing up the telephone pole! I got insane, literally. I
started to run on those long corridors – an army building, no
Germans anymore – and screaming at the top of my lungs – in
German! – "I am free! I am free! I am free!" until finally my own
voice scared me and brought me back to sanity.

We were in dirty rags, some in new prison garb, seven of us Hungarians (six young girls and me). A young Belgian officer opened
up a big store for us and said, "Get some decent dresses."

Then we soon met Ike, who was a captain in the American
Secret Service, and he and Jutka got engaged July 3rd, on her
20th birthday. Ike arranged for Magda to go home to our town of
Kaposvár on a Red Cross bus to see what had become of the town,
our families, and friends. Later, Ike also went to Kaposvár with his
friend Fred by jeep to bring out my husband for Jutka's wedding. I
always was sure my family survived. Ike left two American soldiers
to guard us. We heard those soldiers walking back and forth outside, day and night.

We were so happy, impatient. I was as excited as a young bride.
We just washed our hair, ready to go to bed. We tried to imagine
Ike and the family together. The bell rang. Who can that be?
We don't know anybody. The door opened. The men came in
with dirt-blackened faces. Behind them, instead of my husband
Jani, stood Magda. They had found her all alone, the houses of

Kaposvár occupied by hostile people. Nobody, nobody survived. They had to sneak Magda out of town in their jeep, under burlap, while the Russian soldiers were drunk at the border.

Then I heard, as all separate shots into my heart, one by one, all the beloved names. "Gone. Gone. Gone." I cried desperately. "No! No! No!" My mother. My husband. All my dear four brothers. My husband, at 45, was the oldest of them. Only then did Magda tell us the horrible, unbelievable, evil truth. For the first time, I heard the words 'gas chamber', even though I have lived three weeks under its flame and smell. I am not ashamed. How could I ever imagine anything like that?

Jutka and Ike married in Germany in December 1945 and later moved to Auburn, Maine, together with Rose, where they raised three children.

Jutka: So, after my children became older, I decided to go back for my PhD. I got an all-tuition-paid scholarship to the University of New Hampshire in abstract mathematics, at age 43 or so. I started that and I commuted to the University of New Hampshire. In the meantime, they asked me at Bates to offer a course in calculus.

They invited me to become Dean of Women after the prior dean left. The college psychiatrist at Bates met me and asked about my background when I first started. He said, "My gosh, you haven't come up the usual rungs of the ladder!" I said, "No, I haven't." He asked, "Have you ever lived in a dormitory?" I said, "Well, in Auschwitz."

I thought I'll last a year at best because I had very liberal ideas. But I lasted eight years at Bates. First, I was Dean of Women, and then Associate Dean of the College. I ended up in the last year as Dean of Students, responsible for the entire student body at Bates. I did that until the year I started to write the book, when I went back to Hungary, which was 1977.

*Once her youngest son began kindergarten, Jutka re-
turned to school and earned a degree in mathematics
from Bates College. She went on to earn her master's
degree from Bowdoin College in Brunswick, Maine;
taught math at Lewiston (Maine) High School; and
became the first computer science teacher at Bates. She
was promoted from the faculty to Dean of Women and
then Dean of Students. Jutka dedicated the next chapter of her working life to writing her memoir,* Seed of
Sarah, *and serving as a speaker for the Holocaust and
Human Rights Center of Maine, sharing her story in
schools throughout the state. Her memoir has been used
in schools statewide for many years. At the time of her
death, Jutka was survived by her husband, three children, eight grandchildren, and one great-grandchild.*

*After the war, Jutka's Aunt Magda returned to Ka-
posvár, where she found the jewelry and documents
that Jutka had buried just before being transported to
Auschwitz, including a gold watch that had belonged
to Jutka's grandmother. The watch's mechanism had
rusted away while buried, but Jutka had it made into
a locket which she wore for the rest of her life. Inside
she placed a portrait of her father, who had died in
the Holocaust. She was wearing the locket when her
portrait was made in 1997.*

She also recovered her Gymnasium *record which she had buried. When it was later presented as part of her application to Bates College, she was awarded two years' credit because of her strong record in such a broad array of subjects.*

CHAPTER 7

Alfred Kantor

Alfred Kantor

November 7, 1923–January 16, 2003
Prague, Czechoslovakia

M y name is Alfred Kantor. I was born on November 7, 1923, in Prague. My father's name was Leo, and my mother's name was Olga. I had one half-brother, named Hans, and one half-sister, Mimi, from my father's first marriage. His first wife had died, but he remarried and then I was born when Mimi was 14 or 15 years old, and Hans was about 12. My relationship with Hans and Mimi was a very good one. My father was a salesman for a shirt factory. My mother was primarily a housewife – she supervised the running of the house and so on.

At first, when I was little, we lived in an old house which had three stories. But when I was five, we moved to an apartment which was modern at the time. Religion was not practiced in the home, but my father went to the temple for the High Holy Days. I do remember Hanukkah at home, but that's about it.

Basically, I would say I was a sheltered kid. My earliest memories of life in Prague as a little boy are of my father telling me stories. He liked to be alone with me sometimes and tell me stories.

I first went to a German public school, and then I switched to Czech middle school. After four years of middle school, I had to leave because the political situation was turned against Jews. My schooling stopped when I was 15.

First, signs on stores said: "This is Aryan, this is a Christian store," and then later they were sharper: "We don't serve Jews," and things like that. This to me was unthinkable because Czechoslovakia was really a very modern democratic country. I slowly gave up my belief in the decency of man and found that there are some people who are not decent.

My first inkling that life was going to change was when my sister warned me that I should get out of the country. She would try to help me. This was in 1938, that fateful year. What happened in 1938 was that the Germans had occupied the Sudetenland. Things would never be the same as they were. Mimi was the most realistic of the family. I think she saw danger. She knew this – it was danger. I was the eternal optimist, but I was only a kid.

Hitler marched into Prague on March 15, 1939. German occupation of Czechoslovakia March 15, 1939. I was in my apartment when the Germans marched in. It only took a few months before he declared war on us. His main objective was to annihilate the Jews. Things started changing. Before 1939, there were some antisemitic signs on the stores, but life hadn't really changed that much. But in 1939, slowly at first, there were all kinds of restrictions for Jews, started by the Germans. You couldn't shop in the morning. You had to shop at three in the afternoon, and all the stores were sold out. You couldn't go to movies in the theater. You couldn't go to parks. You had to be home at eight in the evening. One restriction after another built up and made life miserable for the Jews. Still, very few realized that Hitler's idea was to annihilate the Jews.

Unfortunately, my parents couldn't make any plans. My father was very ill. He died of cancer two weeks before I was taken to a concentration camp. My mother focused on keeping him as well as she could. My sister wanted me to marry a Christian girl. It wasn't so easy, and to me it seemed preposterous. But maybe it was right. Hans had a Christian wife, and he was saved so far, and Mimi married a Christian and she was saved too. In Hans' case, he loved his girl. As for Mimi, there was a fellow who offered to marry her to protect her. She divorced him after the war.

After the Nazis took over Czechoslovakia, numerous actions were taken against Jews, including restrictions on freedom of movement, seizures of property, and many others. Thus, Alfred was expelled from art school because he was a Jew. Deportations of Jews to the Theresienstadt concentration camp began in November 1941. Notices were sent to individual Jews directing them to appear for 'transport'.

I obediently marched off and was a good citizen. And six million good citizens died. In December 1941, we were marched up to a building with a huge hall. At 5 a.m. we marched to the train station so nobody should see us. But of course, people saw us, and there was a passenger train waiting to take us to Theresienstadt. As a group we were a thousand young men. This was in a special camp. They wanted the world to see how well the Jews were being treated, but it was all a fake because most of the people were shipped from there to Auschwitz and they never were heard from again. But Theresienstadt was supposed to get Hitler a good name, that he was treating the Jews well. It was a big shell game.

After we arrived in Theresienstadt, at first I did nothing. I was hiding. Then I was working on a cleanup crew. Slowly I worked my way into the kitchen. That was a good thing to do because I wasn't hungry. I was assigned to the group that carried coal to the kettles to heat them. One day the cook saw me and asked, "Would you like to work here?" So, then I was heating the kettles with a stoker. There were no barracks. There were houses that had been left by the population and were occupied by Jews. Of course, we were crowded. A small room would provide housing for fifteen or 20 people.

Throughout his time at Theresienstadt, and later at Auschwitz and Schwarzheide, Alfred made a series of paintings depicting life in the camps. The project became particularly challenging and risky as he progressed into increasingly difficult circumstances after Theresienstadt. Many of the paintings were lost or destroyed during these years, but others survived and were published in 1971 by McGraw Hill and republished in 1987 by Schocken Books.

There was a moat around the town. A few prisoners escaped, but somebody caught them and they were hanged. This showed me for the first time that the Nazis were beasts. The food was pretty dismal, but it was still a little better than we would later get at Auschwitz. Potatoes – not enough, of course. Many people, especially old ones, died of starvation. Young people had a way of finding a turnip or something and supplementing their diet, but not all of them. But of the camps where I was sent, Theresienstadt was still one of the better ones. Of course, the idea was not to keep people in Theresienstadt. The idea was to ship them out to Auschwitz and kill them there.

Theresienstadt became an unusually active cultural center. There were writers, poets, musicians, artists. They all came to the fore. Judaism was practiced by those who believed in it. Whether they were artists or musicians or scientists, writers, or poets, they each came forward. It's well recognized today that there was an unusually active cultural center in the camp with musical performances and opera. The Germans encouraged it because it showed that they were giving the Jews freedom to be themselves and to act with freedom. Of course, it was a criminal charade. One day the Jews would have a concert in a town hall, and the next day they were packed off and sent to Auschwitz. So, it was not all that wonderful, but while it lasted, to us young people, it meant something. It was good to listen to music or go to an art class. The sad thing was when the children were sent away to Auschwitz.

Gas chamber
New arrivals don't know the score, and step in voluntarily but gassing of veteran prisoners (uneasy because they are too worn (weak) for labor) is combined with screaming and the occasional bullet.

I stayed in Theresienstadt for two years. I was 20 years old when I left. I was in good shape because of my work in the kitchens.

I had a girlfriend there named Eva Glauber. She was included in the transport going east, meaning to Auschwitz. I volunteered to accompany her because I couldn't see her going alone so I went along. That's how I got to Auschwitz, of course, but I didn't know at the time. Sooner or later, I would have been sent to Auschwitz anyway, so it wasn't so spectacular. Everybody was sent, if not to Auschwitz, then to some other center of killing. Eva was a wonderful woman. She would cheer me up and when I told her, "I think we've had it," she just told me that I shouldn't have such thoughts. She really gave me courage. Unfortunately, she didn't make it. She contracted tuberculosis and was sent to the gas chamber on July 12, 1944.

We went to Auschwitz in a cattle train. There were about 100 people in the car. It was very crowded so we couldn't lie down; we had to stand up. The trip lasted for three days, and the doors were open. There were a lot of lights shining at the railroad station. And then we were boarding trucks. They took us down the road to some barracks, women on the left side, men on the right. Old timers came and would tell us that people are being gassed here. I thought they're just talking nonsense. I didn't want to accept that. We stayed in barracks built for horses and we slept six abreast on some straw. It was pretty primitive.

Suicide : » she went into the fence «

OR : SHE HIT THE WIRE.

A common view in Avschwitz.

The weather that winter was cold and snowy. The first few days were like a nightmare. I was in the barracks. The door was open. I looked outside and I saw people walking by in the snow in wooden shoes. They received wooden shoes from some Dutch transport, and I felt like it was a movie, but it was more like a nightmare. Then I was chased out of the barracks. We had to do some work that made no sense at all. We carried rocks from one place to another, building a road. It took us months to build the road. But the object was to wear people out. We went to the quarry to pick up the rocks.

Once I met my mother coming back. She also carried a rock, a small one. She became thin, but she seemed to be in good shape. She didn't get sick. She was killed in March of 1944. The entire transport of 5,000 people was gassed.

" HOSPITAL "

LAST BUNK IN BARRACKS IS FOR
, Disqualifieds` - prisoners weakened
to death. Toilets are behind dead corpses

Strange things happened. People who had been normal people in Theresienstadt became animals in Auschwitz. Not all of them, but most of them. They became brutal, cruel, and even little children became cruel. I couldn't understand it, that people could change so quickly over a period of six months. I didn't recognize them anymore.

Serving dinner means a few minutes rest.

Punishment for theft of soup.   49

At noon we had a little cupful of some indescribables – a mish-mash of potatoes and rotten turnips that was called 'soup'. In the evening, we got a piece of bread, some margarine, and tea. It was designed to kill a person within three months or so, the diet was so meager. If you didn't get a package from outside, you couldn't make it. My sister Mimi got my address and sent me packages. She saved my life. She sent two loaves of bread, some margarine, and some hot sausage, wool socks, stuff like that – useful things. So, I was able to share the contents with my friends and still had enough and I didn't lose much weight. In fact, I was quite strong. What kept me going was a firm belief that I'd survive because I had a mission to accomplish: I wanted to tell the story about the camps.

But meanwhile, the war had progressed, and the Germans need-ed workers in Germany. I was sent to a camp named Schwarzhei-de.[1] We left Auschwitz on a cattle train. There were German soldiers guarding the train, two soldiers per car. We were quite comfortable with only 40 people instead of 100, and we asked the soldiers to keep the door open so we could see outside for the first time. After six months, we saw people with baby carriages and

---

1. See **Schwarzheide** in Appendix.

farmers going to work. In other words, we saw a normal world outside, and we told the soldier, "You know where we were, you know, with the gas chambers," and he answers, "You have a wild imagination. I wouldn't believe it." They were so indoctrinated by the Nazi doctrine that nothing could shake them.

So, we went to Schwarzheide. There was a sadistic camp commander who forced us to work long hours without food. It was a very bad situation. If I had not received the packages, I wouldn't have survived it. There was a synthetic fuel factory that was bombed, and we had to fix it up, to straighten out the plant. Also, we dug up unexploded bombs. There was sandy ground and often a bomb would dig itself into the ground and didn't explode, so we had to dig them up. An expert would then explode them somewhere. We built a hoist out of wood. It was difficult work. Most of the SS guards were beasts.

In mid-April 1945, as the war drew to a close and Allied troops closed in on German forces from both east and west, a thousand prisoners at Schwarzheide were forced onto a death march back to Theresienstadt. Only 175 survived the march, including Alfred. Following two visits in April 1945, the International Red Cross took over the running of Theresienstadt on May 2, 1945. One week later, on May 9, 1945, Soviet forces liberated the ghetto. Alfred eventually made his way back to Prague and rejoined his sister, Mimi.

What happened to me? I stayed in Prague about a month, but Mimi urged me to leave because it may seem nice to me after the war, but in reality things were not good. She was right. So, I went to a place called Deggendorf[2] in the area from where it was possible to go to the United States. I worked for the joint distribution committee that facilitated the immigration of people.

I went to a man in the town of Deggendorf who was a bookbinder. I asked him to bind a book of 100 pages. Within a week he had the book done for me. I paid him $5. I put in the contents that I drew from day one to the last day in my three and a half years of concentration camps. Years later I sold the book to McGraw Hill.

The Book of Alfred Kantor was published by McGraw Hill in 1970. He is holding the original bound book in his portrait at the beginning of this chapter.

I had seen a lot of movies about the United States. I was impressed by that. Also, I thought there would be room for a commercial artist in the US.

---

2. See **Deggendorf displaced persons camp** in Appendix.

I was alive, and nobody was chasing me anymore.

Alfred came to the United States aboard a ship named the Marine Flasher. *He arrived here on March 14, 1947. He shared the voyage with his future wife, Inge, although they did not actually meet until he encountered her on the street in Manhattan, some time later. They married soon thereafter. Alfred was drafted into the U.S. Army. After discharge, he worked for many years as a commercial artist in New York City. He and Inge raised two children. They eventually moved to Yarmouth, Maine, to be close to their daughter. Alfred died on January 16, 2003.*

CHAPTER 8

Ingeborg Kantor

Ingeborg Kantor

May 29, 1924–September 2016
Berlin, Germany

M y name is Ingeborg Kantor. I was born in Berlin on May 29, 1924. My parents were Arthur and Erna Nattman. My mother's family was Jewish. I don't know much about my father except that he was a Protestant, not Jewish. He was tall and blonde – a real German type – and he was abusive to my mother. In 1929, when I was 5 years old, my father deserted us and left Germany for the United States. My mother and I remained behind.

We lived with my mother's parents, Marcus Israel and Selma Israel Sarah. Due to the circumstances in Germany at that time, we were very poor – we had nothing. The first thing Hitler and the Nazis did was take away my grandparents' social security pension. Hitler took that away from the old people, and so my mother had to work all the time for the family. But still, I was a very happy child growing up in Berlin.

We lived in a very nice neighborhood, in a nice apartment with two balconies – my grandfather raised peas and vegetables on one of them – but we had to rent out rooms because we couldn't pay the rent otherwise. We constantly had all kinds of people living there, so I never had my own room. My grandmother, my mother, and I had one room, and my grandfather had a little cubbyhole near the kitchen.

I started school in 1930, when I was 5½ years old. It was a public school. I was in a program for gifted children, which meant that I learned both English and French. I also studied typing and stenography, which many others did not.

There were other Jewish children in the school in the first years, perhaps five or six. The rest were mostly Protestant, with a few Catholic kids. There was no separation in school in those years. I was friends with Jews as well as non-Jews, and I would visit the homes of all my friends.

During these years our family members were conservative Jews in our observances. I would go to temple with my grandfather on Friday nights. Our rabbi was very outspoken – he was a very courageous man, and we all looked up to him. He said that we must keep our chins up and have hope, even as things turned bad for Jews. And then, in 1937, he left.

When Hitler and the Nazis first came to power in January 1933, nobody believed that they would last. The Nuremberg Laws[1] passed in 1934, which meant that no Jew could work in a Christian household. A Jewish doctor could only treat Jewish patients. Many doctors and lawyers lost their jobs.

But as a little child, these changes didn't immediately affect me – you know, children do not see these things right away. The grownups always shielded me from this. They didn't want me to know what was really going on.

I do remember an incident during these years, though. I came home from school to discover that one of our tenants, an elderly man, had been taken away and would not be returning. In his room the Nazis had closed up a closet with a flimsy lock. Curious as to what the closet contained, I broke the lock and looked in, finding nothing but some shirts and pants. It suddenly dawned on me that I had broken a Nazi law and was endangering my entire family. Incredibly nervous, I set out for Gestapo headquarters to confess my crime. But it seems that my being blond and blue-eyed served me well – the Gestapo officers patted me on the head and told me everything would be fine. I was quite relieved.

Things changed drastically for me in 1938. That is when I was thrown out of school. Up to then, there had been no change in the way I was treated. But one day the principal called my mother and said that he could not keep me in school any longer. By then, the other Jews in the school had already left the country, and I was the only Jewish child left in class. The principal was crying when he told my mother I had to be thrown out. I was 14 years old.

At some point during those years, due to having had a Lutheran father as well as blue eyes and blond hair, I had an opportunity

---

1. See **Nuremberg Laws** in the Appendix.

to be baptized. Though this would have meant I would not be deported to a concentration camp, I refused because my mother and my grandmother both looked very Jewish with dark hair and eyes. They would both have been deported, and my mother and I realized that in particular, my grandmother would not have survived the deportation. So, I chose not to be baptized.

I got a job as a waitress in a little Jewish cafe, and I worked there for a year from 1938 to 1939. It was run by a Jewish woman. All the Jewish guys in the area congregated there and they would talk about emigration and things like that. There was talk about going to China and going to South America, and I always listened, you know, but my family didn't go anywhere. It wasn't possible for us – we had no money. We couldn't afford a ticket to anywhere. Still, there was no feeling of danger. We all thought this is not going to last. There was danger, of course, and the grown-ups knew it, but in 1938 and 1939 I was only 14.

The storekeepers knew we were Jewish and that they might be in trouble if they helped us, but some were very decent, very decent. We were not allowed to have certain foods, as you probably know. We had ration cards, and the Jews didn't get certain things. As Jews, we were not allowed meat, butter, or milk. My grandfather had cancer and couldn't eat any dark bread, but the baker would somehow give him a little white bread. We were also given a little milk on the side, which nobody was supposed to see. I must say we had very good people helping us, some of them.

My favorite things to do growing up in Berlin were reading and going for walks with my grandfather or my girlfriends. There were very nice parks. Of course, after 1938, you couldn't sit on just any park bench, you could only sit on a yellow bench. After a while, even these benches disappeared. You couldn't sit anywhere.

You could hear Hitler's voice everywhere, coming from loudspeakers in the city and on the radio. He didn't say anything of substance, just hate, hate, hate. And then we had to give up our radio. Also, after 1938, we couldn't buy newspapers. We were totally isolated. No newspapers, no radio, no movies, no theater, no concerts.

After the cafe job, I became an apprentice in an office. I had learned a little bit of stenography and typing in school. So I applied and I got the job. I was 15.

Then, after the war started in September 1939, I was sent to work in a munitions factory in Berlin. That's where I stayed for about three years, until 1943. At first it was safe to go to and from work because we were not required to wear a yellow star until 1941. We were about 30 women, I think, in this one department of Siemens. We were all Jewish, and we were being paid for our work. In the beginning, we could even eat in the workers' canteen. I made a lot of friends. We even had a supervisor who was pretty decent.

At that time there was not much food, just enough turnips or potatoes, maybe, but there was no meat. We had ration cards, which had a big 'J' on them, and we were only allowed to shop between 4 and 5 in the afternoon, when most of the things were already gone. But fortunately, my grandfather had a friend who was a baker. Sometimes when we went there, he would pack up a big bundle for us. We had big stoves in every room which we heated with coal, but then we were not allowed coal anymore. Fortunately, my grandfather had a friend across the street who would come at night and bring us coal in the dark.

One day in October 1942, I came home from Siemens in the afternoon and my grandparents were gone. They had dragged my grandfather down the stairs from his bed. They were gone. I found out where they had been taken. They had nothing with them. I was able to see in the window in the building where they were being held. My grandfather couldn't come to the window. He was too sick. That was the last time I saw them.

These were difficult times for many reasons. It was a struggle to work – to stay in the cellar all night with the bombs coming down, and then go to work in the factory at 5:00 a.m. At night I would eat everything that my mother had made for the next day, and then

I would have nothing left to eat. I was always, always hungry. And of course, the bombs came down.

I continued to work at Siemens until the 27th of February in 1943. That was when there was a so-called Factory Action[2] where they wanted to make the city of Berlin clean of Jews. So, they came with trucks to every factory in Berlin on that day and picked up all the Jews. They came with guns. When we were getting into the truck, we wondered what was going on. Many Jews had already been picked up – it happened all the time. The trucks always came at night and picked people up, and the next day you didn't see them anymore. This was nothing new, we expected it. It happened all the time.

We were taken to a huge building on a street called Rosenstrasse. There were a few hundred people there already, all spouses of non-Jewish partners, or mixed, like me. We sat there for eight days. And then we were let go. It was the only time in history that Jews who were already in prison were let go. You see, there was a demonstration going on outside with at least 200 German women standing in front of the machine guns. They wanted their spouses back and their children back, and so the Nazis let us out. One of the women protesting was my aunt. She was not Jewish, but she was very brave. Years later they celebrated the women who demonstrated there. Books have been written about that – about the courage of these women and the Rosenstrasse Protest.[3] When I was let free, my mother was at home.

I then returned to the employment agency. They sent me to work at the railroad station. We had to clean the trains that came back with the soldiers. Where the train stands in the yard, it's very high. We had ladders and we had to wash the windows. They were

---

2. See **Factory Action** in Appendix.

3. See **Rosenstrasse Protest** in Appendix.

all Jewish girls working there, together with another group of us, all mixed Jewish/Aryan.

Usually when the train took off, the engineer would warn us that he was taking off so we could get off the ladder. But one day he didn't. The train took off when we were high on the ladder, and I flew all the way down to the ground. I still have an injury to my back from that. But we got up and worked again.

We worked there every day for three months. And every day when we came home, we were afraid the truck would be there to pick us up. One day, it was. I gave up. I said all right, we have to go. What could we do? We couldn't hide. I had nowhere to go, and I also knew that we were going to be sent to Theresienstadt.

Actually, we were happy to go because I thought we would see our grandparents there. We would be in the same place, and we would also be away from the bombs at night and from this terrible job. So, we went into a train, a regular passenger train. Fifty of us were in this transport. The next day we went to look for my grandparents. That is when I found out they had died very soon after they got there. My grandmother died three weeks after they got there and my grandfather after two weeks. That was such a shock for my mother.

In Terezin we saw a lot of old people, hungry people digging in the garbage. You saw a lot of carriages driven by people with corpses on them. You saw a lot of misery.

We were assigned certain jobs every day, then we would get food. We had to stand in line by the kitchens. The food was not enough. We had mostly soup, clear soup. And then we had maybe sometimes two potatoes and a little piece of horse meat, very tiny. The food wasn't bad, but it wasn't enough. Always I had great hunger.

In the camp we were pretty free. We could walk around. Of course, we had a curfew, I think 8 o'clock. But the camp was in itself a little town. You could easily walk from one end to the other in ten minutes.

We had a cafe house. Yes, we had concerts, we had cabarets there. You could sit there for a few hours and believe that you were somewhere else. Once, we had the Red Cross coming and everything was being made beautiful. The old people were sent away, and only the young stayed. We had dining halls being built. We had children playing in the street. People were allowed to swim in the river. It was being filmed.

> As noted elsewhere, this attempt to beautify There-
> sienstadt was a fraud being staged for the outside
> world.[4] Most of the participants were shipped off
> to Auschwitz and other concentration camps soon
> thereafter.

I was very lucky to receive packages from time to time. My uncle's wife – the one who demonstrated – sent us packages as much as she could. She didn't have much either. At one point I got encephalitis, and I was in quarantine in the hospital for four weeks. We were supposed to get more food, but the head nurse ate it all. It was terrible. I didn't get any medicine for my illness.

In August of 1944, I was chosen to be transported to a work camp at Zossen-Wulkow, outside of Berlin. I had been in the camp prison because I had used an extra ration card that someone had given me. Other girls had been chosen because they had stolen some margarine. One of the men told me he could prevent me from being transported to the work camp, but I didn't want to get out of it. The work camp was near Berlin, and I had thoughts – who knows, one might run away, right? One might do all kinds of things. I was able to say goodbye to my mother, who stayed in Terezin. So, I went into this transport, and I remember we had 20 girls waiting for the train. I made friends with one of them. We

---

4. See **Theresienstadt Red Cross deception** in Appendix.

were friends until recently, when she died. Her name was Toddie Schumann.

It was just normal going on a train ride. It was a nice trip. But then we came to the railroad station and there was a truck for us, and all the nice things ended immediately. We were being harassed and yelled at. We were taken on the truck to this work camp. There were already 200 Jewish boys, most of them half-Jews.

There was an overshadow of fear of the camp commandant, Franz Stuschka.[5] He was a demon. I mean evil, unbelievably evil. You never knew what he was up to. I can't explain what he did, the terrible things he did. He was a sadist. Whenever he could harm people, he would do so. He would hit people. He had this iron thing he would use to hit people with. Mostly the guys got hit. He sent many people to Auschwitz.

I remember there were pine trees in the camp, and we had to pick up pine needles in big sacks. There was no purpose, no purpose at all. And then we had to carry rocks. It was for nothing. We washed the guys' clothes, for instance, in ice cold water, and we didn't have any soap or anything, but we did that.

There was no heat in our barracks, and it was snowing in there through the windows. It was very cold. They would come into the barracks in the middle of night and get us all out to exercise in the woods – calisthenics in the middle of the night.

Once, I became sick. My throat was very bad, and I went to the doctor. I didn't have to work, and I stayed in the barracks. And then the doctor came in, picked me up out of the barracks, and said, "Come with me." I thought this would be my end. This was the worst moment there for me – I thought this was it. What would he do to me? He walked me to the woods, to where he had all the food, and he packed my arms full of pasta and sent me back

---

5. See **Stuschka, Franz** in Appendix.

to the camp. I couldn't believe this. I was so scared. He didn't do anything to me.

We stayed at this camp until we heard the Russians' machine guns in the distance. I think that was around the 9th of February 1945, I don't know exactly. In any event, we were marched back to the railroad station and put into cattle cars. And then we began a journey of nine days. They gave us salt pork and no water. I warned everybody not to eat this. This journey took nine days back to Terezin. The train stopped frequently because of bombs coming down. Things were very bad for our morale.

During the time I was away from Terezin, my mother was always an optimist – she thought that I would come back. When we got back to Theresienstadt, I saw her. And the strangest thing was that our relatives who stayed in Theresienstadt – the relatives of the people sent to Zossen-Wulkow – were not sent to Auschwitz.

We got a job in the kitchen and suddenly we got to eat right. One day, I was in the kitchen giving out food, and somebody comes in and tells us, "The Russians are here."

The Russians came with their tanks – it was the most wonderful sight for us. The Germans had all run away. There was not a German uniform in sight, only the Russians. They came with the Red Cross, with doctors, nurses, and food. There was typhus in the camp.[6] We also had gotten a lot of trainloads of survivors from Auschwitz. Hundreds of people came in this way. Those other prisoners marched back into Terezin, and they also came on trains that had a lot of dead people aboard. They were all starved and we had to go and feed them.

We were asked to stay a few months to help to feed the people there and to cook, and we did as we were told. I think we stayed from May to July, about two months. And then my mother and I made our way back to Berlin by truck and by train, where we found

---

6. See **deaths after liberation** in Appendix.

my uncle and my aunt. They were fine. They had been kicked out of their apartment a few times. They lost their piano – my uncle was a musician. When we got our apartment back, it was totally empty. The furniture was all gone.

When I went back to Berlin, I was very hostile. I worked for the American government for a while in an office, and then I worked for the German government to help the other victims. I worked in that office until it was said that whoever wanted to emigrate to America could apply, so we did. My mother and I were called to the consulate. We made our application before the end of 1946.

We came to America on a ship named the *Marine Flasher*. We arrived here on the 14th of March 1947. I met my future husband on the boat, but not formally – we only saw each other.

The ship landed in New York. All night long we stood on the railing and saw all the cars going by. It was a fantastic feeling! But we were also very apprehensive. We didn't know what to do in this country and we didn't know the language. It's not easy to come to a strange country, but we had to leave Germany. We couldn't stay there with all the hatred. The strange thing was that the Berliners were more hateful to us after the war than before or during it. I think it was because the Germans were very hungry after the war. You know, before the war they weren't hungry.

We were met by the JDC.[7] They took us to the Hotel Marseille at 103rd Street and Broadway. They gave us coupons for food. We walked on Broadway day and night and saw all these things that we had never seen before. We stayed there in this hotel for a while, then they put us into another hotel, and then we rented a room in a rooming house. My first job was at Sunshine Biscuits.

One day I just ran into my future husband walking on Broadway. I invited him for a cup of coffee. That's it! We got married on the 28th of July 1950. We raised two children, Jerry and Monica,

---

7. See **American Jewish Joint Distribution Committee (JDC)** in Appendix.

and later several grandchildren. We lived in New York for many years. Eventually, my husband and I moved to Maine to be near Monica, who was teaching music in Falmouth.

In order to avoid what she perceived as an embarrassing episode, and to simplify her story, Ingeborg Kantor retreated from admitting to a short-lived marriage prior to her marriage with Alfred Kantor. Her first marriage was to another Holocaust survivor, Kurt Tusk, the biological father of her son Jerry, whom Alfred Kantor 'half adopted' when Jerry was 13. Ingeborg Kantor died in 2016.

CHAPTER 9

Manfred Kelman

Manfred Kelman
October 20, 1928–February 7, 2004
Bremen, Germany

M y name is Manfred Kelman. I'm commonly referred to as Fred. I was born and raised in Bremen, Germany, a town of about 450,000 people in those days, right on the coast of northwest Germany. I was born of a Jewish father, who was born and raised in Ulanov in Poland. He emigrated from Poland to Austria, and then to Germany, where he met my mother. My mother was an Aryan Lutheran. However, once they married, she took the Jewish religion. As far as the Germans were concerned, I was a *mischling*, basically a mixture: I was half Jewish and half non-Jew.

Until 1933, when Hitler took over in Germany, there was very little problem. My father had his own tailoring business. He was an artisan. He sat at the table and did his sewing. He was a well-known tailor both in my hometown, and of course in Europe. In those days most people wore tailor-made clothes. From 1933, when Hitler took over, things of course became much worse because of his being Jewish.

I remember one time when we were standing on a road. We had been visiting some friends and we were trying to cross the road when a parade went by, and as it went by the German flag was being carried. I was a small child, probably 6 years old. We watched, and since my father did not take his hat off as the flag went by, a Nazi stepped out of the line and not only knocked his hat off but just about knocked him for a loop.

I remember *Kristallnacht*,[1] November 9-10, 1938. This is when the Nazis went after Jewish businesses. This was the first time that I saw the Gestapo. Two Gestapo men came to our apartment on the night of the 9th of November. My father was taken to prison at that time. My mother was told that he would have to give up his tailoring business. My dad was in the Gestapo prison for about three or four days, and he was then sent back to Poland to the

---

1. See **Kristallnacht** in the Appendix.

Warsaw Ghetto[2] from the latter part of November 1938 until about August of 1939. Since he was born and raised in Poland, there was very little he could do, I would assume, and the Germans were trying to take the majority of Jews and send them to the east. This was the beginning of their eastern evacuation.

My mother and I had to give up the apartment. She also had to give up the business, which she sold to a man who had worked for my father. My dad came back in August of 1939 from Poland, ostensibly to clean up his business affairs. Then, he and my mother went from embassy to embassy in Hamburg and in Bremen, my hometown, to see if they could get an exit visa from Germany into any country. Of course, on September 1, 1939, World War II started, and on September 2 my dad was taken again to the Gestapo prison in my hometown, at which time the Germans called my mother in and asked her to divorce my father. Although she had taken the Jewish religion, they did not consider her Jewish because by blood and by birth she was not Jewish. But my mother refused to divorce my father. He was sent from the Gestapo prison in my hometown to the Buchenwald[3] concentration camp. My dad died in Buchenwald in June of 1940. My mother and I were now completely alone. I was 11 years old.

My mother had to go back to work. I was still going to school. My mother, in order to make sure that I would not be considered Jewish, had me baptized Lutheran and it was backdated. But in either November or December 1942 my mother was called into the Gestapo office. She was told that because I had been a member of the Jewish Sports Club, I was declared Jewish. Thus, I had to wear the Star of David and I fell under what the Germans called the Nuremberg Laws. That meant that in the city of about 450,000 people, I could not use any public transportation. No buses, no

---

2. See **Warsaw Ghetto** in Appendix.

3. See **Buchenwald** in Appendix.

streetcars. How one gets along in that time without a streetcar, I don't know, especially in those days, during the war years when there were very few cars. I could not own a bicycle. One of my aunts gave me one of her bicycles, which was a lady's bicycle. And of course, it was 'lent' to me, if anybody would have asked.

I could not own a pet, I could not have a canary in my room. I could not use a German barber. I could not go to a German doctor. Of course, there were no Jewish doctors left in those days. Most of them had either emigrated or they had already received their orders to go to concentration camps.

This was very difficult. I was a young kid, 14 years old in those days. I was afraid to go on the streets with the Star of David. My mother used to take me for walks in the evening when it was dark, and people couldn't see me. I had played with the gentiles all my life, and this was now very difficult. The fact that I could not use a streetcar hurt because winter or summer, I had to bicycle from place to place. In addition to this, I was then told to get out of school. I completed seven and a half years of schooling, but I was never given the opportunity to finish school. This was difficult.

Not only were these restrictions physical, but they were mental. You cannot go out, you cannot meet your friends, you cannot go shopping. There was one hour a day where Jews that were still in my hometown could go shopping. The rest of the time you couldn't even go into a store. Among other things, as a Jew I could not go into a public air raid shelter, which gets a little hairy for a 14-year-old kid during an air raid. I remember many times sitting in the cellar of a two-and-a-half story building by myself during an air raid.

There were times during the apple season at the beginning of the war when you could get apples. I would stand in line, and just by the time I'd reach the front of the line, somebody would walk up and make the 'Jew boy' go to the end of the line. You were at the end of the line. You had to start all over again. By the time you get to the front of the line, the apples were gone. The front of the ration card had a big 'J' on it, standing for 'Jew'. By law, I was given an additional name and as a Jew my middle name became Israel. So, I became Manfred Israel Kelman.[4]

When I was bounced out of school, I had to get a job. I was given a job by people that knew my grandfather and I worked in a soda factory to cork soda bottles, which in those days was done by foot. I stood on one foot and the other one kicked the soda bottles into the cork. I had to wear long leather jackets because of the glass splinters and the bottles bursting. The jackets covered the Jewish star. So, if people came into the shop they didn't see it and did not have an opportunity to really make fun of me. The people that I worked with all knew that I was Jewish. I received very little harassment from those people. This went on until the latter part of 1944.

In the beginning of December 1944, I was still in my hometown, which to me was lucky. If the Germans would have taken me in, say, the beginning of 1943, and sent me to a concentration camp, I doubt very seriously that I could have survived. I was fairly skinny and very small built. I doubt very seriously that I would have been selected for the workforce in either Auschwitz or Treblinka.[5] I probably would have gone the other route – to the gas chamber. So, the fact that I was left alone until the latter part of the end of 1944 probably saved my life. Up to this day, I feel that somebody way up there kind of held his hand over my head and said, 'Let's keep this guy around for a while,' until December 1944.

Thus, I was called to the Jewish commander,[6] and given the names of several Jews. Most of us who were still in my hometown

---

4. See **Executive Order on the Law on the Alteration of Family and Personal Names** in Appendix.

5. See **Treblinka** in Appendix.

6. See **Judenraete** in Appendix..

were half-Jews like me – probably the last of the Jewish community. In the middle of the night, I had to warn these people that within three days we had to report to the railroad station to go by transport to Theresienstadt, the prison camp in Czechoslovakia. I still remember doing this in the middle of the night. I was 16 years old, driving through darkened streets on the bike because of the air raid problem, going all over town and warning people that they had to go on transport.

We met at the transport train in the evening at probably 8:00 or 9:00 p.m. My mother took me there. The guards at that time were police, not SS. We were put into cattle cars, 35 to 40 people per cattle car. I had work clothes on, and extra shoes, boots, that type of thing, and we left.

I remember my mother had always considered me a survivor. And I am a survivor. No matter how tough things get, I'd find a way. In addition to that, she also had the feeling that no matter what, I would come through it one way or the other. An uncle of mine went with us to the railroad station, although he got in trouble later on because he was supposedly a 'Jew lover'. He was not a Nazi party member and never had been. He was the type of guy that couldn't have cared less, really.

I remember saying goodbye. I remember being sad about it. My mother had tears in her eyes as any mother would, although she tried not to show it to me.

After the train left from Bremen, I met a man who was fifteen or 20 years older than me. We discussed whether it would be possible to escape. But we realized that if we did escape, our family, our mother, or grandparents – whomever we had at home – would probably have to suffer.[7] When we got to Hamburg there was an air raid. They had stopped the train at the freight yards, probably to change the engine, and there was an air raid. The police opened

---

7. See **Sippenhaft** in Appendix.

the cars and let us get underneath so that we wouldn't be hit by the splinters from the flak. At that time, I thought there was a chance to escape. But having already discussed it with this other gentleman, I thought that our families would suffer. So, we did not try to get away. Now, I did have another uncle in Hamburg. I could have gotten away – I could have gotten to him. He was very much an anti-Nazi. I'm sure he would have hidden me. Yet at the same time I felt that my mother would have suffered.

The next stop was Theresienstadt, an old garrison town in Czechoslovakia. I was given a bunk with this gentleman that I had met on the train who was from outside of my hometown. I think he had the bottom bunk. I had the top one. There were a couple of people in the middle. One of them was a camp policeman. Every day we had to report for our twelve-hour shift to a certain place where we were given duties, anything from sweeping the streets to working in the carpentry shop making wooden boxes. One day I volunteered to work in the blacksmith shop. I lasted about four hours. I then worked in the bakery for ten days.

I mentioned a camp policeman who was in one of the bunks below me. He had his 53rd birthday during this period when I was working in the bakery. To keep us from stealing, we received an extra quarter ration of bread per day while we were working there. So, on his birthday, I gave this man the extra quarter of my bread ration. And I saw a 53-year-old man cry. That's the memory I won't forget.

I was still in Theresienstadt on or about May 8, 1945, two days before the war was over in Czechoslovakia. That's when we were freed by the Russians. We could hear the artillery fire coming close. From what I can gather, a battalion of Russian troops was sent in to free us because they knew we were there. They turned us pretty much loose, whatever we wanted. Of course, most of us were interested in food, which the Russians provided, and provided plenty of. Probably too much food, because our system just was not used to what they were feeding us – the fat, the meat, the eggs, this type of thing. There was an epidemic of typhus and typhoid fever.

The Russians brought in a medical battalion with nurses and doctors. Prisoners were given stretchers, and with Russian soldiers or nurses were then sent throughout the camp to pick up those people that obviously were sick. They were then taken to a building that had been cleaned out completely and they were shaved of every hair that could be found, then washed, cleaned, and carried around by nurses because most of them couldn't walk. Then the whole camp was quarantined. During the worst days, we had a death rate of up to 300 per day of typhus and typhoid fever out of the roughly 30,000 prisoners that were still in camp at that time.

Sometime in July, I came home to my mother. We waited there until roughly June or July of 1946. I remember coming home one night – it was the last day of the month before the new ration card started, and there were three slices of bread left in the house for the evening meal. My mother said, "Why don't we go to the United States?" And I said, "Why not?" I didn't think she could really pull it off. She wrote a letter to an uncle and a nephew who had left Germany in 1936.

We then had an interview with an American consul. Neither my mother or I spoke a word of English, and I will never forget the day we came in. He was sitting in a room in a villa that had belonged to a Nazi and which the American government had taken over. We went in with the interpreter. I thought it was rather rude – my mother at that time was 50 years old, and we were standing in front of the desk like a bunch of school kids. This man was sitting behind his desk writing. I looked across and probably 20 or 30 feet away I saw some chairs against the wall. I went over and got a chair for my mother and told her to sit down, and she sat down. The minute she sat down he asked her some questions. The interview probably lasted three minutes, and we went back out to where the secretaries were. I was very chastised by my mother because I had gone over and gotten her the chair. "Why did you have to do that?"

And I said, "Well, if this idiot is that impolite that he can't ask a 50-year-old lady to sit down, I don't want anything to do with it." Within about five minutes, the secretary called us over and she said, right, here are the papers.

On August, 31, 1946, we landed in the United States. I spent 13 months as a civilian, working as a butcher. I had to learn the language. My mother worked as a cashier in a restaurant to learn it. After 13 months, I joined the Army. I went from a private in the 82nd Airborne Division to acting first sergeant, and then I went to officer candidates' school. I was commissioned in 1953 and spent 30 years as an officer.

Yes, I am a survivor.

Manfred Kelman joined the U.S. Army in 1947. His thirty-six military career included service in Korea and Vietnam, and various peacetime postings. While serving as a Lieutenant Colonel with the 1st Battalion (Airborne) of the 505th Parachute Infantry Regiment in Vietnam, he was awarded the Silver Star for his distinguished service and valor. He lived in Gardiner, Maine, until his death on February 7, 2004.

CHAPTER 10
Emil Landau

Emil Landau

November 9, 1925–August 23, 2007
Witten, Germany

My name is Emil Landau. Up until 1935, life in Witten was pleasant and peaceful. Our home consisted of two large adjoining apartments with a total of about ten rooms on the third floor of a building in the middle of the city, above a bakery and a tobacco shop. We had two maids, we owned a car, and we took nice vacations, including skiing holidays in the nearby mountains and weekend trips to the Baltic. In those years, my grandfather Karl lived with us, and the thing I remember most about him was that he taught my sister and me all of the English he had learned in the United States during a visit he and his brother had made there just before World War I.

While those around us in the community were aware that we were Jewish, we were very comfortable with and proud of our religion, as all of our family members had been before us. We were Germans first and foremost; our faith just happened to be Jewish. Our situation was probably quite typical of the approximately 600,000 Jews who lived in Germany at the time (less than one percent of the total population). This was the period of cultural and social 'enlightenment' in western Europe, following centuries of violent antisemitism, and in the late 1800s and early 1900s Germany was the most advanced of the European nations, including the acceptance and integration of its Jewish citizens.

My immediate family was only moderately active in religious life. Although we attended synagogue with some regularity, it was primarily on the holidays. I went mainly to please my parents. We observed the major religious holidays in our home, such as Yom Kippur and Hanukkah, but we did not keep a kosher home, and, of course, we did not wear any of the symbols of Orthodox Judaism – hats, long coats, and beards.

Adding to my parents' concerns at the time, I'm sure, was the growing impact on our lives of the extensive new and ominous legislation that was emanating from the Third Reich. Ever since Hitler's appointment as Chancellor[1] of Germany early in 1933, there had been a steadily increasing number of restrictions placed upon 'enemies of the state' – Socialists, Communists, Jews, Gypsies, people with disabilities – essentially anyone who was a non-Aryan, who was deficient in mind or body, or who was not a supporter of the Nazi regime.

In Hitler's first year alone, for example, laws had been written that established special courts to prosecute political enemies and prohibit Communists from taking seats in the new Reichstag.[2] All German labor unions had been dissolved and strikes of any kind had been strictly prohibited. An official boycott had been issued against Jewish professionals and businesses, and Jews had been banned from holding all professional civil service jobs. As the year went on, Jews had been banned from public schools and there had been overt efforts to eliminate them from all aspects of public and cultural life.[3]

As I approached my tenth birthday in 1935, and as I prepared to leave for a private boarding school called Herrlingen, the deluge of new legislation continued. Germany introduced universal military conscription, in direct violation of the Versailles Treaty.[4] Jews were forbidden to enter most restaurants, shops, and many public buildings. The Nuremberg Laws which were passed 'for the protection of German blood and honor' prohibited marriage and extramarital sexual relations between Jews and Germans, and stripped all Jews of German citizenship. It was at this time that signs appeared in the windows of the first-floor shops of our apart-

---

1. See **Chancellor** in Appendix.

2. See **Reichstag** in Appendix.

3. See, for example, **Nuremberg Laws** in Appendix.

4. See **Versailles Treaty** in Appendix.

ment building, reading 'Jews Not Allowed'. Many years later, I learned that during this period my mother's brother was arrested and jailed briefly for courting a gentile woman.

There was a tendency on the part of most of the Jewish people we knew to accept and rationalize what was happening to them. Somehow, they wanted to believe that the hardships were not being imposed to punish or control them, but rather to protect the country from 'Socialists, Communists, Gypsies, Misfits, and Avowed Enemies of the State'. I can remember clearly my father's non-Jewish friends saying to him that, "They don't mean this for you, it's for those people in the East." Moreover, the members of our immediate family drew strength from the assumption and the hope that because my father was one of the 10,000 Jews who had fought for Germany in World War I and because his brother had given his life for the Fatherland, we would somehow be granted special treatment.

In spite of such wishful thinking, I'm sure that Hitler's announced agenda and its growing effects upon our town had a strong influence on my parents' decision to send me away. It also stimulated what was to become a continuing effort on my father's part to find a way to get our family out of Germany, preferably to the United States – a preference that eventually gave way to his seeking asylum in any country outside of Europe that would let us in. Initially, my father believed that he had developed several promising contacts in New York who would vouch for us and help us secure visas. Unfortunately, all of these early efforts failed to materialize as our potential helpers chose not to get involved when actually asked for specific assistance.

In July 1938, 32 nations of the free world met at a conference in Évian,[5] France, to discuss the problem of racial, religious, and political refugees from continental Europe. The principal purpose

---

5. See **Évian Conference** in Appendix.

of the gathering was to consider helping Jewish refugees resist Nazi aggression and assist their resettlement in countries that were allowing permanent immigration. The conference had been conceived by President Roosevelt in response to pressure by influential American Jews. However, a poll of all U.S. citizens at the time indicated that 77% were opposed to American support. As a consequence, the conference was attended by neither U.S. Secretary of State Cordell Hull, nor by his undersecretary, Sumner Wells. After three weeks of deliberation, the conferees as a whole decided not to get involved.

During this period many additional laws and constraints were imposed from Berlin, indicating that Hitler was focusing more and more on getting all of the Jews out of Germany. We knew from his speeches and writings that he believed the Jews had betrayed the country in World War I, and he therefore wanted them gone before the next war began. All Jewish newspapers were banned. All Jewish organizations of a political nature were dissolved. All Jewish lawyers were forced to retire. All Jews were required to carry identification cards. All Jewish men had to add the middle-name 'Israel' to their official identifications, while all Jewish women were required to add the middle-name 'Sarah' to theirs. As far as the Nazis were concerned, I became Emil Israel Landau.

At the same time, it was decreed that all Jewish stores and businesses would be sold to Aryans. This required my father to 'sell' his clothing business for what turned out to be less than a nickel on the dollar. It was during this period that Jews were prohibited from owning or driving cars, which led to the confiscation of our family automobile. It was also during this period that Jews were forbidden to employ non-Jews, which forced us to discharge our maids, who over many years had practically become members of the family.

Most threatening of all, it was during this period that deportations of Jews out of Germany began. At first, this forced exodus was limited primarily to Polish Jews, but we feared that others would soon be included, as indeed was the case, starting about one year later. These actions caused my father to make a second serious attempt to arrange for our emigration to the United States. This time he went to Stuttgart and succeeded in getting the American consul to put our name on the waiting list for visas to America. Unfortunately, the U.S. immigration quotas for Germany were very limited, and we estimated that our assigned number 1508 would have no chance of being considered until 1943 and would clearly be much too late to do us any good.

The Nazis finally ordered my school, Herrlingen, to close in late 1938, an action that was accompanied with an offer from the school to transfer at least some of the students to an associated school in Scotland. After careful consideration, I rejected this offer to continue my education abroad because of my strong desire to remain with my family in Germany.

Toward the end of my stay at Herrlingen and my return home, the gradual buildup of prejudice, cruelty, and destruction that we had been witnessing since 1933 exploded on the night of my thirteenth birthday, November 9, 1938. It was nothing less than a brutal assault on Jews and all of their institutions throughout Germany, Austria, and parts of Czechoslovakia, carried out primarily by the SA,[6] members of the SS (*Schutzstaffel*),[7] and the Hitler Youth[8] organization.

This was *Kristallnacht* ('Night of Broken Glass'). It was the first overt, state-sponsored action of Nazi hatred and intention to annihilate all Jews. Over 100 Jews were killed outright, and more than 30,000 were injured, arrested, or sent to concentration camps. Jews were attacked by Nazis in their homes. Approximately

---

6. See **Sturmabteilung (SA)** in Appendix.

7. See **Schutzstaffel or SS** in Appendix.

8. See **Hitler Youth** in Appendix.

7,500 Jewish shops were looted and almost 1,000 synagogues were destroyed.

When I returned home from boarding school in January 1939, I found that the rest of the Landau family, my mother, sister, and grandfather, had been personally subjected to the harsh realities of *Kristallnacht*. Our home had been broken into, wrecked, and robbed. My father had been brutally beaten in the presence of my mother and sister, and imprisoned in a concentration camp. My sister, Helga, who witnessed all of the carnage, was deeply affected by the experience and carried the emotional scars with her for the rest of her life. My mother, on the other hand, seemed to cope with the situation rather well and carried very little of the experience with her into later life. In many respects she proved to be the strongest one in the family.

After about four weeks in captivity at the Oranienburg[9] camp near Berlin, my father had been released and had come back to our home in Witten, just before my return from Herrlingen. We never learned what had actually happened to him during his brief incarceration, but it was clear that he had been seriously hurt both emotionally and physically. He became very quiet and withdrawn. Shortly after this, he visited a hospital in nearby Cologne because of recurring headaches and dizziness, probably a consequence of his beatings and imprisonment. He returned home several days later with the diagnosis of a brain tumor.

By the end of 1941, the urgency to deport Jews had grown considerably as Hitler's continued conquest of Europe had brought more than ten million Jews under Nazi control. This caused the Nazis to begin moving Jews out of German cities and the other countries of Western Europe to camps and ghettos in the East. Each day, in fact, we witnessed the departure of more and more displaced people like ourselves to Czechoslovakia and Poland.

---

9. See **Oranienburg** in Appendix.

While we were only beginning to hear unsubstantiated rumors about the startup of death camps in the occupied countries, we had learned enough to make us very, very anxious.

It was against this background, therefore, that we breathed a sigh of relief when we learned that my mother, father, and sister were going to be sent to Theresienstadt, a concentration camp contained within a walled garrison built by Hapsburg Emperor Joseph II for about 7,000 Austrian cavalrymen, and that now served as a concentration camp. We were transported there on conventional third-class rail carriages. The camp's reputation initially was that it was not as bad as other camps. While we were being denied our freedom, Theresienstadt in the early years was probably the safest place in Europe for a Jewish family to be.

However, we were now exposed for the first time to a group of special prisoners, who in the larger camps and prisons were called kapos.[10] These men and women were given special privileges throughout the Nazi prison system in return for assisting the SS officers in their guard and disciplinary duties. They were selected from the ranks of the prisoners primarily on the basis of their size, their toughness, and their cruelty – characteristics they displayed regularly in most of the camps and ghettos throughout the Reich. We didn't see this kind of behavior very often at Theresienstadt, but it is fair to say that, as a group, the kapos were universally hated by the inmates of Nazi prisons and were the objects of manhunts and reprisal killings by survivors after the war.

By the end of 1943, conditions at Theresienstadt had begun to deteriorate rapidly. There was a huge influx of Jews into the camp from Holland, Denmark, Germany, and Czechoslovakia, as well as a number of non-Jews, most of whom were destined for transfer to the gas chambers of Poland. The Nazi strategy for dealing with the 'Jewish Problem' was no longer to humiliate, imprison, torture,

---

10. See **kapos** in Appendix.

and deport Jews, but to kill them all as soon as possible wherever they might be. This broadly announced policy was called the 'Final Solution', arrived at during the Wannsee Conference[11] in January 1942. It caused the population in Theresienstadt to increase rapidly to almost 60,000 prisoners. It was grossly overcrowded, food was in very short supply, and we were now surviving on a single daily serving of thin soup and one small ration of bread.

Old people were dying like flies. Sickness and disease were everywhere, and despite my occasional extra rations and favorable working conditions in the bakery, I contracted hepatitis which weakened me significantly.

Worst of all, we began hearing rumors that even those of us who had thought of ourselves as somewhat privileged prisoners were going to be sent to Auschwitz. Theresienstadt, which had served as the showplace for Nazi humanitarianism, had now apparently become just a way station en route to the killing centers. Suicides amongst the elderly increased dramatically, as the vulnerable took their own lives rather than having to leave the relative safety of Theresienstadt and face the probability of murder by starvation, hanging, firing squad, torture, or gas.

Auschwitz was an enormous complex located 37 miles west of Krakow, Poland. It was the largest of the Nazi concentration camps. The initial buildings had been converted from an old Polish army barracks in 1940 and had served only as a concentration camp for Russian and Polish soldiers and Jews. By 1944, however, the site had grown to include not only a prison, but a slave labor camp, a killing center, and literally dozens of smaller, outlying satellite camps as well. Birkenau was by far the largest camp within the Auschwitz complex and served as the killing center as well as the largest prison. At its peak, Auschwitz contained well over 200,000

---

11. See **Wannsee Conference and the Final Solution** in Appendix.

prisoners from all over Europe, and in the end accounted for the murder of more than 1.6 million people.

After a tortuous journey of several days in cattle cars, we were unloaded and divided into twos by gender. As the lines crept slowly forward, some prisoners wept, some prayed, and others tried to muster courage so as to appear strong and healthy. When I finally got near the head of the line, I saw a group of SS men who, with flashlights in hand, were scrutinizing the men, women, and children before them. One of the Nazi officers, who looked particularly impressive in his well-tailored black and gray uniform, was wearing what appeared to be a doctor's badge – a serpent wound around a sword. He was tall and slim with a dark complexion. His thick black hair was cut short, and he left no uncertainty that he was in charge. The whispers I heard told me that this was Dr. Josef Mengele,[12] who became known as 'The Angel of Death' because of his lethal experiments on human subjects.

The selection process itself seemed well rehearsed, as the kapos paraded a row of prisoners in front of the Doctor and responded to his quick decisions. It soon became apparent that those being selected to go to the left were the old people, small children, pregnant women, and anyone who appeared to have sickness or disease that would prevent them from working. All were destined for the gas chambers and were taken away directly. Those being chosen to go to the right were being saved for the work crews.

I was chosen to go to the right. Those of us who had survived the selection process were then led away past a long line of three-story brick buildings enclosed in a double-fenced area along which there were towers with searchlights spaced every few hundred feet. These towers were manned by Waffen-SS[13] solders. All of these guards held machine guns that were pointed down directly at us.

---

12. See **Mengele, Josef** in Appendix.

13. See **Waffen-SS** in Appendix.

We stopped in front of one of the largest buildings, where we were placed under the command of an SS sergeant who ordered us into a nearby cellblock. As we entered, we were made to strip and forced to walk through a brackish shower over shallow tubs that smelled of kerosene or naphtha, presumably to rid us of the lice which had infested many of the inmates. Next, we were rinsed off and scrubbed down with what appeared to be another disinfectant. After a final rinse with fresh water, we were led nude and dripping out into a kind of courtyard that had been made into a makeshift barbershop. It was full of inmates sitting on benches, where some eight to ten barbers, all of them prisoners, ordered us to sit, stand, and turn around as they shaved every hair from our bodies. The barbers themselves had crew cuts and wore clean, striped prison uniforms. Many of them were quite talkative and (like barbers everywhere) seemed intent on giving us the latest news, such as the origin of incoming prisoners, the types of work crews being selected, and the unwritten rules of survival. Some of them seemed to enjoy sharing with us the high odds of our never leaving Auschwitz alive.

Eventually it seemed to me that the only real hope for survival was to continue demonstrating my ability and my desire to work. Several days later, therefore, when another work detail of about 300 men was being assembled for transport to a smaller, satellite camp called Czechowitz, I decided to volunteer and do whatever I could to increase my odds of being selected. Accordingly, when we were again ordered to line up in a column five abreast for selection, I positioned myself between two of the oldest and weakest-looking prisoners I could find. The man I believed to be Dr. Josef Mengele motioned me to the right, presumably because I was younger and healthier than my immediate neighbors. I suppose I was also helped by the fact that, when asked about my skills, I was able to answer 'metal worker'. My use of High German also seemed to surprise him.

I have never completely rid myself of the guilt feelings associated with my survival at the probable sacrifice of my fellow inmates.

In Czechowitz, we were in two stables, in bunks, similar to Auschwitz. There were six sleeping next to each other and number seven slept across the feet of the others. There weren't enough bunks. By that time, lice and fleas and other diseases were much a part of your daily life. Food was, in the morning, what looked like coffee and a piece of bread, which was supposed to last all day. I was of the school that what I ate in the morning I didn't have to worry about – losing it, or having it stolen, or whatever. I ate it. There were others who had more strength of character and could keep that damn piece of bread all day and look at it and feel better by looking at it. I ate it.

We built those walls in the winter of 1944-45. As I understand it, this was the coldest period in that part of the world in history, or as long as anyone could remember. We had not enough to wear. You had to keep moving. It was so cold that, to build the walls, they had to put salt into the cement so that it would dry instead of freezing immediately. One of the things we did, at least the group I was in, whenever the guards were not watching closely, we didn't put any salt into the cement. We knew we were not going to be there, come summer. The war was moving in. You heard the rumors. The Russians were coming from one direction, the Allies were coming from the other direction. We thought, well, come the big thaw, this will all come tumbling down.

It is important for young people to know that, even as a prisoner in a concentration camp, you could make decisions every day of your life, affecting you and affecting others.

Then, in January of 1945, the orders came. The Russians were closing in – this was Silesia, the eastern part of Germany – the Allies were coming. All of the prisoners were moved to the center of Germany. We were marched to Gleiwitz, which was a railhead. We marched at night, three nights. I myself had my feet frozen on that march. We lost a lot of people. Then we got to Gleiwitz, and there were the trains. They were not cattle cars any longer – they were open railway cars that we had to go on to Buchenwald. Out of the 500 who left, I don't think 200 made it to Buchenwald, because we were on that train with no more food. The dead froze within hours – it was that cold on the train. We even made benches out of the dead. They didn't let us dump them over the side. My foot hurt already, and I was limping. When the hot water of the shower hit it, I looked down. It turned black. I had third-degree frostbite. I had gangrene. It hurt like hell.

I ended up in Buchenwald in what was known as the small revere, or the small medics' building, which had maybe 20 of us. Remember, there were over 100,000. When the chips were down, I've had quite often pretty good luck that somebody helped, now and later and before. It was run by a German political prisoner, a good kapo, and a Russian medic and a couple of helpers. They knew what to do with frostbite and gangrene, because I was not the only one. So, they peeled my foot down to the bone. You don't have any anesthetic. They peeled it down and you had to put your foot in a warm basin of sodium permanganate, a disinfectant. They said, 'We are not going to put it in there for you. It's going to be up to you. We know it is going to hurt.' It does, but I did it, because the alternative was not acceptable to me.

The camp was now overflowing with more than 75,000 prisoners. Many of them, like ourselves, had only recently come in from the East. Then, for no apparent reason, during the first week of April 1945 about 30,000 prisoners were quickly assembled and marched out of the camp, accompanied by the highest ranking and most elite of the SS guards. This abrupt depletion of the camp population and the departure of the elite guards were our first strong indications that the end of Buchenwald as we had known it was close at hand.

Several days later we were told that another large march out of the camp was being planned for the coming week. I knew that in my condition such an experience would be the end for me since

I would not be able to keep up and would probably be shot as a straggler. I decided to ignore the marching order and when it came, I would just try to make myself inconspicuous and remain in the camp. But this second march never materialized because on the very next day the prisoners staged an armed revolt and took over the camp.

The insurrection was led by Zionists[14] and members of the German underground, many of whom had been inmates at Buchenwald for over seven years and had been planning the takeover for many months. In subduing the Nazis, they used weapons that had been provided by the prisoners who were employed as slave laborers in the local munitions factory. The weapons had been gradually smuggled into Buchenwald in pieces and hidden away for later reassembly and use. I was too weak to participate in the uprising, but I was aware that there were a large number of the Nazis, mostly older officers, who remained in the camp and were killed by the inmates before they could be taken as prisoners of war by the Americans. There were also a few Nazis who had consistently treated the prisoners with kindness and respect, and some of them were singled out by prisoners and protected from the broad scale reprisals. A few days after the uprising, the 6th Armored Division of the U.S. 3rd Army under the leadership of General George Patton arrived at Buchenwald and officially liberated us. The date was April 11, 1945.

Generals Eisenhower and Patton visited the camp shortly afterward. General Eisenhower, in a letter he sent to General George C. Marshall on April 15, 1945, wrote:

'...[T]he most interesting – although horrible – sight that I encountered during the trip was a visit to a German internment camp near Gotha [part of the

---

14. See **Zionism** in Appendix.

*Buchenwald camp]. The things I saw beggar descrip-
tion. While I was touring the camp I encountered
three men who had been inmates and by one ruse or
another had made their escape. I interviewed them
through an interpreter. The visual evidence and the
verbal testimony of starvation, cruelty, and bestiality
were so overpowering as to leave me a bit sick. In one
room, where they were piled up 20 or 30 naked men,
killed by starvation, George Patton would not even
enter. He said he would get sick if he did so. I made
the visit deliberately, in order to be in position to give
firsthand evidence of these things if ever, in the future,
there develops a tendency to charge these allegations
merely to "propaganda"... If you could see your way
clear to do it, I think you should make a visit here at the
earliest possible moment, while we are still conducting
a general offensive.'*

The first special thing that happened to me was that I was moved
to what had been the German officers' quarters in Buchenwald,
where I was treated to a real bed with clean sheets. Another pleasant surprise that came my way quite soon after liberation was that
I was to be spared the experience of being declared a displaced person and either staying in the camp along with fellow prisoners and
many captured Nazis or being turned loose on my own. Instead,
I was visited by a delegation from the Swiss Army and Red Cross
who were inviting young survivors and orphans of the war to come
to Switzerland for rehabilitation.

All told, I remained in Buchenwald for almost two months after
liberation, waiting for my typhus and pleurisy to clear up suffi-
ciently so that I could travel. Our multinational group of young
patients finally arrived at the Marienspital (St. Mary's Hospital)
in Basel, Switzerland, where we found that we were going to be
attended by a very caring order of cloistered Catholic nuns.

Recognizing my Jewish heritage, the nuns also sought to express their appreciation by sending a rabbi to see me, an occasion that turned out to be less than rewarding for all concerned. The rabbi who answered their call was stiff and ill-at-ease. He was totally out of touch with the needs of those of us who had survived the war. He and I established no rapport as he began addressing me as his 'son'. I assured him that I was a son only to my father, Alex, who died in Theresienstadt in 1943. He then asked me to join him in prayer to the Lord, expressing thanks for my deliverance from danger and deprivation, whereupon I informed him that I was not a man of faith and, even if I were, I would not be asking for a blessing on anyone other than the thousands of others who had suffered and died, while I survived.

The nuns, on the other hand, brought me raspberries and continued looking for ways to express their thanks for my help as a translator. So, when two of the younger sisters asked me if there was anything more they could do for me, I again responded with my need for some underwear. The girls giggled at my request but made no specific response, which I assumed meant that they were shocked or embarrassed and would ignore what must have seemed to be a frivolous need on my part.

Three days later, however, much to my surprise, they reappeared with one of those perfectly wrapped Swiss gift boxes, containing a full set of undergarments. As I thanked them for their kindness, they said that as they were a cloistered order, I should thank Mother Superior for leaving the convent in order to buy the underwear. She had never left the convent except on the occasion of her mother's funeral. A random act of kindness – Liberation!

There are two things I remember today, and when I talk to students, that kept me alive. One of them was that when my mother and my sister and I were separated at Auschwitz, we said, "After this is over, we will meet in Witten." Whenever you were ready to let your guard down, you said, "Hey, I promised them I would be there!" The other thing was that my father always said, "Whatever happens, whatever they do to you, don't ever react or be what they want you to be, or what is a caricature they make you to be. Don't ever let them do that." So, when things got very tough, I always said, first, I was going to meet them, and then, that I had promised I would not give in under any circumstances.

Emil reunited with his mother and sister in Bremen, Germany, in 1946, and emigrated to the United States the same year. He became an expert in printing products and technologies, notably helping to pioneer the scanner. With his wife, Carolyn, he settled in Damariscotta, Maine, in 1991, where he dedicated his retirement years to charitable organizations and telling his story throughout Maine. At the time of his death, he was survived by his wife, Carolyn, and their son, Alex. His autobiography, Surviving the Third Reich, *was published in 2013. It is the source for the text excerpted above.*

CHAPTER 11

Kurt Messerschmidt

Kurt Messerschmidt

January 15, 1915–September 12, 2017
Berlin, Germany

My name is Kurt Messerschmidt. All I can say is that Berlin, in my early years, was a fantastic city. There were so many possibilities, Jewish and otherwise, which I haven't found in any other place. I had been involved in Jewish community life in Berlin all my life, as a teacher and a cantor, and as an employee of the *Jüdische Kultusgemeinde* (Jewish Cultural Community) in Berlin.

January 30, 1933, I can never forget – the day the Nazis came to power. The night before, I attended a concert or a theater performance in the *Jüdischer Kulturbund*,[1] which was the fine arts theater group which had been created so Jews would have their own place to enjoy the arts. I remember going by tramway (streetcar) to the theater. I was standing inside of it, when all of a sudden we were stopped. There were marching masses of people carrying torches. This was the great torch march of the Nazis celebrating their taking power. That's when my life took a complete turnabout.

In April of that same year, 1933, I finished my *Gymnasium* and would have been ready to enter the university. My goal was a university career, teaching, and research in languages, since I was such an outstanding student, but my family were not the richest people in the world. My director, who was also the school principal (a philosopher and educator of highest degree, of course a non-Nazi, and all my other teachers were not Nazis) proposed my name as a possible recipient for a complete scholarship from the German Student Affairs Association, *Deutsches Studentenwerk*. It was in March 1933. Hitler had come to power already. These men showed extreme courage to do this even for me and I will always be grateful for that. So, I had an interview with the high Nazi official with his swastika[2] symbol. Of course, nothing could come of it.

---

1. See **Jüdischer Kulturbund** in Appendix.

2. See **swastika** in Appendix.

That brings me to *Kristallnacht*,[3] November 9, 1938 – the so-called 'Crystal Night'. By this time, I was a teacher. That morning, I rode my bicycle through the city of Berlin and all I could see was broken glass. All the Jewish stores, large and small, were completely in ruins. I hadn't seen yet the synagogues. When I got to the school where I taught, some of the children had arrived and were sitting in their seats in tears. All I could do was try to calm them down a little bit. It was an unbelievable situation. Our own conference room had been ravaged. I had in a big closet about ten musical instruments which I owned and I had given to children, and I taught them every instrument we had. I had to fill the afternoons when they didn't have any place to go home to, so we put on concerts and all these things. All this was stolen.

Across from our school, there was a memorial to one of the blood martyrs of the early Nazi days, the 1920s. And this 9th of November was the anniversary of this man being killed. So, there was a guard in front of our school, and at the corner there was a large group of non-Jewish children armed with rocks just waiting for the children to come out. There was nothing that could be done, but the children had to get out. They had to try to somehow get home. I felt like Moses of old, leading the children of Israel through the Red Sea. I stood up to my full height and looked directly at those non-Jewish children. Somehow, I was convincing at that particular moment. They did not throw a stone. They let our children go by.

When I came to what had been my school before we were relocated, the synagogue in the Rykestrasse, I saw flames coming up. But lo and behold, the firemen were there with their hoses. They were hosing. So maybe there was a change of mind, maybe they wanted to not go too far. But I soon realized what they were doing. The synagogue was in the back yard. The front of the building

---

3. See **Kristallnacht** in Appendix.

was part of the whole block, and they had to protect the adjoining buildings from the fire spreading, to make sure the job was well done. After what I had seen that whole day, I didn't know how I could go on living. But you can. At that point, I think my will to live and to outlive everybody became so strong that it helped me later on.

I kept teaching in that school while the transports were going on. The numbers of children began to shrink. In June 1942 the whole Jewish school system the Nazis had helped create was closed down because now it was time to start with the 'Final Solution'. The moment this happened I knew my number was up – I was ready to be transported. Because I had a job with the Jewish community as a cantor and teacher, I was protected as long as possible. Now this was gone. Then, I was called up to the Jewish school administration. It was a lawyer. I remember him like today. He called me in and spoke to me, "Herr Messerschmidt, you know our work is finished and you know what that means for you." I said, "Yes, I'm fully aware of it." "But I have to make a proposition – we want to try somehow to continue the teaching process, and we have to think of ways to do this. We found a front, and we want you to be included in this plan."

Jewish apartments, after the inhabitants had been deported, were sealed. Nobody could enter until the Gestapo came later. The furniture was then removed and stored in various places. They needed people to do this. I was young, I was strong, I was athletic, so they thought of me as one, under the condition that I would try to teach underground. This sounded absolutely marvelous, because teaching and helping these youth was my life, unless I could emigrate.

The deportations of Jews from Berlin continued. In February 1943 the parents of Kurt's fiancée Sonja were deported. Soon thereafter, both Kurt and his fiancée were transported to Theresienstadt.

I had made up my mind, whenever entering a camp, that the thing the Nazis wanted us for – if for anything – would be work. As long as you were able to work, they would find a place for you. So I always volunteered for the hardest things there were. This wasn't too hard, but I had to work outside of the ghetto, digging trenches for the waterworks, and after work I was able to do a few other things.

Kurt and Sonja were married in Theresienstadt. Kurt was able to act as cantor at the celebration of Yom Kippur in the camp in mid-September 1944. But soon thereafter, both Kurt and his brother, and shortly thereafter, Sonja, were transported to Auschwitz.

We arrived in Auschwitz. The eternal standing in line begins now. We were standing in line in front of the first shower area. While we're standing in line, I notice that in front of us, ten people in front of me, there was all of a sudden a big stir, a big to-do among the people who were standing in line there, and of course I could not explain. It was getting a little dark. I could see, all of a sudden, what up to this point I had only smelled. The stench of burning flesh was unbearable – you couldn't miss it. It was unfortunately identifiable. As it got a little darker the eyes got into the act, because I could see huge, huge flames shoot up to heaven. Huge. I'd never seen anything like this. It was all obvious and all very clear to me.

We had been given the striped clothes and wooden shoes, no stockings. It shows again the diabolical intent – they didn't give us stockings, they gave us pieces of prayer shawls which we were forced to use instead of stockings. A prayer shawl is something very sacred to an observant Jew. To somebody who doesn't know anything about it, it wouldn't mean a thing. But they knew where to hurt you, not just physically. So you had to start fortifying yourself not against the physical things that might happen to you, but against the psychological. This was, I think, even more shocking than anything else. But we had to do it.

Then we stood in the line in this new outfit and everything, clean shaven. As we passed, there was a guy sitting next to a pail full of red paint, and he had a brush. Everybody who got through there was painted with a vertical line down his back. All of a sudden, I heard a noise when something else happened. There was somebody who was given a whole design – a whole fence was painted on him, down and horizontally and vertically, a whole gate – and a lot of screaming. I had no idea why. I soon found out.

Next morning, the daily order was standing in line, being counted over and over again, on the *Appellplatz*[4] they called it. A little further away from me there was, again, a big to-do. At this point, the SS wasn't there yet, it was the kapos by themselves – they got us ready for the final inspection by the SS who came a little later. While they were alone, this is what happened. The guy who got this gate painted on his back had been recognized by the painter as one who had acted as a traitor for the Nazis. He had sent the entire family of this man to Auschwitz. The man with the brush recognized this man as the one who did it all, and then there were a few more who recognized him. On that morning the justice of the camp prevailed. It was a jungle justice, of course. This man was, without using any weapons, trampled to death in five minutes or less. And you know, I agreed, as horrible as it was – I was the one who sang classical songs and enjoyed fine literature – but I had to agree. It's something I hoped I would perhaps later on overcome, and I did, but it took a long time. This was a totally new way of life, or, I'd say, of dying.

I stayed in Auschwitz maybe just one week. I was fortunate. Those who were not eligible for work somewhere else immediately would perish, there was no question of it, because Auschwitz was

---

4. See **appell; Appellplatz** in Appendix.

just an annihilation camp, a liquidation camp. That's what they called it proudly, that's all it was. But as long as you were able to work, and were lucky, of course, there might have been a chance.

The first night, the second night, we were in barracks. It was a completely flat cement floor. It was a very, very cold night, below freezing. There were big, wide openings instead of windows all around, so it was not possible for us *not* to see the flames shooting up, and it drove some of the people there absolutely crazy. They went crazy. All of a sudden, somebody screamed, animal-like sounds, and it was the end of that particular person. It was so cold. We had some cocoa mats or whatever on the cement, but we couldn't leave them there – we had to use those mats to block out the view of those flames, so we were lying on the bare floor. It would have been all right for many, but not for some older ones. But even for some younger ones it became impossible because the kapos went to work. They took pails of water – that night I'll never forget – and poured it on the cement. In the morning at least 40 were dead, frozen to the ground. They had many ways of doing those things. But things were happening which a pen would refuse to write down and I may leave some of it to your imagination, or to other people who might be able to talk about it. I prefer at this point not to.

The food we were given was all rotten. It was water with a piece of cabbage perhaps swimming here or there. This was actually water, maybe even dirty water, put it that way. Once in a while we got potatoes. But if there were on that cart with the potatoes any good potatoes, they had been taken by the kapos and those who were constantly working there. For us, all that was left were potatoes of a kind you never saw – they looked like prunes, shrunken black prunes. If you eat it, you die, no question. My brother and I made up our minds we are not going to eat. If we die, we'll die from hunger. That's what saved us – that we had that control over our bodies, that we would refuse to do this.

Then came the big decision day – who will live, who will die, who will stay, who will go to another camp. Both my brother and I were lucky to be selected to be shipped out. Where were we shipped? To a camp named Golleschau.[5] It was a quarry. We were actually shipped out for work, and we were selected because we looked as if we would be able to work. There was a truckload of perhaps 80 or 90 people. After we left Auschwitz, we stopped facing the front of this camp, Golleschau. On the other side, across the street, was another truck facing out, and we saw the people. They looked like the people you saw in those horrible pictures – no face left, deep holes where the eyes would be, dead already. And it was all clear. We might be, a week from that day, in one of those trucks which went back to the chimneys.

Knowing this full well, we went in this more than ever determined to outlive it. We were given a chance to pick our work and I picked the heaviest work, the work in the quarry. There was a cement factory, but I worked in the quarry. My brother was very, very fortunate. He is a carpenter, a very skilled one, and it so happened that on that particular day they needed a skilled carpenter. This was a factory that built, I don't know, beer kegs or bigger kegs of some sort, I'm not sure. He was needed, he was assigned to this, which was a miracle, and I went into the quarry. It had one advantage – I was in fresh air. Of course it was in the winter, and the winters in Upper Silesia are horrible, horrible, and our clothing was nothing. But somehow we managed. Frequently, I worked the night shift.

At one point, I had a kapo who was a criminal – we called them the professional criminals. They had a green triangle, which meant he probably had been in prison for murder or something like this, and he would have been sent to the Russian front. That, of course, he was deathly afraid of, so he was very happy to do his killing right here and then, and he was very, very good at it.

---

5. See **Golleschau** in Appendix.

When we marched, if anybody walked half a step out, he was shot on the spot. We marched to cabbage fields, and if in desperation somebody grabbed a cabbage, he was killed immediately. Dogs were not with the kapos, but they had all the weaponry that was needed.

No matter what my situation in life was, I always either sang or hummed or remembered some melodies or composed in my mind. Once a very strange thing happened. I had noticed that this kapo had an irritable flicker in his eyes at certain moments. There was some mental condition that was very obvious to me. Whenever this happened, I knew he was just waiting to shoot somebody. And I timed it right. It happened: I was humming and he came by somewhat closer. I forgot his name. I never knew his name, I believe. I hummed and he stopped and listened. He went off but he came back again, I hummed a little more. It was around midnight. There was just one little coal fire burning. He said, "Stop everybody, take five." He allowed everybody to gather around the fire. Now, that was wonderful. We didn't know why he did that. He said to me, "You, sing." And, well, I sang something.

I sang a Yiddish folk song which I had sung in Theresienstadt, and I didn't even know how right this choice was, how this would do something to him. It was the story of a blacksmith who is called to war, and he says goodbye to his wife and family. Each night, the wife prays with her son for the safe return of the husband from the front. There are two verses to it. In the last verse, the rabbi enters the house and tells the wife, Esther, be strong, be tomorrow morning at services, you have to say *Kaddish*,[6] the prayer for the dead – your husband is dead. Then it concludes with a very Jewish lesson because the *Kaddish* prayer only reaffirms your faith in God in the face of any adversity. Now that part, of course, didn't touch this one listener. But what moved him was the fact that somebody

---

6. See **Kaddish** in Appendix.

was called to the front. I had to sing this once more and then we went back to work. And then I found out from one other guy who happened to know him from before that he was afraid to be sent to the front.

Whenever I felt he hadn't done anything bad for a while, maybe the time is up for me to sing, I started humming. Sure enough, at least four times a week or so he called a big break for everybody in order to listen to me, and I didn't hold back. My voice was, of course, part of my professional equipment. But I thought only of the moment, and I had the marvelous feeling that I was doing, with my voice, something very unusual. I was actually saving lives. That gave me such a wonderful feeling that, to use a biblical comparison, I felt like young little David who played for King Saul when he was plagued by evil spirits. And that experience in Theresienstadt, when all of a sudden my world ended and all the faith should have stopped, it came back – it gave me strength in a different way.

Well, details of Golleschau are horrible. We were forced to witness hangings; the *Kommandant*[7] made it his business to describe in detail how the arms would get out of their joints and all of this, and forced us to suffer doubly. Then people who tried to escape were brought back by the dogs and were displayed, their bloody bodies. We had to witness it.

Both Kurt and his brother survived the horrific condi-
tions at Golleschau, but their ordeal was far from over.

In January 1945, the Russians finally were so close that we had to flee from our liberators. Horrible as it sounds, that's how horrible it was, because this was the beginning of the death marches. We were given one little piece of bread, a blanket, and set on a march. We marched and marched. Snow that high. Nobody

---

7. See **Kommandant** in Appendix.

plowed any road for us so people stumbled, and whoever stumbled and couldn't get up immediately was shot. This was the idea of the whole thing. The machine gun was in back, and it had to be pushed by some of our half-dead people. That's how it went for days. And food was of course exhausted very soon. We stopped in a place called Gleiwitz, where there was a machine factory. They pushed us in there. The machines were ice-cold. We couldn't lie down, so we stood and leaned on these ice-cold machine parts for the entire night. The next night we were driven out again.

The death march continued. Kapos with whips drove the prisoners. SS guards shot those who could go no further. In the brutal winter of January 1945, they were placed in open cattle cars in which even some of the guards wearing winter clothing froze to death, while Kurt and his brother, lightly clad, survived. They passed through several infamous concentration camps, including Oranienburg and Flossenbürg. They then arrived at a small camp adjacent to two airplane hangars.

I finished up the death march, coming to Traunstein, a city 20 miles away from the Austrian border approximately, near Salzburg. On the way through Traunstein I could sense that there was a change of attitude among the population, because they realized the end was here. Those who hadn't dared speak up until now all of a sudden dared do it openly. We had the SS guarding us with their guns, rifles, and everything. I still see as if today – it was the third floor in one house, a big window, wide open. This window was filled by one tremendous woman, and she had a huge loaf of bread in her arms. She cut large pieces and threw it down to us, who hadn't eaten in days, knowing full well of course that this was a very dangerous thing for her to do. The SS realized it, too. But somehow, the SS didn't do anything to her or to us. They fired wildly into the air. That's all they could do at this point because they felt that the mood of the people was beginning to swing the other way.

We went on and they forced us into a little pigsty, which means the entrance was only that high, meant for pigs only. At this point we were completely unable to do anything. We were hardly able to put one foot in front of the other; it was just the very last efforts on everybody's part. Talk, we couldn't – it would have been too much effort. They forced us into this pigsty. We saw them drive out the pigs, so all the mud was still in there. That's where they forced us in. Now I realized, this is it, this nobody can survive. At least I wouldn't be able to. Somehow I waited for it to get light and I watched the SS guard. He was in a half-crouched position so I could actually see his face. I heard American planes, Canadian planes, in the air. Our senses were, of course, very, very sharpened. When you are down to... when there is no flesh on your bones, your senses are heightened in an unbelievable manner, in an unbelievable way. We could distinguish who was going there. We heard tanks roll by, which meant that the big *autobahn*, the superhighway leading to Austria, went right by us – and those were definitely American tanks.

I tried, with my little physical and mental power, to put two and two together. Maybe that's what it is. I still haven't found out what prompted me to do what I did. But I knew it was the end for me, and I think I discovered a little uncertainty in the face of the SS man. I could have been wrong, but I think if I had stayed another hour there I would have simply collapsed and that would have been the end. So, with the last effort I could muster, I got up, forced my way through all the people who were lying there in some form or other, and I went by the SS guard, and just looked at him. I don't know what I said. I don't know whether I asked permission to go to the bathroom, because that wouldn't have made sense, because then I would have had to go around the corner to the other SS man. Somehow I just walked by him.

May 1st, 1945: Fresh snow on the ground, and my tracks were not covered. There was no need to. I had this uniform on, so I was easily identified – but I knew he would not shoot me. That's what they had done throughout the entire tour – constant shooting – but I knew he wouldn't shoot. At times I feel this may be my greatest moment of faith or whatever. I just knew. And he didn't, he didn't.

So I walked. It was at the edge of the forest, so I walked into the forest, and stayed overnight with a farmer. I never had a chance to meet the man again afterwards. He had very young SS men with him. They were so young, they were listening to the radio, I could hear, and they just heard that the German army in Italy is surrendering. They were crying – they wanted to go home to their mothers. But still that wouldn't have stopped them taking an easy way to kill somebody, to do something for the Führer. But there was a sergeant who was a little older, and I did the thing that saved me before: I started talking in German. It so happened that this sergeant was an educated man and he realized that I was somehow educated, and he listened to me. He took me aside, told them not to touch me, gave me his jacket, and intimated to the farmers that I would stay overnight. Of course, he couldn't tell them where, so I stayed in the stable with the cows. But it was very clean.

Then, the next day, I could go on, and I finally came to the place which they considered at that point to be the American military government, which was on top of a huge hill. There was an inn, and a church of course, and at the fence there was one little piece of paper: Eisenhower's proclamation of Germany's surrender.[8] This piece of paper was at that point America. Now the innkeeper and his wife took me in, and I stayed overnight.

The first or second night, I woke up in the middle of the night from horrible shooting, for about fifteen minutes. I couldn't ex-

---

8. See **Eisenhower's proclamation of German surrender** in Appendix.

plain it – I thought the war was over in this area; it was already May. But in the morning I found out. The 64 of my group were let go by the SS about two hours after I had left on my own. Townspeople told me later it was very moving, because they stayed together – they sang together, whatever, and started their march into their newly won freedom. They came in the middle of the night or about that time to a large farm across the road from where I was, and Ukrainian SS were in that farmer's home. All the Ukrainians had to see were the striped uniforms, and with their machine guns immediately mowed all of them down. Out of a total of 64, 62 went in that direction. Two of them went into another direction and had the same fate – they were also killed. And I survived. The whys, I asked myself. I never got an answer. The answer I had to give myself, because it meant I had to... it placed some obligation on me. And I have tried to fulfill it by exercising my profession.

Months later, in the chaos of post-war Germany, Kurt found a handwritten note Sonja had left weeks earlier on a bulletin board at a refugee center in Munich, a city neither had ever visited prior to the war. With the assistance of the American military, he secured transportation to find her and reunite. Kurt was an accomplished musician and singer. He had a successful career performing opera, lieder, *and religious pieces with a professional choir on Radio Munich. However, in 1950, he decided to emigrate with his family to the United States to escape the Nazi influence still prevalent in Germany. Kurt accepted a position as cantor of Temple Beth El in Portland, where he served for the next 34 years. Kurt was predeceased by Sonja in 2010, and by his brother, Henry Oertelt, in 2011. He died on September 12, 2017, at the age of 102½.*

CHAPTER 12

Sonja Messerschmidt

Sonja Messerschmidt

May 27,1925–October 25, 2010
Berlin, Germany

M y name is Sonja Messerschmidt, and my maiden name was Kolbelsky. I was born in Berlin, Germany, in 1925, and that is where I grew up. That's where I went to school, and where I lived until I was arrested and deported. I went to schools in the beginning, until 1935 or 1936. By then Jewish children were not allowed to attend publish German schools anymore, and I attended a Jewish parochial school. I was 10 or 11 at the time. It turned out to be just wonderful to be with all Jewish children, especially after the treatment we received during the last year or so in the public school.

The problem in the German schools wasn't so much the teachers. It was the hatred of the children. They teased us or told us that we really didn't belong, that we were only guests, so to speak. It was very hard for a child to understand, one who never lived anywhere else, that all of a sudden you didn't belong anymore. My parents didn't dare explain too much to me because they were afraid of what I might say, and that could endanger them.

I could see that my father was lost. He traveled a lot and he lost a lot of his business financially. Even then I could understand that we were under a great deal of trouble. The Christian friends I had withdrew, probably because their parents told them not to play with me anymore. That's why it was such a relief to be in a school with all Jewish children. All of a sudden you were so much a part of everything, and you could have friends again who would come to visit you and would ask you to come to their house. That didn't exist anymore with the other children.

My family was a very assimilated family, so we really did not observe. For holidays we would go to other relatives and spend holidays with them. I was introduced to a lot of Jewish customs in the school and loved them. I would seek out relatives or friends who were observant. You were always welcome in somebody else's home for holidays.

Before the outbreak of the war, there was still a possibility for children to leave in transports. I, for instance, was assigned to a transport to go to England. Some cousins of mine did go. I refused. I was an only child, and I just couldn't tear myself away. I stayed in Berlin until 1943 working at the Siemens cable plant.

It was a war effort. I didn't apply for it. We were just assigned. Yes, it was forced labor. As long as we had that work, we were protected. And at least we could go home to our apartment.

> *On several occasions, Sonja narrowly avoided arrest and deportation by the SS; on one occasion hiding under the bed to avoid discovery. She moved in with Kurt Messerschmidt (see previous chapter) and his brother Heinz. Kurt enjoyed some protection on account of his work, but that protection eventually ran out for all three of them.*

The influence of Kurt's boss with the Gestapo could not save us from deportation, but he arranged for me to be deported with Kurt and his brother Heinz, which got me to Theresienstadt. Otherwise, I would have gone straight to Auschwitz like everybody else. This was in June 1943.

Theresienstadt was dirty and terribly, terribly crowded. But it wasn't terrifying, at least not to me. We were immediately separated, men and women, as we arrived there. In time we were all put to work. I had a much easier job than I had while I was still in Germany. I worked in the sewing room of an orphanage since I knew how to sew. We repaired their clothes and repaired the linen and things like that. We did have freedom of movement; in the evening we could get together with friends who were living in different parts of the ghetto. Kurt and I could see each other in the evening. His brother and mother were there also.

Kurt and I got married in the ghetto. At age 19, I was still too young to get married without permission, so a Czechoslovakian Jewish man became my guardian. It was a religious ceremony, which we recognize to this day as our anniversary. But the German government would have never recognized a religious ceremony. You must have a civil ceremony as well. We had that two years later, after the war.

We remained in Theresienstadt until October 1944, but then Kurt and his brother were shipped out. Of course, they didn't tell us they were going to Auschwitz – we were told they were going to a work camp. Afterwards they told us that women could volunteer to go also to assist the men, so I volunteered. I remember the little food that they gave us for the journey. I didn't eat because I saved it. I wanted to give it to Kurt. When the train finally stopped, we were in Auschwitz-Birkenau, and we were told to get off the train and leave our baggage. Whatever we had on the train would be brought to us later on. And there were the SS with dogs. We were very bewildered. When we got out, we were told to separate – women and children should go to one side. We were separated old and young as well. I had been traveling with a young woman who had two small children; one was 3, and one was an infant. I had helped her with this, primarily with the 3-year-old, for most of the trip.

As we got off the train I held on to this child because she was busy with the baby. We were told that the women with children would not have to work; they would go into a much nicer place where they would be cared for. I had this little 3-year-old on my hand. But suddenly I decided to let go of him and to tell his mother, "You better take him." I don't know to this day what made me do it. Because they never asked you 'is this your child?' – they just assumed if you had a child holding your hand, it was yours. I let go and she took the child and that saved me, because the mother and child went straight to the gas chamber, which we didn't know at the time. We learned of that later. The promises of a much nicer place where they would be cared for' meant nothing, of course. That was just to keep everybody calm so nobody would get hysterical.

Then we were herded into barracks. There were ten or twelve people on a slab of wood in three layers where we had to lie down. You had to mold yourself to the one who was next to you, and some would lie this way and some the other way in order to fit on that slab. There were constant roll calls. The minute you sat down you were called to stand outside to be counted constantly. And there was screaming. You didn't even feel like a person in that place. We had no idea what they were trying to do with us. Every so often they pulled people out for no reason at all, and of course we never saw them again.

At some time later on, we were again put on a train. This time it was cattle cars, and we were taken out of Auschwitz into Freiberg, which is in Saxony. This was another camp, but it was just really a work unit. Our group was working on airplane wings, and I have always said that no plane ever took off that we worked on –we didn't know what we were doing, and we were doing a terrible job. It was such a last-minute war effort that I don't know whether they really thought this would ever work. But there we were guarded by SS. In the meantime, it was winter, and still I wore the same things that I was given in Auschwitz – just a dress and those wooden clogs. We had to march from the barracks to the factory through snow, and I don't know why I didn't get pneumonia. We were forever hungry because the food we got really consisted of watery soups and a little piece of bread, and in the morning some black water that was supposed to be coffee, and that was all.

In the winter of 1944-1945 I was back on German soil. We could hear the American planes go over in broad daylight towards the end. All the Germans who were guarding us would go for shelter and we had to stay. But this was music to us. There was no fear. We could have been killed by the bombs, but somehow that never entered our minds. We were just so delighted to know that to us it was help on the way, and we could also tell by little things. For instance, we had a German foreman when we first got there. I watched him eat his lunch, which always looked very delicious, especially to us.

He had salami and cheese and really nice-looking sandwiches. Well, towards the end there was no more salami. There was no more cheese, just a little jam on it. Little things like that. He didn't talk to us ever – I guess he was not allowed to – but he also didn't mistreat us in any way. He wasn't mean. He left that to the SS. We just went to work and starved.

Then one day we were again herded into cattle cars, and for days there was never any explanation. You don't know where you're going or why. For days we went without any food or water or anything. Sometimes the train would go very slowly and there were people outside in the road who tried to throw bread into the cars; the SS at that point let them. I don't know where we were at the time, whether it was in Austria or Germany. We ended up in the Mauthausen concentration camp. As we arrived there, we were really scared. But we saw a lot of people who told us that the SS had fled because the Americans were very close. The SS were not there anymore, so nobody should be afraid, nobody would be killed. When we arrived, we again were stripped and taken to a shower, which really was a shower – we were so full of lice. Then the next thing, I got to wear good clothes for the very first time. That was in the spring of 1945.

The Americans set up soup kitchens. That's the first thing they did. And with their kindness they killed a lot of people because we were not used to food, especially not rich food or a lot of it. Some people just ate and ate and died. Thankfully, hungry as I was, I wasn't capable of eating very much, so it helped me. They also opened the gates and told everybody to go out and steal whatever they could from the Germans or from the fields. So, people went out and dug up potatoes and cooked them over an open fire and that killed them too, just eating too much.

In the meantime, the camp was taken over by the Russians. The Americans retreated and the Russians took over this whole territory. The Russians were not much nicer to us than the Germans. To them, it didn't matter if you were Jewish or not Jewish. You were

German, and they hated us. They raped the women and beat up the men who were there.

Fortunately, some American forces were still in the area. At some point, a friend of mine came with an American officer in a jeep, and they came to my door and said for me to leave immediately, and to take as little as possible. I only had a little to take away. They put me into the jeep on the floor, covered me up with all kinds of blankets, and went back through the gate where there were Russians. The American officer spoke only English to the Russians – they didn't understand a word. He showed them some papers which they couldn't read, and the American held them upside down, but he looked very official, and he was in his uniform, so the Russians let him go. They just didn't know what to do with him. Then he hurried out and I was out of the camp. After we were out of Mauthausen, I could come out from under the blankets.

Sonja eventually made her way to Munich. She was suffering from tuberculosis.

We were under the protection of the Americans. We really were, for the first time, privileged. We were given an apartment of former Nazis, and we had more food stamps than the Germans did.

Sonja and Kurt were reunited and lived in Munich for a time. They confirmed their wedding vows in a civil ceremony In November 1945, and had their first child there. They moved to New York in 1950, concerned about the residual antisemitism they observed in post-war Germany.

We decided that we would never be happy raising our child in Germany – there was always the fear that, you know, anything could happen again there.

I have recurring nightmares. It is always the same. I'm always running and always trying to find a place to hide. Always, there's very little time and no way of preventing anything. But the thing that makes it so difficult is that I'm trying to protect my children, and this is what is strange because, at the time, I only had myself to worry about, no children.

The Messerschmidts came to New York and after a year moved to Portland, Maine. They raised two children and were both active in Jewish affairs in the community. Sonja Messerschmidt died in 2010, at the age of 85.

Chapter 13

Edith Pagelson

Edith Pagelson

September 20, 1926–October 7, 2023
Worms, Germany

M y name is Edith Pagelson. I was born and raised in the city of Worms, Germany. For the first eight years of my life (1926-1934) things were normal, just as you might imagine. We were a family of four. My sister, Suse, was four years younger than me. We lived in a nice apartment, and my sister and I slept together in one bedroom. My parents, Albert and Flora Herz, owned and operated a retail and wholesale hardware business. I helped out in the store after school and on weekends. My parents worked hard, and they made a good living. We were comfortable.

We were religious people with an active Jewish life. We attended *Shabbos* (Sabbath) services every Friday and Saturday. I belonged to the children's choir in the synagogue and enjoyed every minute of my social interactions there. Jewish and non-Jewish families lived in our neighborhood, and I attended the local public elementary school. I had lots of friends. They came to my house, I went to theirs. There was no distinction between Jew and non-Jew. On Sundays, as was the custom with many families in Germany, my parents opened our front door for visitors, much like the modern-day open house. Lively conversation and laughter filled the walls of our house. It was an open and welcoming home.

The city of Worms is located on the west bank of the Rhine River, and has had a rich history as a center for Judaism since the Middle Ages, when Worms was the home of the great Jewish scholar Rashi. The Jewish community was established in the late 10th century. The first synagogue was erected in 1034. The Jewish Cemetery in Worms dates to the 11th century, and it is believed to be the oldest in Europe.

In 1933, just a week after the Enabling Act[1] made Adolf Hitler the dictator of Germany, Hitler turned his attention to the driving force that had propelled him into politics in the first place, namely his hatred of the Jews. It began with a simple boycott of Jewish

1. See **Enabling Act** in Appendix.

businesses on April 1, 1933, and would end years later in one of the greatest tragedies in all of human history. My life began to feel different. The teachers put the Jewish students in the back of the class, gave us tardy notices even when we were on time (I was never late a day in my life), and generally harassed us. They looked for any reason to give a Jewish student bad marks. It became impossible to learn. This was my first experience with antisemitism, although 'antisemite' was not the word that was used. People said 'Nazi' or 'pro-Hitler.'

My social life also changed. My non-Jewish friends were no longer allowed to associate with me, and many of them joined the ranks of the Hitler Youth.

At home, I don't remember being fearful of impending change, although I do recall my parents whispering in the bedroom. I guess they were trying to protect us. I don't think anyone, including my parents, realized the potential repercussions of Hitler's power. They said, "After all, he's a small-town guy. What could he really do?" My parents thought that it would all blow over. Some Jews in Worms opted for emigration abroad, but my parents weren't among them. My mother's parents were still living, and she couldn't imagine leaving the country without them.

By the beginning of 1935, when I was nine years old, we were no longer allowed to attend public school. The Jewish school, the *Jüdische Volksschule*, was established in Worms, and all Jews attended. It was the best education a person could have. The school attracted young, passionate, smart teachers from the nearby seminary in Würzburg.

My parents wanted my younger sister Suse and me to become broadly educated, so that if and when we emigrated to another country, say America, Palestine or wherever, we could be safe. We would be prepared for anything that might come our way. In addition to Hebrew, Chumash,[2] Talmud,[3] and English, we were taught the basic subjects. This was the equivalent of a modern Jewish day school. I walked to and from school with groups of friends and enjoyed both my educational and social interactions. Retrospectively, I think my life was fairly typical for a normal 12-year-old child.

But over time, things began to get worse for the Jewish citizens of Worms. The Jewish school was denied tax exemption, mass arrests of Jews occurred, Jewish doctors lost their professional status, and Jewish lawyers were disbarred. Special identity cards were issued, all Jewish passports had to be stamped with a large red letter 'J' and, as a further measure, an ordinance was enacted which required all Jews to adopt 'Sarah' or 'Israel' as an additional name to clearly identify them as Jews.

Our family continued to live our lives the best we could in Worms while investigating the possibility of emigration. My father went to Stuttgart to apply for a visa and was told that he was number 49,000. Other Jewish families received their visas and were able to emigrate during the years 1935-1937, until November 10, 1938, when the orderly, voluntary process of emigration turned into a reign of terror. The end had come to the Jewish community of Worms, and my life was eternally altered.

November 10, 1938. I know it was a Thursday. I was 12 years old. My father returned home from the synagogue, just as he had done each day, to say the traditional *Kaddish* prayer for my grandparents, who had passed away earlier in the year. But that morning was different. As he walked through the door, he turned to me and said, "You don't have to go to school today. They burned the synagogue." This was the morning after *Kristallnacht*. And it was my first experience of actual terror, my first real blow. Somehow,

---

2. See **Chumash** in Appendix.

3. See **Talmud** in Appendix.

deep in the recesses of my soul, I grasped that life, as I knew it, was
going to change forever.

In that one night, November 9 to 10, 1,350 Jewish synagogues
were desecrated or burned to the ground; over 91 Jews were killed;
30,000 Jews were thrown into concentration camps; 7,000 Jewish
businesses were destroyed; and thousands of Jewish homes were
ransacked. This night became known as *Kristallnacht*, "the Night
of Broken Glass." It came to stand for the final shattering of Jewish
existence in Germany. To give you an idea of the extent of the
devastation, Germany did not produce plate glass at the time, and
it took every one of Belgium's plate glass firms six months to replace all the windows that were broken. To add insult to injury, the
Jewish community was collectively fined one billion reichsmarks
($400 million) to pay for the damages.

The synagogue was burned, community records seized, museum contents impounded, Jewish property and homes looted
and destroyed, and 87 male Jews from Worms were arrested and
incarcerated. My parents had to figure out their next step. What to
do? They knew other things would happen, but they just didn't
know what. The son of my mother's vegetable vendor mentioned
in passing one day, "Go away. Go away. You will all be imprisoned,
and everything will happen to you." He obviously shouldn't have
conveyed this to my mother, but he did. But how can you make
major decisions about where to go and what to do at a moment's
notice?

My father had to choose the lesser of two evils: one, to stay
put and run the risk of arrest, and be taken from his wife and
daughters, perhaps never to return; or two, flee, leaving them behind, and hide until it was safe to come back. He chose the latter,
and no sooner did he than we saw the hordes of paramilitary SA
Storm Troopers, clad in brown jackets and shirts with swastika
armbands, knee breeches, thick woolen socks, and combat boots
approaching our store. From our apartment behind the store, we
watched the destruction unfold. Our inventory of tools, which we

had been required to give to them, provided all they needed to make the place a shambles. Hearing the terrible noise and fearing for our lives, we hid in a room in the attic where my mother stored vegetables, jams, and fruits. We locked ourselves inside.

Then we heard footsteps come up the stairs that led from the store into our apartment. This was next on their list. They made a feast of damaging our whole apartment. My mother wanted to unlock the door and try to stop them. While her bravery was admirable, and I had seen her demonstrate this positive trait on more than one occasion, this wasn't the time to take such a risk. Somehow my sister and I convinced her to stay put behind the locked attic door. We heard the heavy footsteps of the SA soldiers' boots looking around the apartment, searching for the Jews who lived there, but they didn't discover our hiding place. After several hours, the noise subsided. We no longer heard footsteps.

It was a miracle. Perhaps they were impatient, wanting to leave quickly so they could cause more destruction elsewhere. Perhaps they figured we had already left. Who knows? That fateful day could have ended with our capture or worse, but instead, my mother, sister, and I were safe for the time being. Where was my father? Somewhere in the forest, cold, hungry, and fearful for us. After a while, my father returned to the apartment, but, unfortunately, a little too early. Moments later, two SA men burst through the door, pushed me aside, and arrested my father. No crime had been committed except he was Jewish. That's all.

So, there we were, Mother and Suse and I, just standing there in the wreckage of our home. Not a window left. Not a lock on the door. The furniture was smashed, upside down, and strewn all over the apartment and in the street. The trolley car that came down our street couldn't help but run over our bedding, and hundreds of feathers slowly drifted upward into the sky. I can still see the crooked keys on the busted cash registers. Utter devastation. We had no way to contact anyone. It was now just the three of us, bewildered and fearful of the unknown, a young woman not knowing whether she would ever see her husband again, and her two juvenile daughters not knowing if they would ever again see their father.

Somehow, we were able to board up the windows and clean up the entire store and apartment. I can't recall any friends or neighbors helping. Everyone must have had his or her own troubles and horrors. We had to clean up everything because 'we' had made the mess. If we didn't, we would be in violation of the legal code and subject to arrest. We did every detail, but I do remember thinking "where were all the people? In church praying?" Not helping us, that was for sure.

Every day, my mother went to the Gestapo (police) in an attempt to get my father freed from his jail cell. On November 12, he spent his 50th birthday in the city jail. How's that for a celebration? Then one day my mother went to see him, but his jail cell was empty. He had been sent to the Buchenwald concentration camp.

Suse cried all the time. Imagine a seven-year-old girl living in constant fear about what would happen next, seeing our belongings broken and thrown all over the street, living in an empty apartment, knowing that the Nazi soldiers might knock on the door at any moment. All of the sights and smells were overpowering. Suse just couldn't take it. She had a nervous breakdown. The butcher and the baker were our friends, and they gave us food when they could. I had to be strong, both physically and emotionally. Although I was only 12 years old, I was laden with the responsibilities of an adult. I grew up overnight.

Once again, my mother exhibited her bravery. She went to the Gestapo every single day, pleading with them to get my father out of Buchenwald. I think it was four to six weeks before he came home. I have no idea why he was let go, whether it was a result of my mother's persistence, or because he fought for Germany in

World War I and was awarded the Iron Cross[4], or perhaps yet another miracle. So many others died there. But when my father came home, I hardly recognized him – he had aged ten years. He came back a broken man, but never talked about it, at least not to me. He saw things. He knew the worst was yet to come, and he knew in his heart that he would never make it through. After *Kristallnacht*, Jews were banned from all economic life, and they were forbidden to attend public functions. They were denied welfare benefits, evicted from their homes, and permitted to live only in designated Jewish areas. All adult Jewish males were subject to labor conscription. Curfew was imposed. My grandparents died that year, I suspect of grief, pressure, and fear.

It was now time to make decisions for our own survival. My parents talked about the *Kindertransport*[5] [children's transport] as a way for my sister and me to get out of Germany. The *Kindertransport* was a series of rescue efforts that brought 10,000 Jewish children to Great Britain between 1938 and 1940. Spurred by British public opinion and the persistent efforts of refugee aid committees, British authorities agreed to permit an unspecified number of children under the age of 17 to enter Great Britain from Germany and German-annexed territories.

Private citizens or organizations had to guarantee to pay for each child's care, education, and eventual emigration to Britain. In return for this guarantee, the British government allowed un-accompanied refugee children to enter the country on temporary travel visas. It was understood at the time that, when the crisis was over, the children would return to their families. Parents or guardians could not accompany their children.

My sister was one of the fortunate few to be able to go on one of these transports. In July of 1939, at 8 years of age, Suse left our

---

4. See **Iron Cross** in Appendix.

5. See **Kindertransport** in Appendix.

home to travel to a non-Jewish foster family by the name of Perry, in Coventry, England, where she stayed for the remainder of the war. She didn't know the language. She didn't know the people. She didn't know the geography. I didn't know if I would ever see her again.

A similar but much less formal effort transported a small number, about 1,000 unaccompanied Jewish children, to the United States. My parents awaited the final papers for me to travel by ship to America where I would live with a family in Cincinnati, Ohio. My bags were packed. We were all sure I was going, but I never left. My father suspected that another family bribed someone to get their children out of Germany, and I lost my spot. No other opportunity presented itself, in large part due to the American government's shameful refugee policy.[6] And perhaps this was meant to be. For who knows what would have happened to my mother if we had not been together, physically and emotionally, for the remainder of the war?

***

In July of 1942, we got the word. My mother and I were being deported along with several hundred others. The scene was calm with no uproar or anything, because, like the others who remained, we knew it was coming. We were numb, and completely accustomed to people coming and going. It was just our time. We had to go and we hoped for the best. There really wasn't any other way to think about it. We were taken in trucks to the train station, but then we were loaded onto cattle cars. I won't ever forget that scene. No seats, no food, no sanitary facilities. Hundreds of women crammed in like sardines in a can. At least my mother and I were together.

---

6. See **Immigration policy of the United States** in Appendix.

We promised each other that we would always be. I was 17 years old, and my mother was 42.

After what seemed like a couple of days, the train stopped during the night. All the transports arrived at night. It made the arrival scene and first encounter that much more eerie and threatening. The door of the cattle car opened, and I knew just where I was. I saw the lights, the barbed wire, the SS guards with their dogs, machine guns, and rifles, the building towers with weapons menacingly aimed.

We had arrived at Auschwitz, the camp from which no one came back. It wasn't good, but we were among the lucky ones. We survived the trip. Too many others, in poor health when we left, had succumbed to the angel of death in the darkness of the cattle car.

We were ordered to get out of the cattle car and leave on the train whatever small luggage we had taken with us from Terezin. As we did, I heard someone call my name. I was so surprised and thought, who knew me in this place? It was my friend, Honza Popper, who had been transported to Birkenau a few months earlier! He had been assigned the work detail of meeting the trains. Coincidence, miracle, fate, whatever you want to call it, I was glad to see a familiar face. I figured if he was still alive, then we had a chance.

Leading us into the camp, whispering beyond the earshot of the SS, Honza gave us the rundown on everything we could expect. He didn't spare any of the details. He told us about the gas chambers, the tattooed numbers, the daily routine, and he shared his suggestions on how to survive. He told us about people killing themselves on the barbed wire fences surrounding the camp.

As Honza walked alongside us, he said, "Give me everything you can. I'll save it for you. Otherwise, they will take it." I gave him the one thing of value I still owned, my watch, and some miscellaneous clothes and other items. What happened to that watch? Honza traded it for food. Fortunately for us, one of his jobs was to load the food barrels on to carriages and schlep those carriages, as if he were a draft horse, from the "Gypsy" [Romani][7] camp to the other camps. From time to time, he was able to get us some bread or a little blood sausage to supplement our meager rations.

The Auschwitz complex was divided into three major camps: Auschwitz I, the main camp; Auschwitz II or Birkenau, established in 1941 as an extermination camp; and Auschwitz III, established in 1942 as an *Arbeitslager* or work camp. Each of these had several subcamps. Birkenau included a camp for new arrivals and those to be sent on to labor elsewhere, a Gypsy camp, a family camp, and a women's camp. Everyone from the Terezin transport was placed in the family camp. The barracks were empty when we arrived. All the prisoners had been taken somewhere, either to another camp or the crematorium. We didn't know. We didn't ask questions. Once again, women and men were placed in different barracks.

Thank goodness my mother and I could remain together in the female barracks. The interior of this barn-type building, partitioned into stalls, was originally designed to hold 52 horses. Now several hundred women lived in these barracks on two-tiered wooden bunks, with five women in a row on each tier. We selected the upper tier bunks to shield ourselves from crawling vermin and rats. A constant shortage of water for washing, and the lack of suitable sanitary facilities aggravated the risk for disease. A brick ledge ran through the middle of the barracks.

The next day we received our numbered tattoos. We stood in line with the other new transports, waiting for non-Jewish fellow inmates to inject an indelible identifying mark onto our forearms.

My mother's: A-2674.

My number: A-2676.

You'll note that these numbers are not consecutive. I let an elderly woman go ahead of me in line. My mother was so upset

---

7. See **Romani ("Gypsies") and the Holocaust** in the Appendix.

with me. She said, "That could have been our end. When they go by the numbers, we won't be together."

Getting the tattoo wasn't painful. It was really just a prick. Throughout the years, I have had many surgeons offer to remove the tattoo. I have always refused. For me, it is a badge of honor, of survival, and a visible reminder to the world of the atrocities that the Nazis committed. It is also one of the ways I can reinforce the vow that we must never forget.

Next came the red triangle fabric badge sewn on our garments. We already had the yellow star from Theresienstadt, and the red triangle was added to identify us as Jewish political prisoners. Other prisoners wore different colored triangles.[8] The red triangle was typically given to political prisoners: communists, trade unionists, libertarians, social democrats, Freemasons, anarchists. A black triangle was given to social misfits (drug addicts, the mentally retarded, and the Gypsies, although they later received a reddish-brown triangle); a green triangle to habitual criminals, including the kapos; a pink triangle to sexual offenders; a purple triangle to Jehovah's Witness Bible students; a blue triangle to foreign forced laborers or emigrants; and several other variations of the above.

We were permitted to remain in our own clothes from Terezin. For some reason, they didn't shave our heads. I don't really know why. The Hungarian women arriving the very next day had their heads shaved.[9] We looked at each other and felt fortunate. It was impossible to understand the Nazis' rationale. You certainly didn't ask!

Every day was the same routine. It would begin with the morning: *Appell* (roll call) in front of the barracks at 5:00 a.m., before the sun came up. SS women marched up and down with their

---

8. See **colored triangle patches** in Appendix.

9. See **head shaving of women prisoners** in Appendix.

menacing German shepherds. We stood in line, five in a row, until every inmate was accounted for. No prisoner was allowed to move or speak during roll call. Violators were beaten or killed. When the count was complete, we were given a cup of dark water (coffee) and a single slice of bread for breakfast, then taken to the public latrine. The latrine consisted of a long wooden bar (allowing for multiple prisoners to do their business simultaneously) positioned over a ditch. Can you picture the balancing act needed to go to the bathroom? I was absolutely petrified of falling into that deep, dark trench. One time and one time only, while my mother held on to me, I used this latrine. After that, I found a more private and safer place amid some trees.

We didn't drink the coffee; we used it to wash ourselves. Some people were marched to their workplaces, but we had no work of any kind. In their words, we were quarantined. In ours, we were just waiting for the Nazis' next move. None of the foreseeable options were particularly good ones, but at least two of them would keep us alive, either to a work detail or transport to another concentration camp.

The looming probability of the third option, the crematorium, pervaded our thoughts. Every day we watched the smoke wafting from the gas chambers fill the sky and smelled the overpowering stench of burning flesh.

Punishment occurred for the most mundane things and was entirely arbitrary. One day during daily inspection, my mother left her shoes in front of the lower bunk. She was forced to kneel on the cold, hard, uneven brick wall of the barracks for an entire day. Women were given "medication" to lower libido and disrupt the menstrual cycle so that they couldn't reproduce. This may have been saltpeter (potassium nitrate) or something else. In any case, it was really a blessing in disguise.

The German concentration camps depended upon the cooperation of inmates who supervised the prisoners. Known as kapos, these trustees carried out the will of the Nazi camp commandants and guards, and they were often as brutal as their SS counter-parts. Some of these kapos were Jewish, including the one who ran our section of the family camp, Mr. Fischer. I can still see him in front of me, hunchbacked and walking up and down the barracks, relentlessly swinging his bat. It was hard to believe that other Jews, our people, would be willing to inflict harsh treatment on fellow prisoners. Understanding that failure to perform their duties would have resulted in severe punishment or even death, it was still difficult to believe. Similarly, the *Blockälteste* and room supervisors wielded their power against their fellow prisoners. I wasn't used to this kind of behavior, and it made me angry. But my mother, always understanding and non-judgmental, told me, "There are people like this in the world, and you just have to learn how to cope with them. Forget about it and go on." She was so pragmatic. For me, it was another lesson in human character.

All the children 16 years or younger were placed in children's barracks, which were essentially holding tanks. Children were con-sidered too young to work, and unless they were selected for med-ical experiments by the camp medical staff, they were sent to their deaths. At one point, I was assigned to work in the youth program at the children's barracks. Caring for and playing with these inno-cent children, but knowing that they didn't have a chance, was the ultimate Nazi cruelty.

Days ran into each other, but somehow we kept our sanity. My mother held me up, and I did the same for her. We were togeth-er. That was the important thing. There was no point crying or wishing circumstances could be different. They weren't. We were in a Nazi concentration camp without a foreseeable way out. You couldn't complain, you couldn't talk back, and you did what you were told. The squalid conditions were a fact. During the night, inmates died from disease and starvation, and when you woke, either you saw them next to you on the bunks, or their dead bodies piled up next to the latrine where we began each day. After a while, you became desensitized and thought, *At least it wasn't me.* Each day's selection decided your destiny. Thousands were sent to the gas chambers.

Rudolf Höss,[10] the first commandant of the Auschwitz concentration camp, was responsible for putting the sign *Arbeit Macht Frei* ["Work Sets You Free"] over the gate. By his own admission in his autobiography, written while imprisoned and waiting for his execution, Höss explained what that sign was intended to mean: that work could liberate one in the spiritual sense, not that a prisoner literally had a chance of being released if they worked. In our minds, work was a salvation. It meant we could live another day. With each new day came additional hope that someday, some way, somehow, we could survive this hell.

Part of the routine at Auschwitz-Birkenau was selection: selection for work or selection for death, to live another day or be sent to the crematorium. While my mother and I remained in the Birkenau family camp, some of the inmates were called for selection based on their date of birth. This happened to me – the arbitrary age cutoff did not include my mother. I had to report for selection. I was without her. For the first time since we left our home I was without my mother, my buddy, by my side.

A man I believe to have been Dr. Josef Mengele, whose reputation preceded him, was in charge. Known as "the Angel of Death" or "the White Angel" for his coldly cruel demeanor, he was very tall, slightly built, not a hair out of place, and extremely handsome. I was directed to march, naked, in front of Mengele, while he stood there in his polished black boots, neatly pressed green tunic, and thumb resting on his pistol belt staring at his prey with deadpan piercing eyes. He was the master of my direction and fate. Life to the right, death to the left.

I was short, scrawny, and by all appearances not capable of working. Therefore, being selected to go right that day was indeed

---

10. See **Höss, Rudolf** in Appendix.

another miracle. I had a momentary sense of relief until it hit me – my mother was back in the barracks. We would no longer be together. More than likely, she would be sent to the crematorium. Without any further thought, I, a little, bony, malnourished girl, said to Dr. Josef Mengele, "I have a mother. She is strong. She can also work." He responded, "Bring her here."

I ran back to the barracks and couldn't believe that fate would allow us to remain as one, united in our fight to stay alive. My mother wasn't convinced that she should come, but after what must have been just a few minutes of our talking it through and determining that we would either live or die together, she decided to walk back with me to stand before Mengele and go through his selection process.

It has been reported that 400,000 souls, including babies, small children, young girls, mothers, fathers, and grandparents, were casually waved to the left-hand side by the flick of the white glove of 32-year-old Dr. Josef Mengele. We went to the right and stayed alive. The people left behind were all gassed.

Following their selection in July of 1944, Edith and her mother were sent as slave labor to a number of labor camps in Poland, including Stutthof (July 1944), and others near the Russian front. In January of 1945, their Nazi guards fled and Russian troops advanced westward. Edith and her mother eventually returned to Duisburg where they had relatives before the war. The mayor informed them that of 809 Jews living in the area before the war, only six had survived. In 1947, Edith and her mother came to New York, where they were reunited with Edith's sister, Suse. They lived in Brooklyn for many years and Edith married. Edith's first husband, also a Holocaust survivor, died in 1973. She remarried. After her second husband died in

2005, she moved to Falmouth to be near her daughter, Ruth, and remained there until her death in 2023.

CHAPTER 14

Charles Rotmil

Charles Rotmil

Born October 29, 1932
Strasbourg, Alsace-Lorraine, France

My name is Charles Rotmil. I was born in Strasbourg, a city on the border between France and Germany. It was French when I was born there, but it became German after the Nazis invaded France in 1940. Now it is French again. My parents were Adolph and Dora, and I was one of three children. My brother, Bernard, and my sister Henriette, were both older than me. My father was an art dealer who negotiated the sale of paintings and other valuable art objects. Our family was Jewish.

I was born in October of 1932. Hitler came into power three months later, in January of 1933. During my childhood, the Nazis would fill gymnasiums with supporters. The crowds went crazy, just cheering. The Jews were always scapegoated. We became a target, and it got worse and worse. Joseph Goebbels was the Nazi's propaganda minister. He often said, "a lie told a thousand times becomes the truth. Make the lie big enough, and they'll believe you."

My family was living in Vienna, Austria, prior to the day in March 1938 when Hitler came to the city. The Germans had just taken over the country. On that day he came in a parade. My sister and I went to see him. She was curious, and we saw him come by in a Mercedes-Benz. Everybody acclaimed him. They absolutely adored him. Then, in November of that year, we were in Vienna during *Kristallnacht*. The Nazis smashed and burned Jewish shops and temples, not just in Vienna, but in Berlin and other cities as well. They set fire to synagogues, broke the windows of Jewish shops, and arrested many Jews, including my father.

After my father was released, the family moved to Belgium, which he thought would be safer. But then in May of 1940 the Nazis invaded Belgium, Holland, and France, and we had to flee. We joined the refugees on the road walking from Belgium into

France, trying to get away from the German army. There were mass executions of civilians while everyone was fleeing.[1].

We joined the throng of people, carrying our suitcases, trying to escape. While we were on the road, the Germans attacked us with their *Stuka* airplanes, which were equipped with a siren that made a terrifying noise as they dove toward us. They would come down low above the road and shoot at us. At the last minute we would run to the side of the road to avoid the bullets, and those who didn't were killed. One time, we were walking and there was a couple riding in a cart with a horse. They stayed on the road, and they were killed. The horse was killed also. My father said, "I can't carry these suitcases anymore." He left us to find a wheelbarrow, but he didn't come back. We didn't know what to do.

So, my mother, brother, sister, and I moved to a little town, a village. We slept in a barn on top of the hay. In the early morning, my sister woke me up and said, "Come on, we're going to get a train." We walked down the hill and got on board. It wasn't like you had to pay your ticket, they were loading everybody up. Once the train was moving, I played in the corridor while everybody was sleeping. All of a sudden, I was lifted off the floor. I was flying across the length of the car, and I could see the floorboards come apart... and then I was unconscious. What happened is that the train crashed into another car that had been left on the track.[2] When I woke up, I jumped off the train on the side of a hill and there were bodies scattered all around. I found my mother, who was badly hurt, on a stretcher, and then I found my sister. She was injured, and her face was crushed to the point that I hardly recognized her. I remember that it was the Red Cross that came to our rescue. My mother and sister died from their injuries, and

---

1. See **Vinkt Massacre** in Appendix.

2. See **Morgny-la-Pommeraye train disaster** in Appendix.

my brother's legs were injured and twisted when he was thrown off the train.

At that point, a nurse from the Red Cross picked me up and took me to a waiting train to take us to a hospital in Rouen. Eventually my brother and I were returned to Brussels, Belgium, which was now occupied by the Germans. The Red Cross found my father in Brussels, and we moved in with him. We were in danger now because the Germans were rounding up the Jews of Belgium and France and sending them to concentration camps. One day my father came home with the Jewish star that we were supposed to put on our clothes. My father decided that we weren't going to do that, and I watched him burn the stars in an ashtray. Then there was a Nazi edict in Belgium that said Jews were no longer allowed to go to public school. So we couldn't go to school. If you did you would get arrested.

At one point, my father moved us to a room on the top floor of a house. One morning I was in bed at dawn when suddenly there was a man standing over me with a Luger pistol to my head. It was the Gestapo, and he's yelling at me, "*Aufstehen!*" – stand up. I heard slamming of doors. We went downstairs. I was shivering. I looked around me and saw standing there all of the people who I thought were part of the underground. They had been betrayed. A man saw me shivering and took his jacket off, putting it around my shoulders.

Then we were called in one by one and interrogated. My turn came, and they asked me, "Are you a Jew?" I couldn't talk, I was completely mute. Luckily, they had enough of me, and told me to get out. I ran upstairs. My brother had been interrogated in the basement and they let him go, too. We looked out the window and saw other people were being put on a truck. My brother said they're probably going to be interrogated and executed.

My father was arrested and taken to a prison in the town of Mechelen[3] just outside of Brussels. Not that long ago I wrote to the museum there asking for information about my father. They sent me a photograph of my father taken as a prisoner, his mugshot. You can see the face of despair. He knew he was doomed. I now have his passport. This had been put into a file in Belgium at the city hall and kept there all these years. I also found the Gestapo record of my father, and if you look at it, on the left-hand corner there is the number 77921. That means that he was on train 21 from Belgium. His prisoner number was 779. Years later I found the record that shows that on July 1, 1943, 1087 people from that train were gassed upon arrival at Auschwitz. They went from the train right into the gas chamber. Only 40 survived, but my father was not one of the lucky ones. Two hundred children on that train were gassed upon arrival at the camp.

After my father was arrested, my brother and I had to find a hiding place. We didn't know what to do. A neighbor told us that we had to hide. My brother said, "Sit here and wait for me. I'm going to find something." He went to a church for help, but the priest said, "I can't help you. I'm not equipped. I can't hide anybody in this church. But I know somebody, a monk in the abbey in the town of Louvain who might help." My brother took a train to Louvain. It was only about 30 miles away. He went to the monastery, and there he met Father Bruno Reynders[4] ('Père Bruno') who said he could help.

A short time later, I was sitting outside on the stoop, and there stood this monk, wearing a robe and sandals. "Are you little Charles?" he asked. When I said yes, he replied, *"Prends ma main et ne dis pas un mot"* – take my hand and don't say a word – like an angel rescuing me from the fire. I put on my best Sunday suit. I had

---

3. See **Mechelen assembly camp** in Appendix.

4. See **Reynders, Father Bruno** in Appendix.

no other possessions. Then I took his hand, and we walked to the train station. We got on board and went to Mont César Abbey in Louvain, where my brother had remained. But it wasn't safe to stay there, so Père Bruno found us hiding places. My brother was sent to a farm. To hide me, he went to a man named André Luyckx, who was a a an engineer and a professor of engineering at the University of Louvain. Père Bruno told him, "I have a child who's being persecuted. Can you take him?" Mr. Luyckx said, "I have to ask my wife." She came over and heard the story, and said, "When are you bringing him?" They had four children of their own. This was very courageous and dangerous for the entire Luyckx family – it was forbidden to shelter Jews. If they were caught the whole family could be deported to a concentration camp.

I moved in with the Luyckx family, and I became an 'instant Catholic'. I attended Catholic school, and I learned to pray. You had to pray at every class. One time, I was in the back of the class actually praying. I was praying for my mother, my father. I was praying for my brother, my sister. When I opened my eyes, the nun was on the other side of the classroom with all the kids lined up. She was waiting for me to stop praying. Then she pointed to me and said to all these kids, "That is how I want you to pray." I became a model Catholic, and an acolyte.

I lived with the Luyckx family in Louvain for many months, and by this time the Americans and the English were beginning to get involved in the war. Among many other things, they were bombing cities. One Allied bombardment of Louvain in May of 1944 pulverized the city, but we were in the basement of the college, so we were protected.

We were liberated by the Allies in September of 1944. The war was still being fought out in other places. First it was the British and the Canadian soldiers who arrived. It was not until a couple of days later that we saw the Americans. After the liberation, I left the Luyckx family and moved to a group home for other orphans. I'd never seen anything like it. You lined up for a meal and you were given a mound of mashed potatoes and large quantities of other food. We hadn't seen food like that throughout the war. My brother and I stayed in the group home for almost two years.

There was a German-language Jewish newspaper called *Aufbau* at this time. In the paper, there was a column connecting survivors with people living in the United States. That is how my aunt and uncle found me. They lived in Peekskill, New York. My brother left first for the United States on a Liberty ship. Finally, in December of 1946, I sailed aboard the ocean liner *Ile de France* to New York to live with my aunt and uncle, who drove me to their home in Peekskill.

Years later I went back to visit the Luyckx family. I am still in touch with some of the Luyckx children to this day. The Luyckx parents died in 1999. I also visited Père Bruno several times until his death in 1979. He was heavily decorated, but one of the medals that he had was for saving me, given to him by Israel's *Yad Vashem* to the just. He's called one of 'the Righteous Among the Nations.'

After the war, Charles emigrated to the United States, initially to Peekskill, New York, to live with his Uncle Herman and Aunt Regina. He became a commercial photographer and painter. He later came to Maine, where he still lives. He has four children and remains engaged and active, making art and speaking to school groups about his experiences during the Holocaust

Yad Vashem is Israel's official memorial to victims of the Holocaust, and the repository of a tremendous archive of photographs and objects documenting the Shoah. It is located in Jerusalem. Among its goals is to honor non-Jews who risked their lives to aid Jews during the Holocaust, designating them as 'Righteous Among the Nations'. More than 27,921 individuals have been recognized as such, including Père Bruno.

CHAPTER 15

The Singal Family

Malka Muz Singal

April 12, 1909–April 20, 1999
Lishnivka, Volyn Province, Ukraine

Judith C. (Singal) Catz
April 12, 1938–April 2, 2004
Manyewicz, Volyn Province, Ukraine

George Singal

Born October 27, 1945
Florence, Italy

GEORGE: I am a child of the Holocaust. I was conceived in February 1945 in territory only recently recaptured from the Germans. I escaped within my mother's womb when she made her way across the Alps to a displaced persons camp in Italy, where I was born in October 1945.

My mother, Malka Muz Singal, was born on April 12, 1909, in the region called Volyn in Ukraine. Her parents were Hersh Muz and Udel Lorber Muz. They were Jewish. By 1938, when my sister Judith was born, Malka and my father Zvi Singal lived in a small community in what was then eastern Poland. When the Soviet Union and Germany divided Poland in 1939, my family was fortunate to be in the eastern part, which was occupied by the Soviets. But in 1941, when Germany attacked the Soviet Union, German soldiers invaded Manyewicz, where my parents and sister as well as grandparents, multiple aunts and uncles, and other Jews lived. All Jews were required to wear yellow stars whenever they were outside.

JUDITH: I was born in a small town which was part of Poland when I was born, but which is now part of the Ukraine. It was a small town that was mostly Jewish. It had a population of about 600 people, with about two-thirds of them being Jewish. Most of the Jewish people in the town were shopkeepers, a few professionals, but mainly shopkeepers. My parents were married in January of 1937. My father was in the lumber business. He would go out to the woods and signify which trees were to be cut down.

I was born in 1938, so I really did not have much of a chance to enjoy a normal life before the Germans entered in 1941. When the Germans came into our town, our neighbors, the Ukrainians in the surrounding areas, flocked into town and robbed the Jewish homes of absolutely everything that wasn't nailed down. They even took the beds.

The Germans took the men to forced labor outside of town. They would go to work for the day and then they would come home for the night. We were all wearing yellow stars. My father was quite a delicate man. He had never been used to heavy labor. One evening he had come home and was sitting on the front porch. He was very tired, and it was a hot day. He had taken off his jacket and placed it beside him. A Ukrainian walked by and saw that he wasn't wearing his jacket with the yellow star. That man went to the police, and the police came and dragged my father to the police station. When my mother and I came to get him to try to buy his freedom, the policemen turned on the gramophone record player. They were playing a record and beating my father to the music.

As time progressed, there were a few older German soldiers who had been in World War I and who were not in accord with what was going on under German occupation all over Europe. There was one soldier especially, my mother mentioned he had told somebody in the town that within the next few weeks there was going to be a roundup of Jews. Rumors started coming to us that in surrounding areas, Jews were being rounded up and killed. Of course, this was something that is beyond human comprehension – that people would just be rounded up and shot. The mind cannot absorb that, and the people in my town had a hard time believing this. People felt, well, it's not going to happen here. So, they became a little bit more complacent. But then the rumors became more prevalent. Finally, it became known that within the next week or so they were going to round up the Jews. There was no ghetto in our town, we were left to live in our own homes. So, people started inquiring as to what they could do. Some arrangements had been made by my family. When the day came, my mother and father, as well as my aunt and her family, went to this place where there was a man who was willing to take us, but that man never wanted to tell his wife because she was a real antisemite. He was doing this because he had had good dealings with our family. He hid us for a while outside in the woods, and he would bring us food once in a while. Outside in the woods was not easy. The climate in that area was very similar to New England, particularly to northern Maine, where there are large deep forests

with lots of pine trees. This all happened at about the time of the
Jewish High Holidays of Rosh Hashanah and Yom Kippur, which
was the end of September or the beginning of October in 1941.
The weather was turning cold. We didn't have that much to take
with us, but whatever we could, we did take. I was 3½ years old.

GEORGE: One day, when my mother heard that the next day
the Germans would round up everyone in the community, she
went about to various family and told them unless they fled the
next day they would all be rounded up. Many people didn't believe her. Many people who lived in eastern Poland were used to
pogroms – they were used to being beaten, but assumed that life
would continue after that. Many people just didn't believe that
their end would come. But my mother did believe it, and she
convinced my father and several other sisters to leave. Sadly, the
warnings she gave went largely unheeded and most of our family
and Jewish neighbors were soon killed by German *Einsatzgruppen*
(death squads).

JUDITH: None of the farmers were willing to take us in. They
were just willing to supply us with food. This first man we went
to took care of us only for a few weeks because his wife threatened
to reveal our presence. So my mother and aunts decided that they
would seek another place, and we had to walk to the bogs.

I remember the mud. Very deep mud. And I remember walking
on shoes made of tree bark. I was given a pair of those because that
was the only way to stay on top of the mud, otherwise you would
sink. The mud was as deep as my waist.

At one point we came to another man's house who kept us in the
barn. His name was Ador. He would supply us with food. At times
he would bring us some cold potatoes. He would give one potato
per person. My parents shared one potato and gave two to me.
We were in the attic of the barn, and sometimes German soldiers
would come around and stay in the barn downstairs. In addition
to the Germans, we also had to be very careful about the Ukrainian
nationalists who were their allies. The Ukrainian nationalists hated

the Jews just as much as the Germans did. Whenever they would capture Jews, they would shoot them just the way the Germans would.

I recall that food was very difficult to come by and we were living out in the open. Some of the people in the group went and stole a heifer from a farmer and slaughtered it. We were sitting around the fire one evening, cooking some of the meat. After we finished eating, my mother and a young boy who was living with us decided to store leftovers to avoid spoilage. They moved away from the fire with a torch. All of a sudden, we heard shooting. It seems that the farmer who owned the heifer had reported us to the Germans, and the Germans came looking for us.

My father grabbed me since I was sitting beside him, being ready to go to sleep, and he started running with me. At that time, we didn't know where my mother was, whether she had been killed or captured. Everybody just ran in a different direction, and we had to run through town to get to the other side where my aunts were being hidden.

My father carried me on his back. I was not dressed very well because we had no time to grab anything. I was just wearing whatever I had been wearing while sitting at the fire. As we went through town we passed by a clothesline. I can remember the clothes on the line like ghosts because they were frozen stiff and they were moving in unison with the wind. To my young eyes, it looked like a band of ghosts was attacking us. My father grabbed some things that were on the clothesline.

We ran for a long time. I don't know exactly how far it was or how long it was that we ran. To keep me warm, my father had my feet in the pockets of his pants. When we finally came to where my aunts were, I was cold and sick and extremely hungry. All they had to eat was some green pears that they had been given. The pears weren't ripe. It was the beginning of winter, and that's what I ate. I remember that I was very sick with a stomachache after that from those pears. I'll never forget that when we came to my aunts we didn't know whether my mother was alive or dead. Fortunately, she was alive and we were eventually reunited.

GEORGE: About a year after they went into hiding, they came across a partisan group. This was a non-Jewish, Russian group that was in the business of harassing and killing Germans, not sheltering Jews. My parents asked that they be taken into the group, but the leader told them that children could not join. He gave my mother a choice: "You can join us, but you must give up your child." My sister was about 4 or 5 years old at the time, and my mother knew that 'giving her up' meant abandoning her – a death sentence. My mother was not going to do that. But she argued so forcefully and effectively that the partisans finally agreed to take them in as a family. Soon, other families were allowed to join the group.

JUDITH: At first, we lived out in the open and we would sleep on the ground. That first winter we slept on the ground. I had a little coat that was the only warm thing I had. If my parents put it under me to sleep on top of, I would wake up in the morning covered with snow. And if they put it on top of me, I would wake up and couldn't get my hair off the ground because it was frozen to the ground.

The first year was extremely difficult. We lived mainly on roots and berries and whatever food we could get from the surrounding areas. We were constantly under attack. German parties came looking for us or the Ukrainians came looking for us. And it wasn't just a fear of the Germans and the Ukrainian nationalists – sometimes there was also fear from our own partisans. The leader of the group was named 'The Gare', which I believe means a crow. He was a Russian. There was a little boy who was just a couple of years older than me, and, in front of my eyes, The Gare shot him because he wasn't quiet during the time we had to move from one place to another. He just was a child who was not as quiet as he should have been. And this was not the only incident – some other people would be killed for a coat or for a jacket.

We came out of the woods at the end of 1944. When we came back to our town, there was really no good place for us to live. My grandmother's house was occupied by a Russian officer. He did agree to let us have one room and we lived there for a while. All of the people who had remained behind in my town had been killed. The only people who survived were the ones who had run away like us. Our life wasn't that great either because we were still being bombed constantly by the Germans. My cousin was on her way to Kavla by train when she was killed just outside the town when the train was bombed by the Germans. The Russians were trying to conscript Jews into the Russian army and my father was supposed to have been conscripted to be sent to the coal mines. And I was sick – I had whooping cough, measles, and pneumonia. My mother said that if my father was sent to Russia, she and I would also have to go. That's when my parents, in the beginning of 1945, decided that we would leave the Ukraine and try to go more towards the west. So, around April or May we went to Lublin, which is in Poland. That was when my father became very ill. He died in July in Lublin, and my mother was pregnant with my brother. The war had just ended. I was 7 years old. We had some relatives with us then. Everybody was trying to get out and it was very difficult. My mother had to go to Warsaw to talk to the members of the Jewish Brigade who had come from Palestine – there were people from the Warsaw Ghetto, the leaders of the Warsaw Ghetto, who were active in trying to get people out of Eastern Europe to Israel. Everything had to be done clandestinely. You couldn't cross borders openly. No country would let you. But finally, we did. We were told that we were going to pretend that we were Turks trying to get back to Turkey. The women had to put on scarves on their heads and turn them up to make them look like turbans. We had to be searched at the border. You couldn't speak at all. The border between Hungary and Austria was especially difficult because we had to walk through the mountains by foot. We were being shot at by the guards. My mother, who was at that time quite advanced in her pregnancy, had difficulty walking. She was also carrying a pack on her back and had to hold me by the hand. It was extremely difficult. But we did get into Austria with a brigade. They took us to a military camp that had been used by the British Army and had been abandoned. There were a lot of Jewish refugees there. Then we had heard that one of my mother's sisters and her husband were living in Florence, Italy, so my mother wanted us to join them. We were taken in a convoy of lorries to cross the border from Austria to Italy. They were not supposed to be doing this, of course, so the trucks were closed tight. There were people inside packed like sardines and we weren't allowed to speak or sneeze even, because the British soldiers were not allowing Jews to cross into Italy. The British were afraid that the Brigade was bringing Jews to go to Palestine.

We traveled for what seemed like hours until we came into a town in Italy called Mestre, which is right near Venice. We were in a displaced persons camp there for a few days. Then my mother and I and one of her other sisters were taken to Florence where other members of my mother's family were staying. One of my aunts was also pregnant. Two weeks later, my brother George was born in Florence. We lived in the house in Florence for about a year and a half, and then we came to Cremona. We stayed in Cremona and then another DP camp in Barletta, and then another one. In all, we lived in Italy for four years.

GEORGE: In order for us to get visas to enter the United States, it was necessary for us to have an American sponsor who would financially guarantee that we would not become public charges. Finally, my mother located relatives in Bangor, Maine, who agreed to act as sponsors. At this time, I was actually a stateless person because I had been born in a displaced persons camp. We were put on a train carrying our very meager belongings and taken to Naples where we boarded a converted troop ship called the *Marine Jumper*. We sailed on November 10, 1949, and arrived in New York harbor on November 21, 1949.

*Malka Muz Singal and her children, Judith and George, in the
displaced persons camp, November or December 1945.*

None of us spoke English upon our arrival in the United States
– Yiddish was the language spoken in our home. My mother spoke
five languages, but English was not one of them. We shared a tiny
apartment in Bangor with another family. My sister was put into
the Bangor public schools, where learning English was done on a
'sink or swim' basis. There was no formal instruction for English

as a second language. I started school two years later. My mother started a small grocery store, and we joined the local synagogue. We struggled, but we got by. We had a safe home, and we had a future.

My sister and I did well in school. My mother was astonished to learn that in this country we did not have to pay for schooling through high school. Both Judith and I attended the University of Maine on scholarships. I went on to Harvard Law School, again on a scholarship. Judith left to study in Israel during her junior year in college and remained there for almost a decade, starting a family and teaching English at a boarding school. She remembered that when her husband went off to fight in the Six-Day War in 1967, she would protect her children in an air raid shelter, assuming a role similar to that which her mother had played with her 25 years before. She came back to the United States and had a very successful career as an educator in the Boston suburbs.

My mother died in 1999 at the age of 90, in Chestnut Hill, Massachusetts. Judith died in 2004 at the age of 65, in Belmont, Massachusetts.

After practicing law in Bangor, Maine, George Singal was appointed to be a judge in the U.S. District Court in Maine in 2000. He served as chief judge from 2003 to 2009, took senior status on July 31, 2013, and continues to preside over both civil and criminal matters. On May 15, 2019, Chief Justice John Roberts appointed Singal as one of ten judges on the Foreign Intelligence Surveillance Court. His favorite duty is presiding over naturalization proceedings in which he welcomes immigrants who have achieved U.S. citizenship.

CHAPTER 16

Julia Skalina

Julia Skalina

February 19, 1925–December 13, 2010
Tornala, Slovakia

My name is Julia Skalina. I was born in Czechoslovakia on February 19, 1925, in the southern part of Slovakia, in a little town named Tornala. That's where I grew up and spent the beginning of my life, my childhood. I had one brother. My parents were Emil Lissauer and Elizabeth Lissauer, born Rosenberg. My father was a pharmacist and he owned a pharmacy in the town where we lived. It was quite an old pharmacy; my father bought it before World War I and it was very successful. I can still see it in my mind's eye – when you went in, you'd see the old-fashioned bottles where all kinds of medication were kept. The scale. The cash register, the old type of cash register.

My mother was born in the town where we lived. My grandfather was also born there, and my mother's family lived there, too. Her two brothers, one sister, and my grandparents lived there. I don't remember my grandfather well, but I remember my grandmother. We were very close with my cousins when we grew up.

I had a few very good friends. That's my childhood memories – the very close family life, the very nice friendship with my friends, nice birthday parties. They baked the best pastries. It was a very harmonious, quiet life.

The city had less than 4,000 people and, from that, I think it was 20 percent Jews. When I was born, that was the Czechoslovak Republic, under Masaryk's presidency. It was a real democracy and we all had equal rights. There were no restrictions at all on the Jews at that time. People lived together peacefully. There were cultural events, there were sports events. They participated together, Jews and non-Jews.

At that time, the population of the town was mostly Hungarian, with very, very few Slovaks. There was always a certain hatred between the Hungarians and the Slovaks. They never liked the Jews. There was always antisemitism, but it was 'peacetime antisemitism' – you were 'the Jew', but they didn't harm you for that. You could study, you could be whatever you wanted to be.

I don't remember that there were ever pogroms in that part of the Austro-Hungarian monarchy. There were blood libels,[1] when they were accusing a Jew of killing a non-Jewish girl. There were cases like that, but never pogroms. So, when I grew up, in my early years, I knew we were Jewish. We went to the synagogue, and my parents' household was kosher. But I didn't feel any difference between us and the non-Jews. That came later.

My brother was four years older than me. We were close, but in those early years the four years between a girl and a boy wasn't so close. I had more closeness with my cousins, who were the same age, and with my friends.

We lived in a house that my father built in 1920. It had four rooms, a kitchen, and a room beside it for the help. It was a nice-sized house, and it was very nicely furnished. My mother was a very good housekeeper, who took very good care of the house. I still smell the cleanness whenever I think about the house. We had quite a few beautiful paintings. I don't want to sound as if I am showing off – I am just telling the truth.

I remember we had a big back yard, with fruit trees. That beautiful back yard is what stays most in my mind. Maybe the nicest memories were when we children went into the garden and could eat the fruit. We were very free, very happy.

There were young German girls who went to different houses to tutor us in German – that's how the children learned German in their childhood. One of these girls came to our house, maybe in 1934 or 1935, just after Hitler started. She made up all kinds of lies. I know that she left very suddenly. Much later, when I grew up, I heard that her brother was a member of the Hitler Youth and he didn't want her in a Jewish house. So, he made her do all kinds of things to make the lives of the Jews unpleasant. That was the first time I could sense that there was something wrong that

---

1. See **blood libel** in Appendix.

was going to affect us. I became aware that my family would be in danger much later.

Before 1938, when I was 13 years old, I don't remember that I was so interested in the news. In that year, Czechoslovakia was divided at the Munich Conference.[2] With just the stroke of a pen, they tore the whole republic apart. Naturally, democracy ended. At that conference, the part of Slovakia where we lived was annexed to Hungary. I remember that there were very mixed feelings in the town when they were expecting that change. Most of the population was Hungarian, so I would say most of them were waiting for the Hungarians to come, even among the Jews.

My most vivid memory of a change is when Hungary annexed that part of Slovakia. Before that, there was the threat by Hitler that he was going to 'liberate' the suffering Germans who lived in the Sudeten part of Czechoslovakia. The Czechoslovakian government took the threat seriously. They built bunkers all over and they were really prepared to defend the Czechoslovak Republic against Germany. Across the border, close to our town, they built bunkers. October 28, 1938, would have been the 20th anniversary of the establishment of the Czechoslovak Republic. Now, they were preparing all kinds of big ceremonies for that. Naturally, it didn't come to pass.

I remember the day when the Hungarians came. The night before, the Czechoslovakian army had left. That army was equipped with the most modern military equipment, but they couldn't use it. They had to just leave, without a gunshot. So, for one day almost, we were in a land where no Hungarian had come in yet and the Czechoslovakian army had left.

I was 13 years old and curious about what would happen – standing in the window almost the whole day, waiting for the Hungarians to come. Finally, a soldier came in a shabby uniform

---

2. See **Munich Conference** in Appendix.

with a rifle on his shoulder, on a bicycle. Then again nothing. Then a peasant wagon came and a few tired soldiers in shabby uniforms. They were incomparable with the Czechoslovakian army that had just left. It was around eight o'clock at night when it started to get dark. I wanted to go to my friends and discuss the big event. My father said to me, "You have to realize that the world has changed." I don't remember that he said more, and I didn't ask more. But this scene is still in my mind after so many years. I understood from the tone of his voice how serious it was. Really, that's what happened.

When the Czechoslovakian regime was in power, it held down antisemitism. But just a few days after the Czechoslovakian army left and the Hungarians took over, we had all kinds of antisemitic graffiti on the sidewalks and houses. I remember exactly how it was by our house. Then, a few days later, I was with my father in the living room and a big stone was thrown through the window. I even remember that my father called the police, but they didn't do anything. That was the first expression of the mob. They felt free to be antisemites.

The Hungarians passed Jewish Laws.[3] The first one, which was enacted in 1938, said Jews couldn't go to universities. Stores and licenses were taken away. Mostly it was progressive – not all at once. They went by age groups because they didn't have enough replacements. In 1939, the war started, so they had even less people to replace the Jews.

In the first years of the Hungarian regime, my father's life didn't change, but my father's pharmacy was scheduled to be taken away in May 1944.

I was continuing my schooling, with the exception that in 1940 when I was sent to Budapest. Fortunately, my father could afford to send me there and to finance my studies. In the middle schools and high schools, we could finish our education. They already

---

3. See **Hungarian anti-Jewish laws** in Appendix.

selected and let fewer Jewish boys and girls come into the high schools, but we who were already in could finish our high school.

The real change in my family happened with my brother. He graduated high school in June 1939. My father's dream was always to send him to Switzerland to become a chemical engineer. They applied for passports, my father and my brother. If I remember correctly, they got their passports, but they didn't get the visa to go out – my father was in the age group that couldn't leave the country because they were already at war. They gave my brother an option to go, but they didn't guarantee that he could come back whenever he wanted, or come back at all. I remember very, very clearly the dilemma that my parents were in. Should they let my brother go? It was wartime, the times were uncertain. Unfortunately, my parents decided with their hearts and not with their heads, so my brother stayed. My brother stayed with my father to work in the pharmacy, and he learned it without the university, 100 percent from books and from my father and from the practice.

In either 1941 or 1942, my brother had to join the army. By that time, the Jewish boys weren't regular soldiers. No guns were trusted to them. This was a unit, a labor battalion, where they wore their own clothes. The unit was doing subaltern work for the army. While my brother was in the army, I was in Budapest.

My brother was working in the hospital unit. By an irony of fate, he was sent to Budapest to learn how to detect typhoid bacteria through blood tests. Naturally, because of that, he was vaccinated against this sickness. I'll tell you why it's an irony of fate when I tell you later about his death. My brother was an exceptionally nice man. He had a very good nature. He was clever, a hard worker, and a very devoted friend. Everybody I spoke to later on spoke of him with love and affection.

In 1941, Jews believed that the restrictions of the Jewish laws would be all that would happen. They believed that it would never get to deportation. I think they didn't even believe the deportations would happen. The first time I heard about Auschwitz, it was

from a young woman who came from Slovakia and was married
to a man from our town. She got the news that her father was
deported, and she talked about the deportations. Nobody believed
it, at least not that I know of. That was the reason they stayed.
Then, in 1944 the Germans occupied Hungary.[4] That's when the
German occupation reached us.

My two cousins and my two best friends wanted to come home
the first day. They went to take the train from Budapest. But the
train station was the first place where the Germans looked for Jews
– they arrested my two cousins and my two friends the first day. My
aunt went to Budapest, still hoping to find some connections and
get the children out. My older cousin was 17 by that time and my
younger cousin was 14 or 15. My uncle loved his children. A few
days after that happened, I went to their house and I found him
sitting with the pictures of the children in his hand and crying. For
the first time, I saw a grownup man like him – he was a tall, big
man – sitting there, ruined, looking at the picture of the children.
That was the first time that the reality hit me. I knew that that's
the end.

A few days later, we had to wear the yellow star already, but we
still could go out. Then, at the end of April, they closed in the
ghetto. Now we could not leave. They took one street. Fortunately
for us, it was the street where our house was. There were eighteen
houses on the street. Mostly Jews lived there. They moved out
the few non-Jews, and other Jews moved in. We stayed in our
own house. We didn't have to move out. We had everything there.
Naturally, the situation was hard with so many people together,
but it wasn't tragic yet. We were still all together. It was a hard
situation, but we were all together.

Now they took the girls to work, first in the brick factory. We
were hoping that would be it – going to work. But we were only

---

4. See **German invasion of Hungary** in Appendix.

a few days there. They then took us to sweep the streets, guarded by the gendarmes. That was much harder to take. I had always one feeling: that to wear the yellow star was not my shame. That was the shame of those who did it to us. This feeling accompanied me through the whole deportation.

Then they closed the ghetto. Until then, maybe some people could go out with permission, but now they closed it completely. They came all the time to look for something, to make all kinds of house searches. At first, we could have wedding bands, but everything else had to be handed over much earlier to the authorities. But one day they came and took all the money and any jewelry that was left – now they took the wedding bands and the money. When they left, my father said, "That's it. We'll be deported. They won't leave us here."

Maybe two days later, they came to our house and made a search from eight o'clock in the morning to four o'clock in the afternoon. They searched everything, from the attic down. We were sitting outside and they didn't let us in the house. While we were sitting, I made little figurines from clay in the yard. They came and broke the figurines as if I was hiding something there.

At four o'clock in the afternoon, they took my mother, my father, and me for interrogation. My father was taken separately, and I was in a room with my mother. We heard noises – not pleasant noises. I knew that something was going on, but I was thinking, "No, we live in the 2oth century. No torturing." Then the interrogator came in and asked me and my mother questions. He lifted his rubber stick and came to me and was so close to me. In that moment, he was thinking something else and he left. He didn't hit me. Maybe he went back to my father to torture him more, telling him about me. I don't know. Probably that's what happened. Then they let my mother and me go home. My father came home later. No child should see the father as I saw mine, his hands and feet swollen, dirty – a terrible picture. My mother prepared him a soup. He couldn't hold a spoon to eat it. The next day, they took him for another interrogation. That time it was much milder. It was a Saturday when they took him the second time.

On Sunday morning, the commandant of the army unit came from house to house. He took all the men, from 15 to maybe 50 – I don't remember exactly the limit, everybody who looked able to work – and took them to the labor battalion. The commandant had been years in the town and he knew my father. I think that, in a certain way, he had respect for my father. He said to him, "You don't have to go, but please go away from here." So my father said he was going. He discussed it for a very short time with my mother and me, and he volunteered that he was going. The next day, a Monday, he was at home. We were saying goodbye. He told me, "Stay with your mother as long as you can. If you cannot, go with your friends." Judging from that, much later on I realized that my father maybe knew much more than I thought he knew. The next day, they left. My father could hardly walk. He was in the group with a few doctors from the town. When I saw him marching, I was afraid that he wouldn't make it.

At first all the men were concentrated in one place in the ghetto, so I could run there to see him for the last time. That was the first and last time I saw my father crying. Then I went home. They were marching before our house, so I could see it from the window. They left, and my mother and I looked at each other and said, "It is time to pack." We had a knapsack already prepared with the necessary belongings we wanted to take with us. I remember that I took a shower and brushed my hair and I said, "We are prepared." The next morning, a policeman came. He was an old policeman from the town. He said very nicely, "Get prepared. You have to go." He went to my mother and whispered, "The Allied forces have landed in Normandy, in Europe." That was June 6, 1944. What I lived through in the last three days had been so terrible. Now, all at once, we got hope. Maybe, maybe, they won't have time and everything will be all right.

They took us first to one of the Jewish houses. They made another search, a body search, to see if we were taking something with us. From there, we were taken to the outskirts of the city. There were three or four barracks they were using for drying tobacco leaves. That's where they took us. There are pictures that stay in your mind vividly. One of them is of seeing my uncle and his family. I loved them very much. They were sitting there so hopelessly, just desperate. We stayed there one day.

The next night, very early in the morning, three or four o'clock in the morning, I don't know, my friend woke me up and asked me what message my father brought from the labor camp where her father was also. My father was not here, so I was running out and begging the guard to let me go to the other barracks, which they allowed. I remember one woman, when she saw me, she was yelling, "It's terrible! It's terrible!" Then I went to the barracks and found the body of my father lying on the floor. When they took him for the third interrogation, he took his own life. He left a note in his pocket that we should blame him for everything. With that, maybe my mother and I wouldn't be tortured, or even my brother, who wasn't there. Maybe the other reason why he did it was that he was determined not to be killed in a terrible way. Maybe he wanted to be the one who decided to die.

It was very hard to take his death. Later on, I said that what he did was the right thing. Now, after I found my father, I had to go back to my mother and tell her that my father was dead. We had to tell my old grandmother that her son was dead. He was the first victim of the Holocaust atrocities in our town that we knew about. I see the picture of how the police came to take my father away, my grandmother holding his hand to the last second that she could walk with him. Maybe I am telling that because those are my worst memories.

They took my father's body away. He was buried by policemen. Two Jewish men from the labor camp were in town for something and they were allowed to go to the cemetery. Naturally, all that I found out much later.

After that, they took us back to the barracks. There we were told to get ready, because we would be leaving from there. They didn't say where or how. The cattle cars were already prepared. I remember very clearly that I was standing there with my mother and her sister. The Hungarian gendarme was watching us. All of a sudden, he came to me and said, "Go away. Go to the woods. Go wherever you want. Just don't step in the car." I looked at him and said, "How can I go? I wouldn't leave my mother and the family. I'll go where they go." I don't know, we were naive or stupid. I don't know what we were. Not that I could save myself at that time, because where would I have gone without any money? Who would have helped me? Yes, I went with my mother because I'd like to be with her.

The next day we arrived at Miskolc ('Mishkoltz' in Yiddish), a bigger town close by. There again a brick factory had been converted to a detention camp. The Jews from a few counties were concentrated in that camp. Every day, I don't know how many hundreds of people went on a transport to Auschwitz. Naturally, we didn't know that when we arrived there. The situation there was terrible. The big buildings where they dry bricks were half open, with maybe a yard-high wall, then a roof on pillars. That's where we had to find our place.

As soon as we arrived at Mishkoltz, there were completely different Hungarian gendarmes. They were beating us and pushing us. Before, except in interrogations, we were not beaten when we went from the ghetto to the barracks. But when we arrived in Mishkoltz, they started to beat us. When our group left, I had time to run to my grandmother in another barracks to tell her to please stay with them, because they always announced through the loudspeaker that the sick and old ones should stay behind – that they would be taken by car, and it would be better. So, I was running to my grandmother to beg her to stay. I remember the scene, how we were pushed and I was hit with the butt of a rifle. I looked back and my poor grandmother was coming after us. She couldn't pick up her few belongings. She was just pulling them behind her. Her hair was loose. I couldn't help. I couldn't go back. I couldn't help her to come with us. That scene has haunted me my whole life. She lived through the journey to Auschwitz. Naturally, she was killed there right away.

The real bad memories are the travel from Mishkoltz to Auschwitz. It took two and a half days to get to Auschwitz. We were terribly crowded. The children were crying, naturally. The old ones were moaning. It was a terrible noise to hear. The smell was unpleasant. The lack of fresh air made the whole thing more and more unbearable. There was one bucket with water and the other bucket for a toilet. I remember on that trip, maybe the second day, my mother looked out the window and she said, "Look, they are killing people. Dead bodies are lying by the railroad." I looked out and I saw that they were only stones. I tried to calm my mother, but I don't think I succeeded.

After my father's death, and after we had to leave, I was in such a state of mind that I didn't feel. My pain inside was much bigger than anything else. I will never tell you that I was hungry, or I was freezing, because I was suffering much more from the loss and from what I lived through in those days. Maybe that's why I cannot remember if I was hungry there. I know that we missed air. We still hoped, in that terrible situation, that we wouldn't be killed, that we were being taken somewhere to work.

When we got to Auschwitz, the scene there I think many, many have told you about. They opened the wagon and the inmates in striped uniforms came and told us to leave everything behind and get out, so we left everything behind and got out. Now we got to a selection place, where my mother was sent to the left and I was sent to the right. I told the German officer, "That's my mother. Please, I'd like to go with her." He said to me, "Don't worry, you'll see her later," and they pushed me away. I went to the right; my

mother was told to take my little cousin's hand and go with her
to the left. My older cousin and my aunt went to the right. We
were so confused, in a daze. The only thing I clearly remember
is my mother's last look at me. Her eyes, the expression on her
face, is something I will never forget. I try to pick out those things
which are accompanying me through my life. That's the last of my
mother.

Now we were led to the place where we had to take the shower. There were barracks behind the barbed wire. In those barracks, there were women standing and looking at us. They were so
strange. They had terrible clothes on. They were all bald, shaved.
The expression in their eyes was empty – almost like insane. We
said, "My gosh, where are we? Maybe that part is where they put
the insane people." We had no idea where we were going. So we
went to the place where we had to take a shower. We were shaved
all over. Then we went to the shower room.

We were shaved by Polish and Slovak inmates, girls. They were
the ones who were there already for a few years in Auschwitz. The
SS men were just going in and out, standing there and watching.
We weren't human beings anymore. You know, we were always
saying with one of my friends, Auschwitz had the sign, '*Arbeit
macht frei.*' Much more appropriate would have been the sign, 'All
hope abandon, you who enter here.' But we didn't know. Anyway,
when we took showers, as the water started to run, we started to
drink. Then we washed ourselves. We didn't have soap or a towel.
Then everybody got a dress. Nothing else – no underwear. The
dress that was thrown to you was whatever they had in their hand.
No size, winter or summer. We could keep our shoes.

Now we went to the camp. I found out much later on that it
was Camp C. The barracks had been prepared for the Hungarian
transports, and they were quite new. They were expecting the
mass transportation from Hungary. There were ten barracks and
approximately 1,000 women in each. There was a barracks with a
big Red Cross sign, like a hospital barracks. We found out much

later that it was not a good idea to even get close to it – whoever went there was really sick and never came out. Every day, we saw a black truck come and take away sick ones and dead ones.

In this camp, we didn't do anything. The camp was only like a selection camp. Almost every day, selections were held. During those selections, we went with our dress in our hand. We had to hold it up and go before the SS soldiers. Now they selected. Sometimes they selected the very thin ones, and they were taken right away to the gas chambers. Sometimes they selected younger and stronger ones, and they were the work transports. One of my terrible memories of that is that one woman from our town was there with her 13-year-old daughter, who was big enough that she got through the first selection. The child was sick very soon. The food, the conditions, it was very hard to endure, so the mother, very anxious to take care of the child, took her to the hospital. The next day, we saw the black truck and the child on the truck. She said, "They are taking my child to a better hospital." A few days later, at one of the selections, she was selected out with the very thin ones and put on the truck. I was going between the barracks, and I saw her on the truck. She was yelling at me. She said, "If you get home and if you meet my husband, please tell him that we were together, and I was with my child and I am going after her and I'll take care of her." I had to tell her husband. That wasn't easy.

During the nine weeks I was in Auschwitz, the daily routine was to get up very early, go for roll call, and stand there for hours if we were lucky, and kneel for hours if we weren't lucky. Because it was a new camp, stones on the streets were rough – we had to kneel on those rough stones when they punished us for no reason at all, for hours sometimes. That was very rough. Don't forget the climate in Auschwitz: It is high in the mountains, so early morning is very cold. To be in a summer dress and nothing else, that was terrible.

The day we were selected, they put us aside. We were standing close to the gate. It was a very hot day in August and we were again subject to a selection process. I was there with my cousin and my aunt. My cousin and I made it through the selection, but my aunt was made to go back into the camp. My aunt said to us, "You just go. Don't come with me. I'll go back, my daughter is there." So that made it easier for us to leave Auschwitz and leave my aunt behind.

We were to be taken to the Allendorf concentration camp. The next day we again took a shower and got a grey inmate dress, everybody's the same, and one piece of underwear. We were again put in cattle cars and shipped further. Now this trip was easier, easier because there were no children, no old ones. We were traveling light with just the dress we had on. We had no packages. We had nothing. Taking that into consideration, it was a little bit easier, but the circumstances were exactly the same. We were three or three and a half days on the train, but I don't remember that we got anything to eat. We had water, but I don't remember food. Maybe we did, I just don't remember. That's how we arrived at that beautiful camp.

The first thing was a roll call. The SS man who looked at us said, "How could they send to work such a bunch of weak women?" So we got better food. We thought that's how it would be. Better food meant a bigger portion of bread and the soup was maybe thicker. I think we were there two weeks when the selections started to work in the factory.

The factory belonged to a company called Dynamit Nobel. They were filling bombs with an explosive material, then they put a hole in it, and put the ignition in. Some of the girls were working where they were filling the bombs, and some where they were putting in the ignition. The whole factory looked like it would be underground. As we found out later, the factory wasn't underground, but they put the ground over the factory so it would look like underground. Trees and bushes were planted so you could only see the opening.

It was a special work group that took care of the grounds outside of the factory. Fortunately, I got into that working group. I worked quite a few times in the factory with very poisonous material as well. From that material, your hair became red and your skin yellow.

Then it was January 1945, and the front was getting closer and closer. The Germans were very aware that it wouldn't last long. The commandant of the camp was an older man, in our eyes. He could have been maybe 53 or 54 at the time. He knew that well. My birthday is in February. Naturally, I had a very sad day, to know it was my birthday. I was sitting in a corner and crying. The commandant came by and said to me, "Why are you crying?" I said, "It's my birthday and I miss my home and my parents more than ever." He looked at me and said, "You know, I have a daughter your age and she is on the Russian front. I don't know if I will see her. But you will be at home by spring." I always said that was the nicest birthday present I ever got in my life. I got hope.

Another very unpleasant memory of that camp. One of the young women whose child was taken from her went crazy – she was really mad. I was going to the camp, and I just heard a terrible noise. I have to tell you that the punishment in the camp for stealing a carrot or a potato skin was being put in the bunker. In the bunker, there were rats. She was closed in the bunker and probably that's what provoked her madness. She started to yell, "You murderer! You murderer! You murdered my children! You murdered my family!" The voice – I don't know if you've ever heard a mad person's voice, but you could hear that it wasn't a normal voice. So I went there. There was a fence around the bunker. I don't know how many of us were standing there – we had to stay there and listen to it. One of the SS men was a cruel sadist. He was yelling all kinds of obscenities to her. Then he took a hose and splashed cold water on her. That would have been some time in December, so it was really cold already. He did it until she collapsed.

I can tell you that since then, whenever I recall this scene, I think, who was normal? Who was crazy? She who told the truth? Or we, who just tolerated everything quietly? That's one of the memories I have from that camp.

In the camp, the situation was getting worse. The front was getting closer and closer. We heard the bombing much more intensively. Even the artillery fire we could hear, so we knew that it was getting really close. Because of that and because of the bombing of neighboring cities, it was hard for them to get food for us, so the portions were getting smaller and smaller. Then the work details didn't go out to work because of shortage of material in the factory.

On the last day at Allendorf, we were told to pack our belongings and we left the camp. We were marching through the whole night, approximately 25 kilometers. Then we went to a field where there was a big barracks. We were pushed into the barracks and slept there a few hours. In the afternoon, we were told that we had to continue to go further. As we came out of the barracks, we noticed that something was bad because the Germans were very nervous. The women guards had already taken off their hats. I don't know if they thought that was how they would be recognized. They tore off their epaulets that showed their rank. Then they said, "Go!" Now our group, five of us who were friendly, were among the last 50. We started to march. All at once, we looked back and we see that we are the last ones. So where are the rest?

We stood there in the field and started to discuss what to do. While we were standing there, the older German, the commandant of the camp, came back. He took his pistol and he said, "Go! You cannot stay here." I said, "We are very tired. We cannot go." I closed my eyes. I was waiting for the shot. I opened my eyes a few seconds later and he left. He got on his bicycle and left.

Then we didn't know what to do. We were afraid. That was one SS man who was 'good' to us, but what will happen if somebody else finds us? In spite of everything, we decided to go back to the barracks. More of the girls were thinking the same, and by morning there were already over 100 girls.

We were hiding in that barracks for two days, which was very, very hard. That was the end of March. All at once, we are unguarded but not free. Hiding there, we didn't know who was going around. To keep over 100 women quiet wasn't easy. It was much easier not to eat or drink than to keep everybody quiet. I remember once we looked out the window and saw a German soldier coming with his rifle. We got really scared, thinking that maybe he wanted to come into the barracks. But as he got close to the barracks he threw the rifle away and tore off his epaulets and was marching in the other direction. They were maybe thinking more of saving themselves, fortunately, than killing us.

One of the German workers in the factory where we had worked alerted the American army that there were Jewish women in hiding. That's how an American soldier found us. That was March 30th when we saw the first American soldier. We thought, now we are free, now, really, nothing can happen to us. The American soldier told us to go through the field to the road where the American tanks and military were. We were running through the field, not thinking one second that there could be a mine there, that we could be killed or something. No, we were free! A relief, a joy! The end of persecution, of fear of death. It is very, very hard to see. After those few days when we were so afraid of what the Germans would do, if they would let us survive or not, our fear was more intense. But after that, it was such a relief, such a joy. I cannot find other words.

We arrived where the American tanks were. You know, we all thought that they would greet us with open arms. But they said, "Stop! Don't go further!" We were standing there and wanted to tell them that we were not some beggars, that we were degraded to that degree by the Germans, that we are normal people and that's what happened to us. That first moment there was a feeling of disappointment that they didn't open their arms and say, "You are here!" We waited a few seconds and then two American soldiers came. One spoke a little German; I would say more Yiddish than German.

They took us to the neighboring villages and looked for quarters for us in the German houses. The Germans were afraid to let us in. Thinking back at how we looked, dirty and so on, they were really afraid of us. They were swearing to us that they didn't know what happened to us, who we are. They knew about the camp, but they all thought that we were there voluntarily. That it was a work camp. No deportations, nothing like that. One of the German women was holding her children away from us. We could see that she was standing before a china cabinet where she had very nice things. So, we told her, "Don't be mistaken. We are not the ones who are harming children or stealing other people's property. You look at your people." They all said that they didn't know anything about it.

We were there in that little village for three months. It was the end of March when we were liberated and we were there until sometime in June, when we finally could go home.

It was already July when I returned to my hometown. Naturally, the first place I wanted to go was my father's grave. There was only a little sign in the ground that was hard to spot. The whole town was like a ghost town. The Jewish houses were either empty or there were strange people living there. I didn't find anything from our belongings. From four furnished rooms, later, I found a bookcase – that was it. Furniture from one room, a chair from another. No clothing. Nothing, nothing, nothing.

During the time that we were deported, my only hope was that I would find my brother at home. That's why I went back to my hometown. Unfortunately, after I arrived, I found out that he was shot to death in the beginning of April 1945. What happened was that he, who was helping so many people who had typhoid fever, by that time maybe the vaccines didn't work anymore, and he got it himself. In a high fever, he left the barracks that he wasn't supposed to leave, and a 16-year-old SS boy shot him to death.

After realizing that my brother would not be coming back any-more and I cannot expect anybody from my family, I had to go on with my life. The help came when I met my husband and married him. I had been together in the camp with three sisters. After we were released, they told me I should come to where they lived. When I arrived, they said, "We'd like you to meet my brother." His name is Kolmon, and it ended up to be 51 years of marriage. We were married in May 1946 in Prague, and we lived there until 1968 when the Russians invaded the country. We decided to go to Canada. We chose Canada because at the time it was a much longer wait and much harder to get into the United States. We finally moved to the United States in 1975 and lived in Cleveland, Ohio, for several years. In December 1993, we moved to Maine to be near my son and his family.

In 1990, we were invited to go back to Germany for a reunion. We went to Allendorf, where we spent three very pleasant days. I have to say that. One of those days, they took us to the site where the camp was before. You could see nothing from the camp. It was completely destroyed. The only thing that remained was a few yards of the barbed wire fence and some of the posts. It was a long story. Some students did research and found out that there was a camp there because naturally the older ones didn't talk about it. It got to the point that they made a monument of the remaining barbed wire and posts of the fence. That's all that was left there. When they took us there and we were standing there, I looked around and saw how old we all were already. The youngest among us must have been maybe 66 or 68. When I saw that, I said, "Oh, gosh, if we won't be here, who will tell the truth?" I saw that they can destroy all the evidence. That gave me the first push to talk about it. Then I wrote down everything that I remembered, because I said that we won't be here long.

Julia Skalina died on December 13, 2010. She spent the last thirteen years of her life going to schools to speak about the atrocities of the Holocaust in an effort to ensure it would never happen again. In total she spoke over 100 times and shared her stories with countless students.

CHAPTER 17
Jerry Slivka

Jerry Slivka

July 11, 1915– January 10, 2013
Povursk, Ukraine

Jerry Slivka (born Yuri Sliwka) was born in 1915 in the western Ukraine. That area was ceded to Poland under the Treaty of Riga on March 18, 1921. Antisemitism among the Poles who came to control the country was a dominant feature in Jerry's early life.

My name is Jerry Slivka. Life in a shtetl this size was similar to life in any other little town of a similar size. The religious life was quite strong and had quite an influence on the lives of the people living there. It was inconceivable for a Jewish person not to go to synagogue on Saturday at least. Education was very important, of course, and there wasn't a single male Jew who didn't get some kind of a religious (and in later years, secular) education, even though in those times it was not compulsory. Girls not so much. There was always a *cheder*, a little school, not recognized by the authorities. You didn't get any credit. You just went until you could read and understand some Hebrew, and they also used to teach some Yiddish. In Poland, of course, education was compulsory until the age of 14. At that time, our shtetl was in Poland. I lived in the same place in three different countries – Ukraine, Poland and the Soviet Union – without moving.

The oldest of five children, he had two sisters and two brothers. Jerry went to a Hebrew high school in Poland, and then at age 15, moved to Lodz to learn a trade. He then joined a kibbutz with the hope of being able to emigrate to Israel.

When I was about 15, I joined a kibbutz, a farm or work group, planning to go to Israel. I was the youngest one there. We worked in a stone quarry, but it was quite difficult for a 15-year-old kid to work. Most of them were in their twenties. To me, they were old men, and I left it. I just couldn't do it.

During the 1930s we had our own problems besides Germany, because Poland became very bad at that time. There were anti-Jewish laws passed. Besides that, they started a boycott of Jews the same way that the German Nazis did. They stood in front of Jewish stores and told people not to go in, not to buy from Jews, and there were even a few pogroms.

World War II broke out soon after the signing of a 'non-aggression' treaty (the Molotov- Ribbentrop Pact1) between Nazi Germany and the Soviet Union on August 23, 1939. The effect of the Pact was to partition Eastern Europe between the two nations. On September 1, 1939, Germany commenced its invasion of Poland from the west. Sixteen days later, the Soviet Union invaded from the east. At the time the Soviets invaded and occupied portions of Poland, Mr. Slivka was back in his hometown. The Molotov-Ribbentrop Pact remained in place until Hitler launched his invasion of the Soviet Union on June 22, 1941. Named by the Germans 'Operation Barbarossa', it was the largest land offensive in history.

We welcomed the Soviet occupation, firstly because if we were occupied by the Germans, it would have been worse. You probably know about the agreement between Ribbentrop and Molotov at that time. It was agreed even before the war started that they were going to divide Poland. Of course, we didn't know that. We were bombed by the Germans in 1939, and the whole thing lasted a couple of weeks, until Warsaw fell. We were sure that within a few days the Germans would march in, but then we heard from the Soviets – they told us through leaflets that they were going to free us, to liberate us. Sure enough, it was September 17th when they

marched in and we welcomed them. It couldn't be worse than
the Germans, of course, and it couldn't be worse than the Polish
domination.

In 1941, Jerry was mobilized by the Russian Army,
and then demobilized and sent to a labor camp in the
Russian wilderness.

Well, I was mobilized by the Russian Army for six weeks' reserve
duty. The war started on June 22, 1941, and we started retreating
about the 27th. The Germans were quite close, about probably
100 miles. I retreated with my unit, and then I lost the unit. All
those who lived or were born in the western Ukraine deserted from
the army. They went home. The Russians then took us off the
active army and put us into work battalions.

They took us and shipped us by train, but every day the Germans bombed, and later there was no train. So finally we walked
by foot until we came deeper into Russia. Then, by train, they sent
us to near Kuybyshev, the city to which the Russian government
was temporarily vacated after the invasion. Stalin was there. We
were living in tents and the temperature was 40 degrees below zero,
Celsius.

I wound up working in a coal mine for about four years. They
took us to the coal mine walking. There was a yard and the watch-
man's little building, and there were a couple of guards standing
there. They would call you by your last name. There were about
probably 300 to 400 people going to work for the shift. Mine
was the 1A Brigade with about 30 to 40 people. There you stood
outside with the guards and dogs around you. Across the street was
a bread factory. The bread smells were killing us. You're hungry
– you ate already, but you're still hungry. Then they surround
you and you walk to the mine. The mine is working 24 hours, in
eight-hour shifts. It was the only industry that worked only eight
hours. Underground, eight hours is enough. You start digging.

Some folks used the pneumatic hammer to take the coal. I had to put it on a metal conveyor to get it out of the corridors, and then it's shoveled into little wagons and it goes by a cable up to the top.

When the war ended and Jerry was released to return home, he learned that two sisters, aged 15 and 20, had been killed, as well as one brother and both of his parents. Another brother, who had been in the partisans, was the only member of the family to survive. Mr. Slivka returned to Lodz, Poland, after the war, but found no reason to stay there, and many reasons to leave.

The antisemitism was awful. I was ready to go to Israel from Lodz. I was in a kibbutz, and they brought us a group from the Kielce Pogrom. The Jews there had been armed, but they gave away their arms because they were assured by the secret police that nothing would happen. They were all killed by a mob. A few survivors came to me. I met them personally.

When I left Poland, I was on the way to Israel. Groups of thousands of people crossed Czechoslovakia, Austria, and Italy. When I came to Italy, my brother was there already, and we decided not to part anymore. He already had made arrangements with our relatives in America. He got papers to go to America, so we had some discussions and then we finally decided to go. We came to Boston in 1948.

From 1948 to 1953, Jerry spent his time learning English, and he worked as a Hebrew teacher and a truck driver. He met his wife, who had also been born in Poland, while he was in Boston. All of her family except her sister had perished in the Holocaust. In 1953, Jerry graduated from the Bentley School of Account-

ing and Finance with a degree in accounting. In that same year, his first daughter was born. He worked as a foreman in a Boston factory, and in 1953 moved to Portland, Maine. He became an American citizen in 1954.

Jerry was chairman of the Russian Jewry Committee in Maine and participated in the settlement of Russian families. He and his wife had two children. They were founding members of the Holocaust and Human Rights Center of Maine. They were deeply committed to educating young people about the experiences of Jews and others in Europe during the Holocaust. Jerry died on January 10, 2013. He is survived by two daughters, 14 grandchildren, and numerous nieces and nephews.

CHAPTER 18

Rochelle Slivka

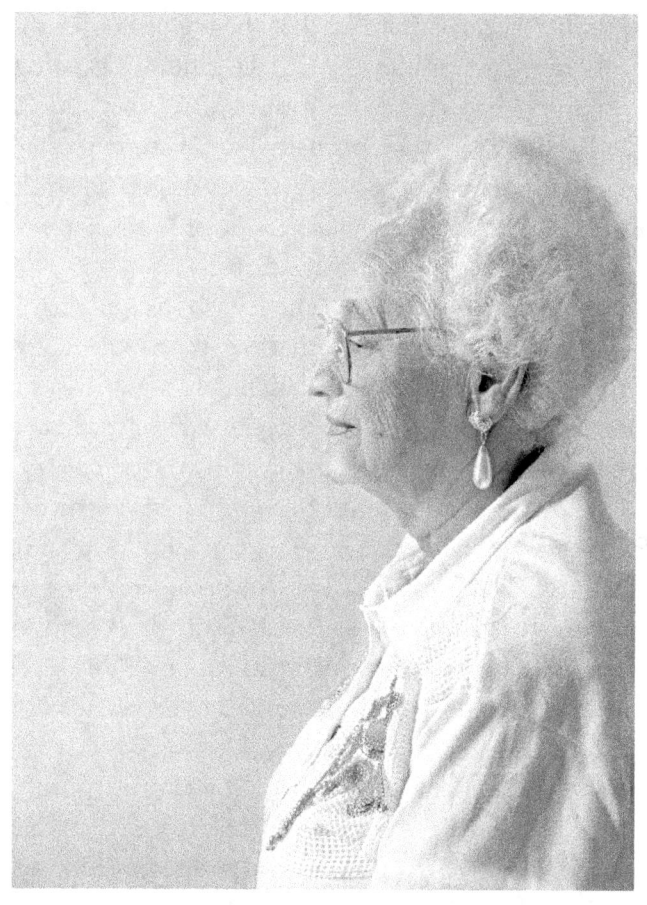

Rochelle Slivka

April 18, 1922–April 3, 2005
Vilna, Poland

M y name is Rochelle Slivka. I was born in Vilna, Poland, in 1922. My parents were traditional Jews. We kept a Jewish home, a kosher home. We knew that the life of the Jews in Vilna wasn't too easy. The public elementary school was compulsory, but the high schools weren't compulsory, and they didn't accept many Jews. They didn't accept many Jewish students to the universities, and those who were accepted were seated separately from the non-Jews, either on the left-hand side or in the back. We were always harassed by the non-Jewish students.

Still, we had our own theater. The Jewish theater was very, very good in Vilna, and we used to go to there. It was subsidized by the Jewish community, by the Kehillah. The plays in the theater were performed in Yiddish. At home we spoke Yiddish, but with the kids on the street we spoke Polish, naturally.

It was going on like this until September 1939 when the German-Polish war broke out. The Germans didn't come into our city right away. The Russians came in, because at the same time Germany and the USSR made a pact to divide Poland in half – one part was Germany, and one part was Russia. We were fortunate enough to fall into the Russian zone, and the Russians came in.

When the Russians arrived, life was going on. We went to school, we had to learn the Russian language. It was quite normal in the beginning. The Russians started to look for rich people. They sent some to Siberia. But it wasn't too bad. They didn't stay too long in Vilna. They decided to give Vilna to Lithuania because the Lithuanians claimed that Vilna belonged to them. When the Lithuanians came into Vilna, there was a pogrom on the Jews. They beat up some Jews and they killed some. Then, after a while it stabilized again, and we went back to school. We had to learn again a new language, Lithuanian. It was a hard language.

After the war broke out between Germany and Russia on June 22, 1941, our Holocaust started. The Germans came into our city of Vilna. In the beginning, it wasn't too bad because they didn't know who was a Jew and who was not a Jew. But after a while, our non-Jewish neighbors pointed out some Jews, and then they started to pick up people on the streets. They used to go into their houses. And they used to pick up some Jews, especially young men. They used to take them away and we never saw them again. We weren't allowed to stand in line for bread. They used to come out and drag us out from the lines.

We weren't allowed to walk on the sidewalks. We had to walk in the middle of the street and bow for every German. We wore yellow stars with the word 'Juden' – Jew. Then they started to recognize that we were Jews. They knew exactly who was a Jew and who was not. There were some people who didn't look like Jews or were hiding, and a lot of people didn't wear the star. But not for long.

We were still living in our house until just before the High Holy Days in 1941. The Germans always managed to have a roundup of Jews or do something to the Jews' rights before the holidays. In September, they decided to make a ghetto in Vilna. But first, they took many Jews from their houses and brought them to a place called Ponary, outside of Vilna, and they shot them there – The Ponary Massacre.

Yes, we knew about this. One night we heard some screaming and yelling and crying, but we weren't allowed to look out the window at what was going on, because whoever looked out was shot. But the next day our non-Jewish neighbors told us that all the Jews from this part of the city were taken away and taken to Ponary to be shot. Then they collected all the Jews from the city and around the city, the suburbs, and put them in the ghetto there

We stayed in the ghetto for about two years. We had to have a yellow card, and those who didn't have the yellow cards weren't allowed to stay in the ghetto. They used to take them out and shoot them. They had just so many cards to distribute, and the rest weren't allowed to work. They couldn't go out to work if they didn't have the card, and so they were taken away and shot. One day the Germans, with the help of the Lithuanian police or Ukrainian police, came in and took away all the children up to 14 or 15 years old from the ghetto. It was a couple of hundred children if not more. We used to see some Germans coming to the ghetto, but we didn't know the difference between Nazi Wehrmacht or SS or some others. There were Germans, and a lot of Lithuanian police coming in, as well as Ukrainian police. Some of them were even worse than the Germans.

In 1943, just right before the Jewish holidays again, they liquidated the Vilna ghetto. They told us over loudspeakers that we would be relocated the next day and only to take what we could carry on us, no more. The next day we were collected at the gates of the ghetto, and we were driven to a field on the outskirts of Vilna. When we came there, we saw three people hanging, a young woman and two men. They told us over loudspeakers that in case somebody had any ideas to run away they will be caught and hanged or shot in front of everybody. Well, we stayed all night in this field. It was a miserable, rainy day and night.

Then we left, by foot. We were walking all the time. When a child or baby cried, whoever was our guard at the time – a German, a Lithuanian, a Ukrainian – would take the baby to their feet and tear them apart and throw the baby back to the mother. Some mothers even choked their own children because they were afraid. This was going on like this the whole night.

The next morning, we had to stay in line and be sorted. They looked in your face and they put you either left or right. Those who went to the left went to an extermination camp, and those who went to the right went to a concentration camp. I was fortunate enough, with my sister, to go to a concentration camp. They looked in your face, and if they felt like you were fit to work you went to the right. Those who weren't fit enough to work, they took to the left. Mostly older people and very, very young children went to the left. You had to be lucky at the time, that's all. That's how we survived – because we were lucky.

They took us by cattle cars, 100 women in a car. We were standing like sardines there. We didn't have enough room to sit down, and we didn't have any bathrooms. We didn't have enough food while we were riding for a couple of days, until we came to a camp in Latvia, on the outskirts of Riga, called Kaiserwald concentration camp.3 We were met by SS men during the night, and they told us that this concentration camp was built on Jewish graves. The Jews from Riga and some from other parts of Latvia were taken there and they were shot. They were buried, and then they built a concentration camp there. They took away everything that we had with us. We had to go through showers. They shaved our heads, so in case somebody wanted to run away, she'd be recognized as a Jew from the concentration camp. They gave us uniforms with numbers. From then on, we were called by number and no more by name. We lived in barracks; we slept on long boards. We didn't have enough blankets, we didn't have pillows, we didn't have anything, only plain boards. Naturally it was very cold, and we didn't have any coats, we didn't have proper shoes, we didn't have any proper clothes. We used to get up every morning – five o'clock in the morning – and stay and be counted. In case our kapo made a mistake in counting, in punishment we had to stay another couple of hours.

I was in the first concentration camp between ten months and a year. It's hard to remember, you know. Our minds didn't work so good at the time. We lived like animals. We never knew what time of the day it was, or what day of the week. We only guessed.

Next we went to the Stutthof concentration camp. I don't know exactly why, but I guess the war was not going well for the Germans. The Russians were coming, and they were nearing this part of the country. Again, they took us to showers and shaved our heads, and gave us different clothes, striped clothes again, the same but different numbers. Most of the guards were very, very bad to us. They were Germans a lot, and it's hard to describe how bad they were to us. A lot of people were sick with typhoid or scarlet fever and other diseases, but we weren't allowed to go to the infirmary. We had to nurse ourselves.

Women were dying like flies all the time. Every day we used to lie down to sleep with a live person and wake up next to a corpse. But we were like animals ourselves. We were happy if somebody died – we could have their clothes to put on ourselves to keep us warmer. We didn't have any shoes, so we could take their clothes and wrap our feet in them. This was going on like that for almost a year in this concentration camp, and a lot of women couldn't take it any longer. They used to go out of the barracks at night, sneak out, and go and touch the barbed, electrified wires and kill themselves because they couldn't take it anymore.

Right before Christmas in 1944 or the beginning of 1945, the Germans decided to liquidate this concentration camp altogether, and they put us on a march. We were walking, and while we were walking, we saw a lot of dead people lying on the road. Men, especially men, dead, frozen. We knew that a transport with Jews went by this road.

We didn't know where we were walking, and our guards didn't know either where they are taking us. But one day we came to a barn and overnight they changed guards. They took away the young ones and they substituted them with older SS men. They were even worse than the young ones. They were so mean, it was something terrible. From then on, we couldn't go any further because they didn't know where to take us, and the old men couldn't drive us any longer.

We were in a barn, and if we had to go to the bathroom we had to go outside in the back of the barn. We didn't have any doctors, we didn't have any nurses, we didn't have medication, nothing. We were existing then, not living. We didn't work and we didn't know what to do. They didn't know themselves what to do with us. They stood there and watched us, until one day one of the guards told us that the next day, you are going to be digging ditches for yourselves because you are going to be shot. They don't want us to fall in anybody's hands, and they were going to shoot us. During the night we heard some bombing and shelling, and we didn't know what was going on.

But when we woke up in the morning, we didn't see any guards anymore. We couldn't go anywhere – we were too sick and too tired. We didn't have the strength to move. We were skeletons. We were so filthy; it was something terrible, not to wash ourselves for so many months. We didn't know what to do, but we didn't have any choice. We stayed there, until a couple of hours later a jeep filled with soldiers came.

We were liberated at the end of March or the beginning of April. I don't remember exactly the name of the city or the place where we were liberated. The Russians liberated us. They told us that the war in this part of the country was over, and we could go wherever we wanted. But where do we go? How do we go? We were so sick, we were living skeletons, that's all – only skin and bones. That's all we were.

Then they sent a truck. A couple hours later a truck came and took us to the village. It was an empty village; all the Germans ran away from there. We started to run into their houses and grab food, whatever we could find. Some were eating too much, or not the right foods. We took sick, a lot of us. Some even died because they couldn't take the food. We were like animals. We didn't know what was going on with us.

We were numb. We didn't know what was going to happen to us. We didn't know what was what. We weren't sure even that we were alive. We didn't know what was going on with us. We couldn't believe that we're free already.

The Russians treated us pretty well. We had enough food to eat, and we had enough clothes. They treated us very good. They told us that when we were ready to go, "You can go wherever you want to." We knew we were somewhere in Germany, but we didn't know where we were. After a while we got used to it, and we started to put on weight and feel better, and we started to think about going home. But where is home, where do we go? Well, my sister and myself decided to go back to the city of Vilna. We didn't have any regular transportation, so we had to hitchhike, by bus, by train, by horse and buggy, by whatever we could find.

We came to the border between Poland and the USSR, and we met some people coming out from Russia, from the city of Vilna. They told us not to go there because the situation there is very bad. There was not enough food and in general it wasn't good there. But my sister was very stubborn, and she said, no, she had to go. So she went back to the city of Vilna. After my sister reached Vilna, they closed the borders and my sister couldn't come back any more. She was left in Vilna, and Vilna was in Lithuania, and Lithuania was part of the USSR. I couldn't communicate with her at all, because Stalin was in power at the time, and it was very hard to communicate with anybody. In the meantime, she got married and had a child, and she stayed there until 1958, when she was permitted to go back to Poland. She went back to Poland with her husband and child, and from there they went to Israel.

Like many concentration camp survivors, Rochelle was among millions of displaced persons separated from their families and pre-war homes, destitute and wandering. The situation was complicated by the shifting of national borders at the end of the war and increasing tensions between the USSR and its former Allies, which made efforts to reunify families very difficult.

I registered with the authorities in the town of Bialystok, in Poland. A Jewish organization supported all the refugees. They gave us food and clothing and money, and they used to pay the rent for us, everything. We lived in private homes at the time, until we came to Germany. When I arrived there, in 1946, I lived in Landsberg in a displaced persons camp. First, I was in a sanatorium – I was still recuperating a little. Then I went to school there and I learned a profession, nursing.

I was looking for my relatives. Three of my uncles had come to the U.S. in the early 1900s, and my grandparents, two aunts, and another uncle came in 1921. My grandmother used to read the Jewish papers in the United States and she found my name and learned that I was still alive. My grandmother notified all my aunts and uncles in and around Boston and some in Maine that I was alive. After a couple of months, I received a letter from one of my uncles saying that they were happy that I was alive, and they urged me to go to the American zone in Germany, and from there, they would try to bring me to the United States.

On May 18, 1948, I came to this wonderful country. The people here in the United States were wonderful to me, the non-Jews and the Jews. People were very sympathetic, and they were very, very good. I went to school, to Brookline High, in Massachusetts. I was in my 20s already. I couldn't work as a nurse because I didn't have the license and I didn't know the language good enough. So, I worked as a nurse's aide in Beth Israel Hospital in Boston, Massachusetts. In 1951 I met my husband, Jerry Slivka, on a blind date. We were married in Boston on June 22, 1952, and had two daughters in the years that followed.

To me, it's very hard for me to talk about my experiences, because the whole picture comes in front of me, what I lived through. But I feel that it's my duty as a survivor, and as a United States citizen. It's important to me to tell the kids, to anybody who wants to listen, about my experience – they are the future generations of this country, the future leaders of this country, and I hope they can prevent it happening again. It shouldn't happen again to anybody, because it did happen to six million Jews and five million non-Jews. And it's still happening in this world.

Rochelle Slivka and her husband Jerry moved to Maine, where they spent many wonderful years. She died on April 3, 2005. She is survived by her husband, two daughters, 14 grandchildren, and numer-

ous nieces and nephews. Together with her husband, Jerry, they enjoined traveling to schools throughout the State of Maine and sharing their stories in hopes of assuring that the Holocaust would never happen again. This was a huge part of their lives. She and her husband, Jerry, were founding members of the Holocaust and Human Rights Center of Maine.

CHAPTER 19

Alan Wainberg

Alan Wainberg

1937–March 13, 2021
Zelechow, Poland

M y name is Alan Wainberg. I was born in Zelechow, Poland, a very small town about 50 or so miles south of Warsaw. My parents were Chaim Meyer Wainberg and Perla Borohovich Wainberg. There were four children before the war, but my eldest sister, Rivka, was killed during it. My parents, my next sister Sarah, my older brother Solomon (Sholem), and I survived.

I will start chronologically from what I remember, what I know. I was born in 1937. When the Germans attacked Poland in 1939, I was very young. I don't have any memories, except somewhere in my mind is a picture of all of us, very many Jews, standing in some big place or square and hearing bombs and bullets exploding. One of my parents is holding me in their arms. This was in 1939 in Zelechow.

Very soon after the occupation by Germany, all of the Jews were pushed into the ghetto. The Jews had been living more or less in one area anyway, but they were just squeezed in. Jews who were living outside of the area were put in there and non-Jews were asked to leave the area. There was some sort of fence so that people could not come and go as they pleased. You had to get special permits to leave, but they were given for commerce.

My parents were in retail business, selling and distributing various foods and staples. My mother's family had lived in Zelechow for many generations. I have very few memories of that period, again because of my age. I know that I attended classes to learn Jewish religion, Jewish history, and to read the prayer books. I know that my first language was Yiddish rather than Polish. I have a few memories of walking to the synagogue on Shabbat. In September or October of 1942 came the *vished lanya*, which is Polish for 'the taking out', 'taking away', or 'moving out'. For some time, the Germans were emptying several villages in the area. Each time there was a *vished lanya* in one village, many of the people would be taken away to the camps; others would leave and run to other cities. By the time of the *vished lanya* in Zelechow, the Jewish population had approximately doubled to 12 or 13,000, with people coming in from other areas. There was a lot of poverty, on the one hand, because there were very many refugees. On the other hand, the locals were always helping.

By this time, there were already many stories around about what was going on all over. There was still not total awareness of death camps, but there was a strong awareness of what the Germans were doing.

Prior to this *vished lanya*, there were many soldiers in town. They were often playing with Jews. I remember them grabbing a Jew by his beard and cutting it off and sometimes taking a piece of his face with it. Every once in a while, I remember, a black car would come at night with Nazis in black uniforms. They would come out and gather Jews and either shoot them or take them out and shoot them. Whenever word would get around that a car is coming, everyone would shut themselves in their homes and turn off all the lights and make themselves a harder target. But there were a number of individuals and groups taken away or shot. I was protected by my parents. I had enough to eat. I had clothing. We were even studying.

Before the *vished lanya*, my father had been taken away to a work camp which was not far away. I asked my father a few times, "What were you doing? Were you building something or making something?" He didn't talk much about it, but the answer was basically that they were moving stones. I don't know if they were really doing productive work or just keeping them busy, but he did tell stories of not having food, of working in the cold, and being submerged in water.

My family had prepared, again knowing that something was coming. They had arranged in one relative's home a hiding place in a false ceiling; that is, between the ceiling and the roof there was a crawl space. They had a place to store some food and hide maybe a dozen or so people. Also, they had arranged with a gentile man who had done a lot of business with my family to have access to a hole in the ground at his sister's farm. It was a room about the size of a normal bedroom, but the walls were bare and the bottom was bare earth. This was under the house and there was a secret entrance from inside the house. There was one small window that was almost below ground, but you could see a little bit and you could get some sunshine into it. There was a second little room for toilet facilities. They had arranged for food and a hiding place for maybe about a dozen or so people.

Another of this same man's relatives had made a similar but smaller arrangement on another farm. The main farm – the one we stayed at – was in a very small village. This must have been maybe three miles from Zelechow, out in the fields. The name of the family that hid us was Sokol.

This was in 1942 that they made the arrangement. I was 5 years old, my brother was 6, and my sisters were 7 and 8. Each of us was about a year or so apart. Now I am going to tell you about how we got there. Before the *vished lanya*, my two sisters had been sent out to stay on another gentile family's farm. So, my mother and my brother and I were in Zelechow when the announcement came that everybody must come to the town plaza together 'so that we can arrange transportation for you to move away.' There was no railroad in Zelechow, so the transportation was to go by horse and buggy, or truck, or whatever, to the nearest railroad station. It was very early in the morning. It was still dark. I have some visual pictures of running around and people running back and forth – complete chaos in town.

My mother took the two of us and we ran to that false attic hiding place right in Zelechow. As it turned out, there was a larger number of people up there than we had expected. I don't remember the number, but at least 30 or 40 people had ended up there. We were there for a few weeks. During this period, the Jews had been taken away. They were searching houses, one after another, and burning down some houses.

We were hiding upstairs with very little food – a piece of bread and a glass of water a day. We couldn't move. I was sleeping where the roof comes down to the floor. I remember one time, in the middle of the night, just raising my head, it hit the roof. Everybody panicked because they thought that was it, that the Germans heard it. Luckily, they didn't. This is a story that's hard to believe, but it is a true story. Some of it may be my own memory, some of it may be just hearing it from my mother so many times.

After a few days, we heard the Germans come into the house. They were searching everywhere. They were really going through. They had with them a Jewish policeman. Some of the Jewish police were good people who were just being forced to do it. So, one man hiding with us just said that he had to take a chance that the policeman who was down there was going to be a good one. He opened the door. It was about the size of this table. He just lifted it and stuck his hand out so that the policeman could see that there were human beings upstairs. The policeman saw it. The Germans didn't. They weren't in the room at that moment. The signal was for him to do his best to get the Germans away from that room, which he was able to do.

He and another Jewish policeman would walk the streets. Beginning the next morning, when they passed the house, knowing that we could hear what was going on in the street, they would speak in a somewhat loud voice – not looking up – just talking about what was going on and, in fact, giving us messages. Basically, they were telling us, 'You better get out of here, because no one is going to survive hiding in town,' because of the way they were doing the search. Also, they gave some other information about what happened.

The one bit that sticks in my mind was that they said that of the 13,000 or so people who had accumulated in Zelechow before the *vished lanya*, only about half were taken away. That means that between 6,000 and 7,000 had done what we did. They were hiding in cellars, in ceilings, in graves, in the fields, and everywhere else.

After hearing this from the Jewish policemen, every night a few people would leave to go to someplace else. One night, I don't know how they picked it, it was our turn. My mother took the two of us and we just walked out and started running, trying to make our way to the farm. I don't remember much. I do remember running and the tremendous fear of being seen or heard by either a German or Pole, because very many of the Polish people were in fact turning Jews in. I had an aunt and cousin who were not with us but were similarly hidden. They ran away and ran into a farmer's barn and were killed by the farmer. So we had that fear, but we made it. We stayed someplace in a barn on the way for one night. The son of the farmer came out to help us and he carried me on his shoulders the second night to get us into the hiding place.

I don't know who got there first or when, but we ended up being there with about 20 or 30 people, so there were many more people than we had anticipated. We were all in one room, sleeping on the ground, laid out side by side. There was our family and another family and some other people. Eventually, my two sisters came over from where they were hiding and hid with us, because theirs was not a safe place. My father, who had been at a forced labor camp, had managed to escape. Those labor camps were not very well guarded. My uncle and my uncle's two sons also escaped and came to another farm while we stayed at the Sokols'.

We were there for approximately two years. Sometimes at night we'd go out just to stretch or get some air, but very seldom, because it was very dangerous. If any one of the neighbors suspected that there were Jews, it was very likely they would give us away – some of them from pure hatred, some from fear, and some for money, because the Germans would give a sack of sugar for every Jew that was turned in. Jews were turned in for sacks of sugar.

The Sokol family provided us with food. For quite a while, we were paying them with things we had brought – clothing, jewelry, whatever. As that was running out, it became tougher and tougher. I will not say they were hiding us for the money. They were hiding us because of the brother, who was a very strong moral person. I wish he had survived the war, but he didn't. He had, through his own will, imposed on his family to hide us. But the money helped get us food. They obviously were a very good family to do it. They absolutely risked their lives. On the other hand, they were sort of taking advantage of having the upper hand. The food was very meager, very little. We were hungry very frequently.

Schooling? Whatever we were learning was from each other and from the parents. My father has always been religious. Even down in the hiding place, he refused to eat bread on Passover. My uncle, who was in another hiding spot throughout that period, created a complete handwritten *siddur* (prayerbook) from memory, doing the script like you see in a modern *siddur*. So, people were praying in there. We were learning something, although I don't remember. We were playing cards. It's amazing what human beings can do without when they have to. The issue was survival. Imagine children not being able to run around – never running around for two years! Occasionally going up into the field, never looking into the sun. We could see some sunlight, but it obviously had to be hidden with bushes and so on.

The season? I only remember the cold. I don't remember the change because we didn't see it, but I just remember being very cold because we didn't have any heating. In the winter it was cold. During that time, we were hearing some news of what was going on, but basically, we were completely cut off. This went on from the period from late 1942 to the spring of 1944, which is just one big block.

Here comes the hard part. It's just too hard to hide. Someone gave us away. One night, the Polish Home Army or 'AK'[1] came. The AK was said to be 'the army of the people', the folk army. They were a bunch of outlaws in Poland. Today some of them, or their children, like to talk about being the folk army or the partisans. It's a big lie. These AK were just a bunch of thugs who were out to

---

1. See **Polish Home Army (AK)** in Appendix.

kill Germans, kill Russians, kill Jews, kill anybody they could that they didn't like. They would take advantage of the situation and rob them.

They came and surrounded the house. The other family hiding with us had two older brothers, in their late teens or early twenties, and they had revolvers. These brothers said they were not going to just die. When the AK said, "We know you're there. You'd better start coming out," one of the brothers opened the door and went out with his gun and started shooting. He was shot. When we heard all the shooting, my father told my elder sister and my aunt who was hiding with us to go out through the window and try to hide. As my aunt got out, my older sister Rivka went right behind her. Then my sister Sarah started going behind them. My aunt and Rivka were shot. So, my father pulled Sarah back inside.

Things got a little calmed down and all of us, little by little, started walking up the ladder to get out. I remember that I was barefoot. I remember walking in blood that was maybe an inch deep from those two brothers who had been killed. There were a lot of things going on. I don't remember too much, except staying there in the middle of the night in tremendous fear.

There was a wagon that we were supposed to get on. My father and mother started negotiating with the men with the wagon. They knew that my parents had been very wealthy. They knew that we had buried jewelry somewhere under the store or under the house. They started negotiating that my father should take them into town – 'Let's go into town. We'll dig the stuff up and then we'll let you go.'

My father did not believe them, for very good reason. Also, he knew that the jewelry was no longer there, because the Germans and the Poles burned down the houses just to dig underneath to see what they would find. We knew it wasn't there. Anyway, he kept on negotiating with them and finally agreed. He and a few others of the men got on the wagon and they started going towards town. But it was getting too close to daylight. Of course, they were just as afraid of the Germans as we were. So, they said, "Why don't you stay here for the night. We'll come back tomorrow and bring some food early in the evening and we'll take you out and we'll go do it. We'll even give you some of the jewelry so you can survive." And they left.

What were we going to do? As soon as they left, my father and my uncle and my two cousins from the other farm decided that we were just going to run away. So, my parents, my brother, my sister, my uncle, my cousins, we all just started walking, hoping that some of my father's gentile friends might be willing to help us. The other family that was with us decided to hide on the same farm, but in a hayloft. Obviously, they wouldn't go down into the cellar, but they said, "We're not going anywhere. We'll just hide here." So my family went out on foot. This was now late spring of 1944. Zelechow and all the surrounding area was completely free of Jews except those possibly who were hiding like us.

We went out and started walking to find another hiding place. We'd walk at night. We'd go into farms, and steal milk or bread. During the day, we would hide in the rye fields. We would just hide in the burrows and eat the raw kernels. If it was raining, or if it had rained, we would be lying in the wet. Even though the temperature wasn't too cold, it was still cool enough to feel. Every night we'd get up and try to walk further. Some nights we'd pass by some farm or village and there were people watching us. My cousin would tell us to walk lively in a row. He would give marching orders so that the people would think we were partisans. Kind of pretending, we'd put sticks on our shoulders. If they thought we were partisans, they'd be afraid to approach us. If they knew who we were, some of them certainly would have approached and tried to get a sack of sugar.

We were thinking about going into the woods, which very many people had done. We were hoping to find partisans to help us, but we didn't. We had heard that the woods were the most dangerous place because that's where the Germans were most active in looking for Jews to eliminate, but also in looking for partisans, because of the threat they presented. We could hear sometimes that the war was not that far away.

We could hear the farmers reaping the fields. In fact, a farmer did see us and started talking to his horses in Polish about the fact that we shouldn't fear him but that we should leave because these fields are going to be cleared this week. So, we left the rye fields and went into the wheat fields. The harvest of the wheat is usually about two weeks later. Again, a different field each day. This was very difficult, because this crop was much lower. During the day you had to be absolutely flat on the ground. Food was a big problem. We were able to get water because every farm had its well. The farmers would milk the cows – remember, this is before refrigeration – and would put a wooden bucket of milk down into the well to keep it cool. So, we did a little larceny occasionally. On a couple of occasions, we actually bought some bread with a tiny bit of money from some of the farmers, but always with the fear that they'd give us away.

We were hiding out like this in the fields for six weeks. This had to be summer because it was harvesting season. When we were liberated, it was about *Tisha B'Av*, the traditional day of mourning in the Jewish calendar, which would be in July. It was getting worse and worse. If we had not been liberated in another four weeks, we probably would not have survived. All of a sudden, we heard rumbling of tanks and cannon going off. There was no actual war. There was nothing to fight over. But suddenly, we found out that the Russians were now occupying Poland. The Russians were moving through Poland towards Berlin in the late summer of 1944. They liberated us and we went back to Zelechow.

We went back to our home and kicked out the people who were occupying it. Now the Russians were on our side and the Jews were, in fact, using the Russians as their protectors. There was lots of talk of revenge against some of the bad gentiles, but none of it happened, at least in our town. I remember acting as a *shochet* – the person who performed the slaughter of animals per the rituals of the Torah – over some chickens because there was nobody else to do it. We started to rebuild a life. Who was left? Of the 6 to 7,000 people who had run away into hiding at the time of the *vished lanya*, only 56 people survived, including my parents with three children – my brother, my sister, and me. That's a hard statistic to think about.

At some point, Mr. Sokol was shot by the Germans. Because the Sokols were found to be hiding Jews, Mr. Sokol was shot by the Germans. So they did sacrifice. They did die.

And how did our old neighbors react when we returned? Well, we were under the protection of the Russians. My father opened up a store and started trying to make a living again, to get some possessions. People were taking properties back wherever they could. There was no joy in the gentile world around us. I remember playing with some other kids. I remember being enrolled in the public school in what would be the first grade, because I'd had no schooling in Polish. I remember having a very hard time with it, and I remember very clearly gentile boys picking on me, calling me names and throwing stones at me. They were definitely not friendly. People were coming in and telling stories of other cities, of Poles killing Jews who had survived. This happened in a few towns. Hearing that this was happening in other cities, a few months later, as soon as the Russians left, we decided, for safety reasons, that we could not live in Zelechow.

We closed down the shop and put all of our possessions on one wagon, drawn by a horse. That was the transportation of the day. We were able to get everything – furniture, pots and pans, et cetera – on the wagon and we started to trek towards Lodz which, for some reason, was the place where many Jews were coming back. It took us a few days and nights. One night we were robbed and almost everything was taken from the wagon. We continued to Lodz and got an apartment.

At this stage, at age 7, I was enrolled in a Jewish school that was teaching both Yiddish and Polish. I was then in second grade. I had never finished first grade but, for some reason, I was now attending the second grade and trying to learn Polish and a little bit of Yiddish. We had an apartment, not big and not well furnished. We also had a little store. However, at this point my father decided that we must get the hell out of Europe. He just doesn't want to be in Europe. He doesn't trust Europe. This was not just his own feeling.

The journey to America was to be a long and tortuous one for the family, lasting fifteen years and taking them to displaced persons camps in Europe, to Paris, and to Costa Rica. They were often separated. Finally, in 1959, Alan and his brother were able to get to the United States.

We came to Miami, found work as bank tellers, and attended night school. After about a year and a half, I switched to day school and to engineering, with a partial scholarship and help from my brother and parents. I finished in three years and my brother continued with accounting at night. Eventually Miami became our base. Our kid brother came to live with us and went to school. Then my sister and her family also moved to Miami with their two children. When my parents retired in 1970, they also came to Miami. I ended up at a shoe company in Miami, and because of the experience with the shoe company there, I was recruited by G.H. Bass to come to Maine. The whole family moved here six years ago.

Alan Wainberg eventually retired to Florida. He had three children and two grandchildren. He died on March 13, 2021.

CHAPTER 20

Walter Ziffer

Walter Ziffer

Born 1927
Cesky Tesin, Czechoslovakia

My name is Walter Ziffer. I grew up in Czechoslovakia in the town of Cesky Tesin. My memories of growing up there, with few exceptions, are very good. Our family life was idyllic. There were four in our immediate family. My father was a very distinguished lawyer in this town. My mother was a wonderful Jewish mother, totally devoted to the father and to the children, and I had a sister, Edita. The town is beautifully located in the midst of the Carpathian Mountains. We would go on excursions on weekends into the mountains.

My father was an outstanding person in terms of culture, though he was not an observant Jew. My mother lighted the candles on Shabbat, but we went to synagogue only on Yom Kippur or Rosh Hashanah. I received practically no Jewish education. We were an assimilated Jewish family. The outstanding memory is that my father was a very esteemed citizen. When we went on a walk on the main street of Cesky Tesin, practically everyone would lift their hat and say, "*Dobry den, Pane Doktore.* Good day, Herr Doktor." Of course, my sister and I would get a big charge out of this. The memories are wonderful. It was a good life.

Things started changing in 1938. That is roughly one year before World War II began, because in 1938 Cesky Tesin and the area surrounding it was annexed by the Polish government. There never has been much love between Czechs and Poles, and our town was about 30,000 inhabitants, divided by a river, half of it Polish, half of it Czech. My grandparents lived on the Polish side. Most of the grandparents' children were on the Czech side. In 1938, the Poles took over.

At that time, my father was head of the Jewish community in Cesky Tesin. I remember how, on that fateful day of October 2nd or 3rd, the whole Polish delegation, including the rabbi of the Polish side, came across one of the bridges and annexed us. The Polish rabbi annexed the Czech religious congregation, and my father subsequently lost his license to practice law. Of course, he also was no longer head of the Jewish religious organization or congregation of Cesky Tesin.

We had to start going to Polish school – I, my sister, our cousins, et cetera – and that was very distasteful to us. It was in the Polish school that antisemitism was quite pronounced. I'm thinking particularly of one teacher who would always, as he called some of us to recite a poem or whatever in front of the class, make antisemitic remarks and sort of imitate Yiddish. Of course, he couldn't because he wasn't a Jew, but that was just a terrible put-down for the Jews in class, and we could not respond.

That is a very bad memory, although at one time prior to that, still under the Czech regime, a friend of mine who was an Orthodox Jew and I were actually stoned on our way home from school. We had to just save ourselves by running away. That was the only overt antisemitic event in my life prior to the Polish annexation. But during the Polish annexation, things were quite antisemitic, and overtly so.

I think it will be oversimplifying to say that we knew nothing about the conditions, say, in Germany prior to 1938 or '39. Let me relate one case to you because it is typical and indicative of how we thought about this whole danger that was approaching.

A cousin of my mother lived in Vienna. I don't remember his last name, but they called him Franzerl. He came to our house in 1938 as a refugee from annexed Austria. He told us gruesome stories about how the Nazis had begun treating the Jews as they entered Vienna, and how many suicides took place immediately after the annexation of Austria. My father was skeptical about the story. He was imbued with the Germanic spirit, and he was cultured – Schiller, Goethe, Beethoven, Grillparzer, and so forth and so on. This is the kind of culture I was brought up in, so he just could not envision that Germans would be treating, say, intellectual Jews in that terrible manner.

At one point Franzerl said, "Well look, I'll show you something." He took his shirt off and he showed us his back and chest, just totally scarred. There were not pinpoint scars, but scars as big as the tip of my finger. We looked at this and, asked, "What in the world are you showing us?" He said, "Well, I was interrogated by the Gestapo, and they tortured me by extinguishing cigarettes on my back and chest. These are the scars that are left over." My mother, being a very compassionate woman, broke out in tears, of course. But my father still was not convinced.

On the first of September 1939, the town was totally deserted. We were now in Poland, remember, having been annexed by Poland, and very close to the former Czech border. I was 12 years old. About two hours later, there was a tremendous amount of noise coming from the retreating Polish army that just came rushing through the main street of our town. Our apartment was on the main street, on the second floor. It was totally chaotic. There were soldiers, there were peasants, there were horses, cows, goats, you name it. I mean a hectic retreat that lasted perhaps for 45 minutes, or an hour. We watched it from our window. We were just fascinated, you know – what's going on? Then I remember a lonely plane being shot at. We never saw that plane. Another hour later it was again total silence.

Then the sound of oncoming traffic and the first sight of a motorcycle with a sidecar and two SS men in their black uniforms. Then various military vehicles – personnel carriers, you name it – just very orderly marching, taking the same paths that those retreating Poles had taken, and just passing through. That's when we knew we were occupied.

On September 1st, on that very first night when the Germans had come in, our synagogues burned, both in the old Czech part of Tesin and in the Polish part of Tesin. We were aware of the burning on the Czech side where we lived – which had now become German, of course – and my father took me to the balcony. It was an eerie night. There was silence, and then there were these crashing sounds of breaking glass, a lot of laughter, just a mob sound you might say. It was about five blocks away from us. The sky lit up red.

The next morning, when we went over there, the synagogue was in ruins. The same thing had happened to the huge temple across the river in the ex-Polish side of the city. These were some of the first signs.

Now, it so happened that the SS command of our town (which took its old Austrian-Hungarian name of Teschen at that point) installed itself on the floor below our apartment. For about four or five days nothing happened. We were scared to death, of course, walking to the second floor always through the midst of these SS people, but they didn't bother us. About two weeks later, the ordinance came out for us to wear white armbands with a blue Star of David – all Jews. Of course, at that point it became terrible, because people started, you know, hitting us, spitting on us, saying all sorts of things like *Judensau, Judenschwein* – Jew pig, Jew sow – to us, et cetera.

Another few days later, we were thrown out of the apartment, and we left without any furniture. We moved into an uncle's apartment about three blocks from there who owned his own house. That liberated us from the terrible situation with the SS, but that was the first point at which we lost 90 percent of our belongings, including a beautiful 3,000-volume library.

We remained in Teschen for roughly another two years, until June 1942. During that time, we were thrown out of apartments successively five or six times, ending up on the periphery of the town in an old restaurant ballroom place. There were 20 families in the big ballroom. We had compartments – the whole ballroom was divided up with curtains. Some people lived on the stage, such as my uncle and his family. That was the last dwelling prior to our deportation.

My first deportation happened in June 1942, when I was 15 years old. We were told to assemble in the morning in an old junkyard on the ex-Polish side of the city, with one suitcase for each person. By then, the Jewish population of Teschen had been reduced slowly. I cannot tell you how many people were involved. Perhaps

1,000 out of 3,000 that made up the population of Teschen. So we went, we got our own suitcase, and we went to the *Sammelplatz*, as they called it, or "assembly place" – the junkyard – only to see a big table with SS people, whips, guns on the table, threatening us and telling us, 'Now you give us all the jewelry, all the money, all the things that have this kind of worth.' Most people gave it to them. Some people resisted, some were searched, and if valuables were found they were beaten to shreds.

The first camp Walter was sent to was in Sosnovitz and was called 'the Dulag'.

The Dulag was a five-story wooden house with these tiered partitions where you slept. Of course, boys were separated from girls. We did nothing. We were counted, we were fed some terrible food for the first time, you know, food prepared in the camp. I remember for the first two days I gave my food away; I couldn't eat it. On the third day I started eating it. During our stay in the Dulag, which was about two or three weeks, one night we heard screams and cries. We were free to circulate in that building, and I remember walking down one or two stories and there were all these corridors filled with stretchers with people who looked absolutely horrible. I mean, they were skeletons, they stank, they were in shreds as far as the clothes are concerned. They howled.

I couldn't make out what that was all about. One of my friends said, "Well, these people are on the way to a convalescences camp. They must have been working very hard or may have caught some diseases, and now they're on their way to a convalescents camp." So much for that. It scared the daylights out of me.

Over the next two years, Walter would be sent to several camps. The first was a forced labor camp (a 'Zwangsarbeitslager') named Sakrau, where he was forced to help build Hitler's interstate highways. He would go through seven different camps before being liberated on May 8, 1945. His next camp after Sakrau was called Brande.

Well, we got to Brande. That was a camp housing probably 400 to 600 people, something like that. It was not a huge camp. When we arrived in Brande, we lined up for the *Appell* (roll call). You've heard about the *Appell*, where you stand for hours and are repeatedly counted, so forth and so on. You must give your name. The *Lagerkommandant* (camp commander) was a man by the name of Pompe. He had one wooden leg. He looked like the spitting image of Hitler. The Jewish commandant of the camp (the *Judeneldester*) was a man by the name of Gebuhrer, who happened to be from a town about 40 miles from my hometown. He came to me with Pompe. I was asked my name and when I said, "Walter Ziffer," he said, "aren't you the son of Dr. Ziffer, the lawyer in Teschen?" When I said yes, he had me step out of the ranks. Then he said, "You're going to be my private servant." Thus, I was very privileged in Brande – so privileged that I saw what went on in that camp.

What I found out was that Pompe was an absolute sadist who took pleasure in killing people personally. There was a rite, as it were, in camp, whereby during selections when we lined up to be counted in the morning or in the evening, he would select his victims. He would take these victims into the shower barracks and kill them – but kill them in a very peculiar way. He had kapos, Jewish camp police, throw buckets of cold and hot water, alternating, on these people standing there until they died. It was boiling water then ice-cold water. He stood there and watched it, and I had to stand there quite often with the Jewish commandant next to him and watch it. That spaced me out – I mean, I don't know how many people I saw killed that way, writhing on the floor and finally just dying of a heart attack or stroke or whatever.

This just demolished me: Once, I had to get up early in win-tertime to make a fire in the stove. I crossed the *Appellplatz* and I saw a lonely older Jewish man in one corner of the camp by the fence, fooling around with his blanket. He must have wet it, that would be my guess, and wanted to hang it up on the fence to dry it, unbeknownst to the Germans. I saw a German guard walking up to the man from the outside. There was a double fence in those camps. He said, "You, Jew, what are you doing?" The man said, "I'm hanging up my blanket to air it out," in Yiddish of course. The guard said, "Well, why don't you do it well, why don't you hang it up on those hooks on the barbed wire, make sure that it's hanging well." The man turned around and hung it up well, and the guard shot him down in cold blood. The old man was laid out during the next *Appell* in front of the whole group, and it was said that he had tried to escape and was shot during his escape.

It was a hell. It was an absolute hell. We stood being counted for three hours. You see, there was no work – it was strictly a circus for that man Pompe. We'd wet our pants, our shoes froze to the snow, to the ice. There were special dust *Appells* where we had to bring out our blankets and he would hit them with his whip, and if there was any bit of dust, you were whipped. That was the first camp, by the way, in which kapos carried whips, long and tapered to a point, about six layers of leather, and in the middle layer there was a piece of steel.

I was caught once during wintertime in the shop where the Jewish inmates made the beautiful black boots for the guards and the kapos. It was warm in there. Those were privileged people for a particular time. I, being privileged myself at the time, walked in there and wanted to warm myself up. Pompe came in and asked me, "What are you doing here?" I mumbled something, I don't know what I said. He had me turn around. A kapo came, took my head between his legs, two kapos held my feet, I was stripped down, I mean my pants went off, and he personally hit me with that whip 25 times. This can't be described, I mean the pain that you experience. I thought I was dying. Then I was detailed to a group cleaning out the latrines for about a week – despite my privileged status, you see – and then I was back on good terms with everybody.

One case that really finished me off involved a man by the name of Bornstein. He was a young man who worked in the camp office. I can see him as today. He was a short stocky fellow with thick glasses. One day I was called to the refectory where we ate, and Pompe was there. He asked Bornstein, "Did you send this letter? Was it you?" When Bornstein said "Yes, it was I," Pompe, Gebuhrer, and the kapos beat that man to death before my eyes. They beat out his eyes. I didn't know what to do. The man finally fell down as if lifeless. They dragged him and dumped him into the coal chute under the wash barracks.

After this hideous ordeal, Gebuhrer took me back to his room. I was scared. I was weeping. On the way I felt his hand stroking my head, and him saying, "My little one, try to forget what you saw." I wish I could forget it.

We heard the man howl throughout the night. That next morning, they pulled him out, put him in a cart, took him to the woods and put him into a mass grave. No markers, no anything.

At that point my spiritual life or existence was in total shambles, I was undone. I mean, this is not to say that we had lost all human individuality or identity. But it was seeing these people being tortured and die that, well, that finished me up. From then on, I was some kind of a being living on a lower scale of humanity, you might say, though physically still in fairly good shape.

Walter was then sent to other camps including Klettendorf and then Schmiedeberg, where German rockets were assembled. His last transport was to Waldenburg near the German city of Breslau.

We arrived in Waldenburg, and at that point, we had no more underwear, just the pajamas. The weave of the pajamas was thin enough to see right through them. Shoes with wooden soles – the top being cloth, but no shoelaces, and only a rag to put into the shoe, no socks. This is how we had to survive. That was a relatively big camp; Waldenburg may have had 2,000 people, I don't know. But there was a triple fence there – the electric fence in addition to the two other fences – and there were suicides on that fence fairly often.[1] There were miradors (guard towers) with machine guns, which were in all the camps. In Waldenburg, we worked for the IG Farben[2] industry, a big German chemical outfit. We were in construction work, extremely heavy construction work, about ten to twelve hours per day, expanding the factory. What they made there I don't know.

We marched through the town every morning. People saw us. We marched through the town coming back at night. The *Appells* were unending, again, and the people were at the end of their strength. I mean, people dropped right and left, on the way to work, on the way back from work. They were sometimes left lying there, they were sometimes shot.

One of the most, most excruciating things that I remember from Waldenburg was these shoes, because in wintertime the snow would build up under the sole of the shoe and our feet. Our legs weren't very strong at that point anymore, you know, and when we walked, we would go this way and that way and this way and that way. We would have to hold each other up and drag each other to work, and even hold each other while we stood up eating. The food at that point amounted to probably less than ten ounces of bread per day. Sometimes one would get eight ounces, depending on who cut the bread and whether he liked you or not. There was one bowl of soup, literally water, at noon – lukewarm water with a few peels on top – and coffee in the morning and coffee at night.

My major preoccupation during that year in Waldenburg was how or what to do with my bread. Should I eat my bread in

---

1. See **suicides by prisoners** in Appendix.

2. See **IG Farben** in Appendix.

one piece when it was given to me at night? That way I had it within me, and it would give me some strength, but then there was nothing for 24 hours. Or should I eat half of it and hide half of it in the straw overnight? Or should I just eat a little piece of it and hold it in my pocket, and eat tiny little chunks of it during those 24 hours? I opted for eating the bread as it was given to me because the danger of having it stolen was so great.

There was at this point hardly any communication with my fellow inmates. We were apathetic. We were totally subhuman at that point. I would like to relate to you one instance to show you how subhuman we were. It's a little complicated story. We marched through town, as I told you. On the march we passed a particular church early in the morning, when it was still dark. A figure came toward us, toward this marching column, and threw a package into our ranks. I happened to catch this package. It was brown paper. I started ripping it open. Shots rang out. There were hands all over me trying to grab what I had, and I retrieved a portion of what was basically two slices of dark bread with margarine. I got some of it down my throat, the other stuff was grabbed from me. I marched on. I spent all that day at work making holes for dynamite and shoveling and working with a pick and what have you. I came home at night. I took off my shoes – I didn't undress my clothes ever during those days. I looked, and there was a hole in my foot, a hole right here. A bullet had gone right through my foot. I had not noticed it; it was bitter cold. There was no blood. I don't understand it. I mean, you can see what's there today.

Becoming ill meant being sent to Auschwitz. We knew about Auschwitz at that time already, what was happening there and in other extermination camps. So I kept on going to work. It was not too much of a burden in terms of hurt. Within six to eight days, this wound started festering, and when I took my rag off it would be glued onto this wound and the thing would turn colors and expand. I finally told myself I had to go see the camp doctor. He was a Jew, of course. I went to see him, a lovely man from Holland.

He looked at it and said, "Now look, this has to be taken care of. You're going to lose your foot, or you'll go even before then to Auschwitz. I'm going to hide you."

There was this camp hospital consisting probably of 20 beds, three-tiered beds again. Not beds, but wooden structures with straw in them, and covers, bed covers. He put me on the floor under one of those and so arranged the blankets of the lowest bed that they would hang down on all four sides. I spent about two weeks lying on the floor there. When the Germans came in to count, he would give a false count. He jeopardized his own life in doing this. I don't know how they dealt with this absent person in terms of counting. I have no idea.

I want to relate to you what had happened to me also. At one point, as I lay there on the floor under those tiered beds, a bowl of hot soup was pushed toward me through these blankets, and I peeked out. Well, I mean I had to. I saw next to the bed a foot whose toes were black. I just saw a hand with a pair of pliers cutting off those black toes with a pair of ordinary pliers. They were gangrene toes. I pulled in my bowl of soup and finished eating it with a lot of appetite. It was some assistant there cutting off the toes of a prisoner who had frozen toes. But I mean, to give you an example of what happens to humanity as we perceive it, by then I was down to 90 pounds.

It was toward the end of the war. I leave it to your imagination that there were daily beatings and daily deaths, and daily there were people found dead on the beds being carted away, I mean that's how it was. It didn't particularly impress me, I must say. I had no sensitivity left. But what happened then on that last day – that was May 8th, 1945 – we were standing again, early in the morning, on the *Appellplatz* being counted by the Jewish kapos and the *Judeneldester*. We stood there, and stood there, and stood there, it must have been two or three hours. Nothing happened. Finally, the *Lagerkommandant*, the German, came in. He was a Waffen-SS man. He made some cynical remark to the Jewish leaders, I don't know what it was. I mean he grinned; it was such an ugly grin on him. He turned around, walked out of the gate, took a ring with keys off his belt and threw this ring with the keys back over the fences. The ring of keys landed in camp. He walked away.

We all stood there at attention another two hours. We did not comprehend what had happened. I do remember looking at these towers, called miradors. Usually, you know, an SS was up there or a home guard. They had all sorts of people guarding us in those days, older people, grandfathers, you name it. But nobody was up there next to the machine gun. I did not understand, nobody did. So we just stood there.

Then we heard a rumbling noise, closer, closer, closer, and one solitary Soviet tank appeared with a Russian star painted on the turret. That tank just went right into the triple fence and crushed it, and then went right on. It never stopped. We still stood there. I didn't have a watch obviously, but it seemed like an eternity. We kept on standing there. There was no fence, and there were no guards.

Finally, the assembly started breaking up, maybe another hour and a half. I mean, it's incredible to me today. People sort of shuffled around. What do we do with ourselves now?

A friend of mine, an Austrian whose name was Karl, decided to go to town, to Waldenburg. Maybe we can find some food. You know, as I give talks, most people ask me, 'Well, what about revenge? You know, this was the time to take revenge!' Well, not a soul thought of taking revenge. It never entered my mind. Food was on our mind, day and night, 24 hours a day.

We walked to Waldenburg, very shakily, and in one of the streets in Waldenburg we saw a truck parked. We scrambled onto that truck, and it was loaded with brown cans and sacks of some sort. Somehow, we found a screwdriver, and we punched holes into the cans. When we opened the first can, there was a layer of pork grease on top and then pork in it. These were rations, German army rations. My friend and I delved into this and we stuffed our mouths with pork. Then he said, "Hey, how about the sacks?" When we ripped open the sacks, sugar poured out. We stuffed ourselves with sugar. And then we passed out.

I remember nothing until I woke up in a bed between two clean sheets in a tiny little room. I looked to my right, and there was another bed there, beautifully made up. I thought I had arrived in heaven. But the door opened, and an old lady came in. She looked at me, saw that I was awake, and she smiled at me. She said to me, "*Jetzt ist das vorbei*," which means, 'Now it's over, it's past.' I stayed with this woman. My friend woke up too within two, three hours. She fed us, and she nursed us back for three or four days until we felt able to stand on our feet and walk.

So now we were humans again, more or less. What should we do? We go back to camp, go back to this damned concentration camp. That camp was still full of people. We don't know what to do with ourselves. Food started arriving, you know; the Soviet army brought in beets, potatoes, bread, and stuff like that, so we were no longer hungry. Maybe a week later women arrived, they were in concentration camp garb. I walk up to one group of these women and say, "Excuse me, please, but did you ever in your time by any chance run into a Mrs. Ziffer somewhere?" One woman said, "Sure, she was my bunkmate, she is in Langenbielau."

Well, I requisitioned a bicycle from the first German that rode by on a bike, and he willingly stepped off. The people were deadly scared of us at that point, although nothing had happened to my knowledge. I don't know how long it took me, but I biked to Langenbielau and walked into the women's camp. My mother wasn't there, but I asked my way around. The women in the barracks knew her and they just lavishly fed me. They took me in like a child of their own.

Then my mother came in, together with my sister and my cousin Ilse, who had lost both her parents in Auschwitz. My mother didn't know me. She walked right by me. I think the women got a charge out of this. They thought that was a joke and then told her, "Hey, your son is here! You walked right by him!" Then we recognized each other, and you can imagine the celebration. It had been almost three years since we had been separated.

By the end of the war, Walter had been in seven camps, beginning when he was 14 years old. He returned to his hometown of Cesky Tesin and became an automobile mechanic. As the Soviet Union began asserting its rule over Czechoslovakia, Walter managed to make his way to Paris and then to the United States, arriving with five dollars in his pocket. He eventually received an engineering degree from Vanderbilt University, two master's degrees from the Graduate School of Theology at Oberlin College, and a doctorate in theology from the University of Strasbourg in early Christian history, Biblical Hebrew, and comparative religion. He has authored several books, including The Teaching of Disdain: An Examination of Christology and New Testament Attitudes Toward Jews *(1990),* The Birth of Christianity from the Matrix of Judaism: From Jewish Sect to World Religion *(2001), and* Confronting the Silence: A Holocaust Survivor's Search for God *(2017).*

CHAPTER 21

Afterward

Walter Ziffer, Ph.D

L et me tell you a story. It is a true story, though not a story about me. The story is told by an Italian Jewish chemist whose name was Primo Levi.

Primo Levi was imprisoned in Italy with other members of an anti-Fascist group. Eventually, he was transferred to the extermination camp of Auschwitz in German-occupied Poland. After a harrowing long train ride in cattle cars during which the prisoners received neither food nor water, they arrived, starved and thirsty, at the Auschwitz camp, and after lengthy arrival procedures, they were assigned to sleeping quarters.

Upon entering the barracks, Levi noticed a long icicle hanging outside one of the windows. Terribly thirsty, he walked over and reached for the icicle to break it off. In the process of reaching for it with his arm, he received a harsh blow. Hurting from this totally unexpected savage blow, one of the few German words he knew came to his lips.

"*Warum*? [Why?]" he screamed.

"*Hier gibt es kein warum!*[Here whys do not exist!]" came the quick answer in a gruff voice.

I am telling you this story because in a way it contains the answer to the often-asked questions: Why the Holocaust? Why is teaching about the Holocaust so very important, even to this day? What does it mean for a society in which 'Whys do not exist'?

I mentioned in my earlier account an episode that I need to return to here. It was the winter of 1944, and I was 17 years old. It was bitter cold. Snow was on the ground. It was the last year of

World War II. The German Nazi government under the leadership of Adolf Hitler still administered 20,000 detention, forced labor, concentration, and extermination camps in Germany and its occupied countries.

As a Jew, I had been deported from my hometown of Cesky Tesin in what is now the Czech Republic, and I found myself in the seventh concentration camp since then, in the camp of Waldenburg, in eastern Germany. At that point in time, I and my fellow prisoners had been reduced to skin-covered skeletons. All of us had lost our humanity and had become the *Untermenschen*, or subhumans, just as Hitler had planned. We even had lost our names. I had become an object: #64,757.

One early morning, after roll call, still in the dark, we marched to the work site through the city of Waldenburg, as usual, flanked by SS guards. Marching through the streets, I often looked longingly at the windows of the homes, dreaming of what might be going on in the warm rooms. Often, I saw the blinds moving. People in those warm rooms peeking down at us, the living dead, marching below.

Still in early darkness, as we passed a church building, a figure emerged out of the darkness, running toward us. The person threw a small package into our ranks. Shots rang out. I caught the package and tried to rip it open. There were suddenly many hands around me trying to wrest the package from me. With the wrapping paper in shreds, I desperately held on to two thin slices of buttered bread. Alas, within a few seconds, all that was left in my hand was a small part of the treasure, just enough for one bite. What happened to our benefactor, I do not know...

It is a simple story. Yet, in my opinion, a very complex one. It is a story behind which lurks the complex necessity of decision-making by human beings like you and me, a necessity crucially important for ourselves, for our fellow humans, for good or for bad. This decision-making falls into the category of ethics.

In these stories we encounter four categories of people, three of whom made choices in thought and behavior: the perpetrators, the bystanders, the heroes, and the victims.

What do we know about the perpetrators? Who were they? The frightening answer to this question is that in many cases they were ordinary people like you and me, indoctrinated into the Nazi culture of hate through constant propaganda in media, in schools, and in youth groups. Following my lectures, I am often asked whether a Holocaust-like catastrophe could happen again, even in our country. While this seems unlikely, my answer is YES – simply because our biological makeup is the same as that of many of the Nazi murderers. Well-run propaganda is a powerful instrument. Democracy is fragile. This is how the Germans under Hitler lost it. Beware! And better still, be aware in time, before it is too late.

What about the bystanders? Martin Niemöller of the German Confessing Church of that time reminds us:

First they came for the Communists, and I did not speak out because I was not a Communist.

Then they came for the Socialists, and I did not speak out because I was not a Socialist.

Then they came for the Jews, and I did not speak out because I was not a Jew.

And then they came for me – and there was no one left to speak out for me.

The Holocaust happened because the German people let it happen. They were bystanders. They refused to be confused by the facts. These men and women ignored the radical evil that was happening in their very presence and under their noses. They did not ask questions when their Jewish neighbors suddenly disappeared. And so over time they came to share the guilt of the perpetrators.

The third category in these stories are the heroes – those folks who resisted becoming inhuman and evil instruments of the Nazi machine. In my case, they are represented by the person who, ignoring the danger of her action, threw the sandwich into our ranks, risking her life. They are the people who sheltered and fed the Jews and other 'enemies' of the Nazi regime, doing so at the risk of their own lives.

The fourth category are the victims. Clearly, the six million murdered Jewish Holocaust victims did not choose that fate. The fourteen innocent members of my family did not choose to be killed. They did not choose to be born to a Jewish couple, either. That simply happened, just as the circumstances and background of our parents happens to all of us.

In reading these accounts of the survivors, what lessons can we learn? What questions can we ask ourselves? How would we have responded if we had lived in the Nazi-ruled portions of Europe in these days? For me, one lesson is this: Let us be cautious but not afraid, remembering that inaction by the German people allowed the Holocaust to happen. The key to preventing a repeat catastrophe is asking questions – seeking out the facts and rejecting the slogans. We need to embrace a healthy skepticism about what we are told, to insist that we live in a world in which whys *do* exist, to be explored and answered. This leads to critical thinking, which in the end, is our best defense against the menace of totalitarianism. And beyond that, we need to have the courage to speak up.

In closing, let me share with you the words of John Schaar, a modern-day prophet-scholar: 'The future is not some place we are going, but one we are creating. The paths are not to be found but made. And the activity of making them changes both the maker and the destination.'

What path will you take?

CHAPTER 22

From Tragedy to Hope

Aaron Rosen, Ph.D, M.Phil

Antisemitism is metastasizing in ways that many Jews, especially in America, hoped had long disappeared, or at least retreated into the margins. Instead, this ancient hatred seems to have a received a shot in the arm in the 21st century. As antisemitism emerges from the shadows on both the far right and the far left, many Jews understandably fear that less and less daylight remains for them in public life. In these conditions, the specter of the Holocaust feels more and more proximate, not just as a recent past but a possible future.

This resurgence of antisemitism comes at an especially precarious moment for Holocaust remembrance. The number of Holocaust survivors still living is dwindling rapidly, depriving us of firsthand witnesses just as their veracity and courage is needed most. What will the future of Holocaust memory be as we reluctantly envision a post-survivor era?

Some aspects are clearer than others. The personal burden of transmission will shift to second, third, and fourth generations who heard the experiences of survivors firsthand, or felt the weight of intergenerational trauma in their own lives, emotionally or even epigenetically. Official structures of memory are already in place at institutions like the U.S. Holocaust Memorial Museum in Washington, D.C., and Yad Vashem in Jerusalem, as well as at numerous smaller institutions around the world, including the Holocaust and Human Rights Center of Maine. Yet, they too will face new challenges as they seek to educate generations with vastly different habits and expectations for consuming information and building meaningful experiences. Creative responses to the Holocaust in art, film, music, and many other modes of expression will continue to germinate in the minds of those who did not experience the Shoah nor even know anyone who did, presenting new risks and fresh possibilities along the way. The links in these chains of transmission will be tested in novel ways, especially in an online ecosystem of rampant disinformation, deepfakes, and other emergent dangers.

Looking at this uncertain terrain ahead, the Maine Holocaust survivors project that has served as the source for this book provides some compelling ways forward. These survivors' narratives accompanying their portraits focus not just on the catastrophe of the Shoah, but on the wider arc of survivors' lives, before and after the events of the Holocaust. They draw attention to the astonishing resilience with which survivors navigated the changed and devastated worlds into which they emerged. Their relaxed yet unflinching gazes in these photographs draw out this quality of quiet determination. While the focus of the project remains squarely on preserving Holocaust memory, the resilience shown in these photographs has the potential to communicate across generations, speaking to multiple contexts. For young people, inundated with bleak projections for a climate-changed world, the defiant fortitude of survivors may sow seeds of resilience in their own lives, cultivating the kind of hope needed to create new worlds.

Aaron Rosen, PhD
Searsport, Maine, 2024

CHAPTER 23

Appendix

American Jewish Joint Distribution Committee (JDC): Together with the Hebrew Immigrant Aid Society (HIAS) and other organizations, provided support to Jewish displaced persons after the war. It played an instrumental role in assisting Holocaust victims to leave Europe and resettle elsewhere.

Anschluss: The German annexation of Austria on March 11-13, 1938. This was accomplished with the connivance of Austrian Nazis, who vigorously supported Hitler's campaign against the Jews. The harassment of and violence against Jews by Austrian citizens, even in the culturally rich city of Vienna, intensified and were widely publicized throughout the world. Among other humiliations, the Nazis forced Jewish women to clean sidewalks. Images of this appeared in newspapers throughout Europe and the United States.

Appell; Appellplatz: The roll call of prisoners [*Appell*] held at a location on the grounds inside the camps (*Appellplatz*). Prisoners were forced to stand in lines, often for hours and in all kinds of weather, until the guards and **Kapos** had finished their counts. The practice is mentioned by many survivors as a daily torment which they dreaded.

Auschwitz-Birkenau: Extermination camp located in German-occupied Poland. At first it housed political prisoners as a concentration camp, but later became a centerpiece of the effort to destroy Europe's Jews and other "undesirables." It was ultimately made up of more than 40 subcamps, including a slave labor camp for a chemical plant run by **I.G. Farben**, the same conglomerate that produced the chemical Zyklon B used to murder Jews and others in the gas chambers. Construction began on the Birkenau subcamp (also known as 'Auschwitz II') in 1941 to greatly expand the capacity of the original camp to kill prisoners. Most of the murders at Auschwitz occurred at Birkenau. On arrival at the train ramp of Birkenau, the Nazis separated Jewish women and children from the men. German camp authorities sent the vast majority of children directly to the gas chambers upon arrival at Auschwitz-Birkenau and other killing centers. It has been established that there were approximately 232,000 children and young people up to the age of 18 among the 1.3 million or more people deported to the Auschwitz-Birkenau camp. The Nazis murdered more than a million deportees there, mostly Jews from across Europe.

Blood Libel: An antisemitic trope with roots in medieval times that has been invoked for centuries as a justification for the harassment and killing of Jews. It is the false accusation that Jews murdered Christian children to extract their blood, which was then used in religious rituals including the baking of *matzah* (unleavened bread used by Jews at the festival of Passover). At various times, some Christian denominations have both promoted and discouraged the myth of the blood libel.

Buchenwald: One of the largest concentration camps established within the borders of Germany. When it opened in 1937, its prisoners were primarily communists and other political prisoners. After **Kristallnacht** in 1938, 10,000 Jewish men were sent to the camp, where they endured concentrated abuse that claimed the lives of at least 250 in the early weeks, followed by many others. The camp's inmate population grew to include Jewish women, Allied prisoners of war, **Romani** and Sinti ('Gypsies'), prominent political figures from countries conquered by Germany, and others. At Buchenwald, the Germans murdered at least 56,000 of the more than 250,000 prisoners who entered its gates. The prisoners liberated the camp themselves as the guards fled in April 1945 before the arrival of the 6th Armored Division, part of American General George S. Patton's Third Army.

Chancellor: The head of state of Germany. President Paul von Hindenburg named Hitler as Chancellor on January 30, 1933. Hitler immediately began consolidating Nazi party control in Germany, expanding the role of the **Gestapo** as a major force in forming a police state, manipulating elections, and targeting so-called enemies of the state.

Chumash: A book-bound edition of the **Torah**, the compilation of the first five books of the Hebrew Bible; namely, the books of Genesis, Exodus, Leviticus, Numbers, and Deuteronomy, also called the Five Books of Moses, or the Pentateuch.

Colored triangle badges: Beginning in 1938, Jewish concentration camp prisoners were required to wear a yellow badge on their uniforms. The system was expanded in 1939 to include colored badges for other categories of prisoners, including, for example, those accused of being gay (pink), common criminals (green), Romani (black), and political prisoners (red).

Deaths after liberation: Many concentration camp inmates died soon after their liberation by Allied forces. Typhus and other diseases ran rampant through every camp, and the fatal effects of profound malnutrition continued to be felt. For example, when the British liberated the camp at Bergen-Belsen on April 15, 1945, they found about 60,000 living inmates, of whom between 10 and 15,000 would die in the following weeks. Similar deaths were repeatedly noted at other camps.

Deggendorf displaced persons camp: Established in the American-occupied zone of Germany after the end of WWII. At its fullest, some 2,000 Holocaust survivors lived there, many of them survivors of the **Theresienstadt (Terezin) ghetto** in Czechoslovakia. It closed on October 18, 1948.

Displaced persons (DP) camps: By the end of World War II, more than 40 million people had been displaced from their homes, of whom at least eleven million were then in Germany. These included former prisoners of war, slave laborers, concentration camp and extermination camp survivors, and others driven from communities devastated by the war. Most were now without a residence to return to, and justifiably feared ongoing hardship, ethnic animus, and antisemitism in their former home countries. Disease and starvation were rampant. The United States, Great Britain, and other nations established a series of camps that were taken over by the United Nations Relief and Rehabilitation Administration (UNRRA) on October 1, 1945. The fortunate among the displaced persons were able to resettle in other countries where they could rebuild their lives, but immigration policies in the United States and other countries created enormous difficulties.

Eichmann, Adolf: Lieutenant Colonel in the **Schutzstaffel (SS)** with primary responsibility for the administrative oversight of the **Final Solution** that was put in place at the **Wannsee Conference** (the decision had been made previously by Hitler; the Wannsee Conference merely set the bureaucratic machinery in motion to carry it out). Like many other former Nazis guilty of war crimes, after the war he escaped from Germany to Argentina, where he lived under an alias. He was captured by agents of the Israeli secret services in 1960 and flown to Israel. His trial was widely televised and brought the horrors of the Holocaust to the world's attention. He was convicted of fifteen crimes against humanity and executed by hanging on June 1, 1962.

Einsatzgruppen: Death squads of the paramilitary **Schutzstaffel (SS)**, responsible for mass murder throughout German occupied territories, especially in Eastern Europe. Their victims were often killed by firing squads. They were key players in the **Final Solution**. Their victims were mostly Jews, but also included non-Jewish intellectuals, Catholic priests, politicians opposed to Nazi rule, partisans, and **Romani** people. As many as two million people died in this 'Holocaust by Bullets' at the hands of these mobile killing units, the vast majority in the German-occupied lands of the Soviet Union.

Eisenhower's proclamation of German surrender: General Dwight D. Eisenhower was the Supreme Commander of the Allied Expeditionary Force, making him the highest-ranking Allied officer in Europe. On May 8, 1945, General Eisenhower announced that Germany had surrendered to the Allies. His 'Victory Order of the Day' was immediately distributed worldwide and marked the end of World War II in Europe. Sadly, it did not mark the end of extreme violence against Jews in Europe and elsewhere.

Enabling Act: The 'Law to Remedy the Distress of the People and the Reich', also known as the Enabling Act, was passed by the German legislature (Reichstag) on March 23, 1933, and became effective the following day. Before the voting, members of the Nazi **Sturmabteilung (SA)** entered the Reichstag to intimidate its members. The law gave Nazi Chancellor Adolf Hitler the power to enact laws, even those in violation of the constitution, without further approval by the legislature. It became the cornerstone of Hitler's absolute dictatorship.

Évian Conference: Held from July 6-15, 1938, in Évian-les-Bains, France. United States President Franklin D. Roosevelt took the lead in convening the conference to consider the plight of German and Austrian Jews seeking to flee persecution. Sadly, the conference was a failure; the only country that agreed to accept these Jewish refugees was the Dominican Republic. The borders of other countries, including the United States, remained closed to the persecuted Jews, with few exceptions.

Executive Order on the Law on the Alteration of Family and Personal Names: Adopted by Germany in August 1938, it compelled Jews to identify themselves in a manner intended to separate them from the rest of the population, specifically, by adding 'Israel' (men) and 'Sara' (women) to their names. Jews were required to carry identity cards that identified their religion as defined by the Nazi race laws. All Jewish passports and many other government-issued documents were stamped with a large 'J'.

Factory Action (*Fabrikaktion*): The last major roundup of Jews in Berlin began on February 27, 1943, and continued into March. It was undertaken in anticipation of Hitler's 54th birthday in April. At the time, thousands of German Jews (especially Jews in mixed marriages) were working in war-related industries in Berlin and throughout Germany. They were taken to one of six collection centers in the city. Jewish men married to gentiles and some Jews with a non-Jewish parent were sent to a factory building on Rosenstrasse (Roses Street). Many of the factory workers arrested that day were subsequently deported to Auschwitz, where they were murdered. Others were sent to **Theresienstadt**. In protest of these roundups, many of the non-Jewish spouses risked their lives and publicly demonstrated for the release of their loved ones. Several were indeed set free as a result. See also **Rosenstrasse Protest.**

'Final Solution' (*Endlösung der Judenfrage*, or 'Final Solution to the Jewish Question'): The Nazis' plan to exterminate Jews in Europe, including Great Britain, Sweden, and elsewhere. While widespread killing of Jews and others had taken place in Germany for several years, after the German invasion of Russia in June 1941, Hitler gave orders to undertake the mass slaughter of Jews in the occupied territories. Technology was refined to increase the pace of killing using poison gas at established killing centers, including Chelmno, Belzec, Sobibór, Treblinka, **Majdanek**, and **Auschwitz-Birkenau**. The mass killings were further implemented through careful planning following the **Wannsee Conference** in January 1942.

German invasion of Hungary: In March 1944, Germany invaded Hungary and installed a puppet government. Subsequently, Adolf Eichmann, who had been given broad responsibilities for overseeing the **'Final Solution'** at the **Wannsee Conference** two years previously, arranged for the transportation of 550,000 Hungarian Jews to the death camp of **Auschwitz-Birkenau** and other camps in the Nazi system.

Gestapo: The German national secret police force, existing from 1933 until Germany's surrender in May 1945. Its members wore both plain clothes and uniforms. They were greatly feared and known for ruthless and sadistic treatment of Jews, political prisoners, and other 'undesirables'. The Gestapo was led by Heinrich Himmler, Hitler's close associate and one of the principal architects of the Holocaust. As Nazi Germany's political police force, the Gestapo was responsible for protecting the regime from its supposed racial and political enemies. The Gestapo used informants, surveillance, house searches, and brutal interrogation methods, including torture, to carry out its investigations. One of the Gestapo's main responsibilities was coordinating the deportation of Jews to ghettos, concentration camps, killing sites, and killing centers.

Ghettos: Areas where Jews and others were forcibly segregated from the general population in a small geographic area within a town. For example, more than 250 ghettos were established in Poland, beginning within weeks of the German invasion in September 1939. Residents were then often moved to larger ghettos, including Warsaw and Łódź. From there they were shipped to the death camps. Some ghettos were initially 'open' in the sense that residents could come and go to a certain extent. Over time, however, they became 'closed', meaning that residents were not permitted to leave except under special circumstances. These closed ghettos quickly became vastly overcrowded, with poor sanitary conditions and insufficient food. Disease was rampant.

Golleschau: One of the first **Auschwitz-Birkenau** subcamps, it was located at a quarry and cement factory. Prisoners were literally worked to death breaking and carrying stone, laying train track, stoking lime kilns, loading bags of cement on trains, and other extremely arduous tasks. Workers were malnourished and barely clothed.

Gymnasium: A European secondary school, roughly equivalent to high school in the United States.

Head shaving of women prisoners: Concentration camps sent women's hair to three processing centers where it was used to make socks for submarine crews and to manufacture felt stockings for railroad workers, as well as for mattress stuffing and other purposes.

Hitler Youth (*Hitlerjugend* or HJ)**:** The Nazi-organized movement for youth 10-to 18-years old, with sections for both boys and girls. The female equivalent was the *Bund Deutscher Mädel* (BDM). It grew from about 100,00 members at the time Hitler took power to more than seven million in 1940. It became a principal means of indoctrinating young Germans in the Nazi ideology of antisemitism, militarism, and worship of Hitler. Its male members were expected to join the army, the females to become German wives and mothers, all supporting the conquest of Europe and other goals of the regime. Strict discipline and conformity were required, including the wearing of uniforms. A few anti-Nazi youth groups did organize, such as the Edelweiss Pirates, but their members risked severe punishment, including transport to concentration camps.

Höss, Rudolf: The SS commandant of Auschwitz from May 4, 1940 to November 1943, and from May 8, 1944 to January 18, 1945. He perfected techniques for efficient killing, including the use of the gas chamber. He oversaw Operation Höss in which 430,000 Hungarian Jews were gassed in 56 days. At his war crimes trial at Nuremburg in April, 1946, he affirmed his affidavit in which he stated as follows: "I commanded Auschwitz until 1 December 1943, and estimate that at least 2,500,000 victims were executed and exterminated there by gassing and burning, and at least another half million succumbed to starvation and disease making a total dead of about 3,000,000." Höss was executed by hanging on April 16, 1947, at the site of the Auschwitz camp.

Hungarian anti-Jewish laws: Between 1938 and 1941, Hungary passed a number of laws modeled on Germany's **Nuremburg Race Laws**. These measures defined Jews as a race, expropriated their property, prohibited them from attending schools and practicing their profession, and otherwise stripped them of their civil rights.

I.G. Farben: A German chemical company that developed close ties with the Nazi regime after Hitler came to power in 1933. It depended upon slave labor for many of its operations and established a factory manned by 30,000 concentration camp inmates at the Auschwitz complex. One of its subsidiaries manufactured the poisonous Zyklon-B that was used to kill Jews and others in the gas chambers. The company was dismantled by the victorious Allies when the war ended. Thirteen of its directors were subsequently convicted of war crimes.

Immigration policy of the United States: During the years of Nazi rule in Germany, it became increasingly difficult for European Jews to escape to the United States. Quotas for immigration from specific countries were far below the number of individuals seeking to flee Germany and other counties overrun by the Nazis. After July 1941, immigration into the United States from Nazi-controlled lands became impossible. In just one example, in February 1939, Senator Robert Wagner of New York and Representative Edith Rogers of Massachusetts introduced a bill that would have granted permission for 20,000 German Jewish children under the age of 14 to come to the United States. At first, it appeared that the bill would easily pass, but opposition was raised by isolationists and other groups alleging that it was a "Jewish" bill. President Roosevelt never uttered a word in support of the bill, but the First Lady, Eleanor Roosevelt, came out in favor. The Wagner-Rogers bill died in committee. Following the end of World War II, President Truman implemented a much more humane position toward Jewish immigration than that which existed previously.

Iron Cross: Decoration given for exemplary service in the German military. Many key figures in the Nazi hierarchy had received the decoration in World War I, as had many of the Jews who fought for Germany in that conflict. Initially, many Jews believed that this decoration might bring them some protection from persecution of themselves and their families, only to be sent to their deaths in the camps or killing fields during the Holocaust.

Jewish Resistance: Jewish resistance to the Holocaust took many forms, including participation in armed groups that engaged German forces. The best-known example of that combat is the Warsaw Ghetto Uprising from April 19 to May 16, 1943, in which Jewish residents did battle with German troops. Underground Jewish fighting groups were active in several countries, including, for example, the Parczew and Włodawa partisans near Lublin. These groups were made of up of Jews who had gone into hiding before being rounded up and, in some instances, included concentration camp escapees.

Judenraete [Jewish council]: Established by the Nazis within the ghettos, the *Judenraete* were responsible for assuring that German regulations and orders were carried out within the ghetto. They also organized basic community services as well as they could for the ghettos' inhabitants. (It is likely that when Manfred Kelman referred to the "Jewish leader" in his account, he was referring to the council's chairman.)

Jüdischer Kulturbund: A cultural federation of German Jews established in 1933, the year Hitler came to power. It initially included about 2,000 artists, musicians, and actors fired from German institutions. Its total number of members is not known but is believed to have been between 70,000 and 180,000 at its height. It was ordered closed in September 1941. Many of its members wound up in concentration and extermination camps.

Kaddish: A hymn praising God, sung during Jewish prayer services. One form of this hymn is a prayer to honor those who have died.

Kaiserwald: Concentration camp built in March 1943 during the period when the German military occupied Latvia. Following the liquidation of the Riga ghetto (and others) in June 1943, the remainder of the Jews of Latvia, along with most of the survivors of the liquidation of the Vilna ghetto, were sent to Kaiserwald.

Kapos: Prisoners who acted as enforcers and guards at Nazi concentration and extermination camps, often with great brutality. Many, but not all, were Jews. They were given special privileges, such as better food and living quarters, as long as they maintained favor with the SS officers running the camp. Some Kapos were killed by their former prisoners when the Germans abandoned the camps in the final days of the war.

Kehillah: The elected local communal Jewish structure in Eastern Europe during Poland's Second Republic and the Ukrainian People's Republic which preceded it, during the interwar period (1918–1940).

Kielce Pogrom: After the defeat of Germany, the Soviet occupation of Poland became extremely repressive in the months and years that followed, and included anti-Jewish measures from both Soviet authorities and their Polish administrators. Moreover, violence against Jews continued long after the Germans withdrew, including a series of organized assaults (pogroms) in the town of Kielce that resulted in 42 people being murdered and many injured at the hands of local Poles. Many other incidents of violence against Jews in Poland and elsewhere were recorded in the years following World War II and were widely reported. As a result of such violence, many Jews began making their way to Israel, South America, Canada, and the United States in the hope of finding a safer home.

Kindertransport [Children's transport]: An organized rescue effort that brought approximately 10,000 children, mostly Jewish, from German-held lands to Great Britain in the nine months prior to the German invasion of Poland in September 1939. The children came from Germany, Austria, Czechoslovakia, Poland, and the free city of Danzig. The children were placed in English foster homes, schools, and on farms. In many cases, they were the only members of their family to survive the Holocaust.

Kitchener camp: A voluntary work camp and community for Jewish refugees established in Sandwich, England, in 1939. It allowed approximately 4,000 men from Germany, Austria, Poland, and Czechoslovakia to escape deportation to the concentration and extermination camps to which they would have been sent had they remained in areas controlled by the Nazis. It was closed in May 1940 and its members were either interned or sent to Canada or Australia for the remainder of the war.

Kommandant: Formally *KZ-Kommandant*, or *Lagerkommandant*, the SS officer charged with commanding Nazi concentration and extermination camps. He directed all camp activities and was responsible for overseeing all personnel.

Kristallnacht [Night of Broken Glass]: A series of violent riots throughout Germany on the night of November 9-10, 1938, during which Jewish places of worship, businesses, and homes were burned, Jews were assaulted on the street and in their homes, and additional repressive anti-Jewish measures were adopted. The widespread shattering of plate glass windows at Jewish stores gave the events their name. These abuses, with photographs, were widely reported in the world press and gave witness to the violent nature of Nazi oppression of the Jews. Most survivors of that night report that it marked a significant and permanent downturn in their already diminishing safety and sense of well-being in Germany. The pretext for *Kristallnacht* was the assassination of a German diplomat in Paris by a Jewish expatriate whose family had suffered severe deprivations at Nazi and Polish hands.

Majdanek: Nazi concentration and extermination camp built and operated by the SS on the outskirts of the city of Lublin during the German occupation of Poland in World War II. It had seven gas chambers, two wooden gallows, and some 227 structures in all, placing it among the largest of Nazi concentration and extermination camps.

Mauthausen: Concentration camp located in Austria, in operation from August 1938 until its liberation by the U.S. Army in early May 1945. Several subcamps were subsequently formed to provide slave labor for a number of activities, including the operation of a large quarry. Other industries included arms factories, aircraft construction, and mines. Conditions were more dire than in most camps. It is estimated that half of the camp's 190,000 inmates died in both the main and subcamps.

Mechelen assembly camp: Established in 1942 in German-occupied Belgium. Served as a site for gathering Jews and Romani before their eventual deportation to Auschwitz and other concentration and extermination camps.

Mengele, Josef: One of about 30 camp doctors at Auschwitz, he was known as "The Angel of Death". He became infamous for his performance of sadistic experiments on camp inmates, including many children. Like many Nazis, in 1947 Mengele fled to Argentina where he was free from judicial extradition. Out of fear that he might be captured by Israeli agents, he later fled to Paraguay and Brazil. Mengele drowned while swimming off Bertioga, Brazil, in 1979.

Molotov-Ribbentrop Pact: A non-aggression pact between Nazi Germany and the Soviet Union signed on August 23, 1939. It included a secret protocol that divided Central and Eastern Europe between the two countries. Seven days after the pact was signed, Germany invaded Poland from the west on September 1, 1939. The Soviet Union then invaded Poland from the east on September 17. After Hitler failed in his plan to invade England in the spring and summer of 1940, he turned his attention to the defeat of the Soviet Union, launching a surprise attack on the Soviet Union on June 22, 1941. The German attack ultimately failed, and the Soviet Union turned the battle in its favor at a tremendous cost in human life (the death toll included more than 25 million Soviet civilians and military personnel).

Morgny-la-Pommeraye train disaster: On May 18, 1940, a train carrying Belgian refugees fleeing the German invasion collided with a train carrying French refugees in the town of

Morgny-la-Pommeraye, France. Fifty-three people died and 128 were injured. The driver of the train at fault was prosecuted for negligent homicide.

Munich Conference: Held in Munich, Germany, in late September 1938, one year before the start of World War II. In addition to Hitler, its participants included Prime Minister Neville Chamberlain of Great Britain, President Édouard Daladier of France, and Premier Benito Mussolini of Italy. The resulting Munich Agreement acquiesced to Hitler's demand for German annexation of a large part of Czechoslovakia (Sudetenland). The agreement was reached without Czechoslovakian participation and stripped that country of its ability to defend itself against German aggression. Additionally, Czechoslovakian territory with Hungarian minorities became part of Hungary in accordance with the related First Vienna Award signed in November 1938. Chamberlain's appeasement of Germany was initially popular among most of the British population, but it was strongly criticized at the time by Winston Churchill (among others) who termed it "an unmitigated disaster".

Night of the Long Knives: A series of arrests and executions in June 1934 that ended the independent power of the Nazi paramilitary organization, called **Sturmabteilung** or **SA.** Among other SA members, its founder and leader Ernst Röhm was murdered at Hitler's orders.

Nuremburg Laws: Two racist laws enacted by the German Reichstag on September 15, 1935. The Law for the Protection of German Blood and German Honor forbade marriages and extramarital intercourse between Jews and Germans, and the employment of German females under 45 years old in Jewish households. The Reich Citizenship Law declared that only persons of German or related blood were eligible to be Reich citizens. The remainder, including Jews, were classed as state subjects without any citizenship rights. A decree defining who was Jewish was passed two months later. These laws provided an important legal basis for subsequent anti-Jewish measures.

Nuremburg war crimes trials: In the aftermath of the war, beginning in October 1945, the International Military Tribunal, made up of jurists from the United States, Great Britain, the Soviet Union, and France, initially put the 22 leading surviving Nazis on trial in Nuremberg, Germany. The United States held an additional twelve trials of major Nazi German organizations and their leaders, including government administrators, military officials, leading medical professionals, and industrial magnates, as well as members of the SS. Of the 199 defendants in the Nuremberg trials, 161 were convicted, with 37 sentenced to death. One of the common contentions of the defendants, subsequently dismissed by the judges, was that Nazi authorities were "only following orders from above", and that they were not responsible for the deaths of millions of innocent people.

Oranienburg: First concentration camp established in the German state of Prussia, established within weeks of the Nazis' taking power on January 30, 1933. Oranienburg was a "revenge camp" established by a local SA unit in a deserted brewery about 24 miles from Berlin. Its inmates were primarily political opponents of the regime, communists, socialists, and Social Democrats. Jews were also incarcerated at Oranienburg, where they were subjected to special abuse. It was closed in the summer of 1934 following the Night of the Long Knives, and the decline in influence of the **Sturmabteilung (SA)**. This camp is not to be confused with the Sachsenhausen Concentration Camp in Oranienburg.

Polish Home Army (AK): The principal resistance movement in Poland, established to harass and fight the occupying German forces, formed in 1942. The role of the AK, and its members' actions toward Polish Jews in hiding, remains highly controversial in Poland today. Many Jewish survivors have claimed that that AK was indifferent, if not hostile, to Jews. However, many statements along these lines have been declared defamatory and misleading in Poland. It appears that the attitude toward Jews varied among units of the AK, ranging from highly antisemitic to supportive.

Ponary Massacres: Beginning in July 1941, German killing squads and Lithuanian collaborators commenced the systematic murder of Jews, Poles, and Russians near the railway station in Ponary, a suburb of Vilnius, Lithuania. By the end of the German occupation, it is estimated that more than 95,000 victims were murdered. Prisoners were marched into carefully constructed killing pits, executed by rifle fire, and then buried.

Reichstag: The national parliament of Germany from 1933 to 1945.

Reynders, Fr. Bruno: Benedictine monk in Belgium credited with saving 350 to 400 Jewish children, at great risk of arrest and death. After the war he continued to provide support for these youngsters and to assist in reuniting them with surviving family members. The state of Israel proclaimed Dom Bruno Reynders one of the Righteous Among the Nations, an honor bestowed on gentiles who risked their lives to help Jews during the Holocaust.

Romani ("Gypsies") and the Holocaust: In November 1935, Germany amended the **Nuremburg Laws**, thereby classifying Romani people as "enemies of a race-based state" and therefore subject to the same persecution as Jews. Estimates of the number of Romani killed by the Nazis range from 250,000 to 500,000.

Rosenstrasse Protest: Following the arrest of many Jewish men married to non-Jewish women in the late winter and early spring of 1943, the wives converged on the collection center at Rosenstrasse in Berlin demanding the release of their husbands. This extraordinary display of courage resulted in the release of their husbands and many others. This was one of very few instances in which German citizens rose up in public protest during the Nazi era; any act of protest subjected the individual to immediate arrest and deportation to a concentration camp. See **Factory Action**.

Rumbula Massacre: The Rumbula Massacre was one of the two largest mass shootings during the war (the other being at Babi

Yar or Babyn Yar in Nazi-occupied Ukraine). The Germans had established a ghetto in Riga in the summer of 1941, where 30,000 Jews were trapped when the ghetto was sealed in October. During three days in late November and early December, at least 25,000 Jews were murdered in the nearby Rumbula Forest by German and Latvian forces. Only three people brought to the Rumbula killing site are believed to have survived.

Schutzstaffel or **SS:** Literally meaning "protective guard", the Schutzstaffel's roots go back to 1923 when Hitler designated 50 men to serve as his personal bodyguard. After Hitler and the Nazi Party came to power in January 1933, the tasks of the SS expanded, eventually resulting in the SS serving as instruments of murder, terror, repression, and intimidation under the direction of Reichs-führer-SS (Reich Leader) Heinrich Himmler through 1945.

Schwarzheide: Concentration camp located approximately 80 miles south of Berlin and operated from 1936 until April 1945, its principal function was as a forced labor camp, where the SS operated several factories and brickworks. However, it also served as an extermination facility where killing techniques were refined, including the use of mobile gassing units. It housed many political prisoners and "undesirables" as well as Jews. Many of its prisoners, particularly in the later years, were Soviet, Polish, and other non-German citizens. Approximately 200,000 prisoners passed through the camp during the years of its existence, with many dying from disease, exhaustion, and abuse, as well as intentional killing.

Siemens: An industrial company that was a major producer of electronic goods supporting the Nazi war effort. It relied heavily upon slave labor, including Jews and others who worked in production facilities constructed in concentration camps. It also maintained an enormous production facility in Berlin.

Sippenhaft: The German term for the concept of collectively punishing families for the transgressions of individual family members. It was often practiced during the Nazi era, during which the families of perceived wrongdoers would be arrested, sent to concentration camps, or summarily executed. Victims included children.

Sturmabteilung (SA): Paramilitary organization also known as "Storm Troopers" or "Brownshirts" because of their brown uniforms. They were the original paramilitary arm of the Nazi Party, and they played a large role in Adolf Hitler's rise to power and consolidation of his dictatorship. Their power diminished after their leader, Ernst Röhm, was murdered in 1934 on Hitler's orders during the **Night of the Long Knives**. The SA were notorious for their bullying and abusive behavior towards Jews and others.

Stuschka, Franz: Notoriously sadistic and rabidly antisemitic SS officer who worked closely under **Adolf Eichmann**, one of the principal architects of the Holocaust. Numerous surviving witnesses attested to his cruelty and erratic behavior towards Jews in the camps he controlled. Stuschka was apprehended in 1946, tried, and sentenced by the Vienna People's Court to seven years in prison.

Stutthof: The first German concentration camp set up outside German borders in World War II, in operation from September 2, 1939. It was one of the last camps liberated by the Allies, on May 9, 1945. It is estimated that between 63,000 and 65,000 prisoners at Stutthof concentration camp and its subcamps died as a result of murder, starvation, epidemics, extreme labor conditions, brutal and forced evacuations, and a lack of medical attention. Some 28,000 of those who died were Jews. In total, as many as 110,000 people were deported to the camp during its existence. About 24,600 were transferred from Stutthof to other locations.

Sudetenland: Region of Czechoslovakia which was home to a German-speaking majority and which Adolf Hitler demanded be given to Nazi Germany in the late summer of 1938. This and other demands became the basis for the **Munich Conference** in September 1938, at which European leaders yielded to Hitler, hoping to avoid the risk of a wider European war.

Suicides by prisoners: Many prisoners in concentration and other camps sought to end their own lives. This was often accomplished by throwing oneself onto the electrified wire surrounding the camps, or by crossing into forbidden territory to provoke being shot by camp guards.

Swastika: An ancient religious symbol adopted by the National Socialist German Workers (Nazi) Party as its emblem in 1920, to associate itself with the concept of a pure Aryan race.

Talmud: A principal text of rabbinic commentary and a source of Jewish religious law and theology.

Theresienstadt (Terezin): A "camp ghetto" located in the fortress town of in Czechoslovakia. It existed for three and a half years, between November 24, 1941, and May 9, 1945. Initially it held many intellectuals and artists as well as others not destined for immediate annihilation. The Nazis used this camp for propaganda purposes to hide their brutal treatment of Jews and other prisoners. It also served as a transit camp for those to be shipped on to the death camps, including **Auschwitz-Birkenau**. Conditions deteriorated over time and many people died of starvation and disease. According to Yad Vashem, the official Israeli memorial to those killed in the Holocaust, more than 155,000 Jews passed through Theresienstadt before it was liberated on May 8, 1945; 35,440 perished in the ghetto and 88,000 were deported to be murdered. Of the approximately 15,000 children sent to Theresienstadt, fewer than 1,500 survived.

Theresienstadt Red Cross deception: In 1944, the Nazis agreed to allow an inspection of Theresienstadt to assure the King of Denmark and the International Red Cross of the "humane" treatment of deported Jews. They then embarked upon an elaborate ruse in order to deceive the inspectors: In the weeks before the inspection, more than 7,500 prisoners were deported to the **Auschwitz-Birkenau** death camp. The Theresienstadt ghetto was then given a facelift, concerts by inmates were arranged, and fresh clothing was distributed. On June 23, 1944, as planned, two delegates from the International Red Cross and one from the Danish Red Cross visited the ghetto. The visit was filmed by the Nazis. Following the visit, the deportations to **Auschwitz-Birkenau** and other camps and ghettos across Eastern Europe resumed. The prisoners who had met with the Red Cross were then deported in attempts to remove any evidence of the lie.

Third Ordinance on Restrictions on Residence (Poland): In November 1941, the German forces occupying Poland announced the first of several regulations providing severe penalties for Poles who gave shelter or any other assistance to Jews residing outside the ghetto. Penalties included confiscation of property, transportation to concentration camps, and in some cases, death. In addition to these penalties, the regulations also provided significant rewards for Poles who turned in Jews found outside ghettos.

Transports: Trains run by the *Deutsche Reichsbahn* national railway system under the control of Nazi Germany and its allies, used for the transportation of Jews and other victims of the Holocaust to concentration, labor, extermination, and other camps.

Treblinka: A concentration and extermination camp located in Poland. Initially constructed as a labor camp, it was converted to a killing center in 1942. By the time it was dismantled about fifteen months later, almost one million Jews and others had been executed there.

Versailles Treaty: After Germany's surrender in World War I on November 11, 1918, the victorious Allies convened a conference to decide upon the terms which would be imposed upon Germany. The resulting Treaty of Versailles was signed on June 29, 1919, at the Palace of Versailles, outside of Paris. Among its many provisions, Germany was forced to disarm and pay enormous reparations to the Allies. Many critics at the time warned that the provisions of the Treaty were unduly harsh and would backfire. Hitler's denunciation of the Treaty was an important factor in his rise to power.

Vinkt Massacre: Violence by German troops against Belgian civilians was widespread. The Vinkt Massacre, during which German soldiers murdered between 86 and 140 civilian hostages between May 26 and May 28, 1940, was one of the most notorious incidents.

Waffen-SS [Armed Protective Squadron]: The combat arm of the SS, commanded by Heinrich Himmler. The Waffen-SS was engaged in combat throughout the war and at its height consisted of over 900,000 members. Many of its units participated in war crimes.

Wannsee Conference and the "Final Solution": The Wannsee Conference was a meeting of Nazi officials held in an elegant mansion in the Berlin suburb of Wannsee in January 1942. The purpose of the conference was to plan for the execution of the **Final Solution** – the extermination of all Jews in Europe (to eventually include Jews in Great Britain, Sweden and elsewhere had those countries been conquered). The conference was called by Deputy Reichsführer-SS Reinhard Heydrich, a close associate of Adolf Hitler and the director of the Reich Security Main Office. Significant responsibility for executing the decisions made at the conference would rest with SS Lieutenant Colonel **Adolf Eichmann**. Heydrich was assassinated in Prague about five months after the conference.

Warsaw Ghetto: The largest Nazi ghetto of the Holocaust. As many as 460,000 Jews were imprisoned there at any one time, in an area of approximately 1.3 square miles. Hundreds of thousands were transported from there to extermination camps, especially **Treblinka**. More than 90,000 inhabitants died of disease and starvation. The camp was dismantled in May 1943 following an uprising among the residents, and all remaining inhabitants were transported to various concentration and extermination camps, with the exception of a few who escaped to join the **Jewish Resistance**. Some of those survivors emigrated to Palestine and founded the *Lohamei HaGeta'ot* kibbutz, which still exists in modern Israel.

Yiddish: A language once spoken by Jews throughout Europe. Though it was largely eliminated by the "cleansing" of Jews during the Holocaust, it has survived and is spoken by religious and secular communities in the United States, Israel, Russia, and elsewhere.

Zionism: Movement for the establishment of a Jewish homeland in Palestine that arose in the late 19th century in Europe. Theodor Herzl founded the modern Zionist movement in the 1890s, and his ideas eventually helped shape the establishment of the nation of Israel in 1948.

Zossen-Wulkow: Forced labor camp established for the building of a temporary headquarters for the SS, away from the intensive bombing of its facilities within inner city Berlin. It was under the command of SS officer **Franz Stuschka**. The Nazis surrendered it to Soviet forces on February 3, 1945.

CHAPTER 24

Sources By Chapter

Julius Ciembroniewicz's account is based upon his interview by Sharon Nichols of the Holocaust and Human Rights Center of Maine (HHRC) on November 16, 1992. Transcription provided to the author by the HHRC.

Tama Fineberg's account is taken from her interview by Dr. Konnilyn Feig on August 30, 1976:

Fineberg, Tama, "Mrs. Abe Feinberg (Tama)" (published 1977). *Portraits of the Past: The Jews of Portland. 14.* Portland Oral Jewish History Project. Retrieved from [https://digitalco mmons.portlandlibrary.com/jewish_oral_history/14/]

Additional source material from her interview by the author, June 23, 2023.

Gerda Schild Haas' account is taken from her interview by Marjorie Goldberg of the Holocaust and Human Rights Center of Maine on June 8, 1987. Transcribed by Cyrille White, November 27, 1987; revised transcription by Nicci Leamon, January 2, 2001. Transcription provided to the author by the HHRC.

Jutka (Judith) Magyar Isaacson and Rose Magyar

Jutka Magyar Isaacson's account is taken from two sources. The first portion, describing her early life through her arrival at Auschwitz (ending with "I returned to my place in line and naively relayed all that false information word for word") is taken from Jutka's published memoir, used with permission of the publisher.

Isaacson, Judith Magyar, *Seed of Sarah: Memoirs of a Survivor.* 2nd edition. 1991. University of Illinois Press.

The remaining text is from her interview conducted by the Holocaust and Human Rights Center of Maine on August 26, 1993. The interview is available at the website of the National Holocaust Memorial Museum. Transcription by the author.

Extensive papers and photographs maintained by the Edmund S. Muskie Archives and Special Collections Library at Bates College in Lewiston, Maine, were also examined, including Jutka's *Gymnasium* graduation certificate.

Rose Magyar's account is taken from a lengthy memoir she wrote more than 20 years after her liberation in 1945. Both that text and her poetry are available as part of the Judith Magyar Isaacson papers at the Edmund S. Muskie Archives and Special Collections Library at Bates College in Lewiston, Maine. [https://www.bates.edu/archives/manuscript/judith-isaacson-papers-1912-1996/]

Alfred Kantor's account is taken from his interview with Ann Bernard of the USC Shoah Foundation, conducted on July 23, 1997. Used with permission.

Additional information was obtained by the author's interview with Alfred's daughter, Monica Churchill, on June 13, 2023, and correspondence with Jerry Kantor. Images are used with permission of Monica Churchill and Jerry Kantor. Used with perission.

Ingeborg Kantor's account is taken from her interview by Ruth Meyer of the USC Shoah Foundation on July 23, 1997. Used with permission.

Additional information was obtained by the author's interview with his daughter, Monica Churchill, on June 13, 2023.

Manfred Kelman's account is taken from his interview by Norma Kraus Eule and Paula Marcus Platz of the Holocaust and Human Rights Center of Maine, on November 10, 1987, transcribed by Steve Hochstadt and Cyrille White of the HHRC. Transcript provided to the author by the HHRC.

Emil Landau's account is taken from his book, quoted with permission of the publisher:

Swanson, David S., *Emil Landau: Surviving the Third Reich*. 2013. Skidompha Press.

Kurt Messerschmidt's account is taken from his interview by Katy Beliveau and Paula Scolnik of the Holocaust and Human Rights Center of Maine on November 18, 1987. Revised transcription by Nicci Leamon for the HHRC, April 16, 2001. Transcript provided to the author by the HHRC.

Sonja Messerschmidt's account is taken from her interview by Margaret Meyer and Gerda Schild Haas of the Holocaust and Human Rights Center of Maine on November 18, 1987. Revised transcription by Nicci Leamon, January 29, 2001. Transcript provided to the author by the HHRC.

Edith Lucas Pagelson's account consists of excerpts from her book, quoted with permission of her heir and publisher, Ruth Finegold

Pagelson, Edith L. *Against All Odds: A Miracle of Holocaust Survival*. 2012, published byMaine Authors Publishing.

Charles Rotmil's account is taken from a speech he gave at Sanford High School, Sanford, Maine, on October 15, 2019, as well as interviews with the author in the summer of 2023. Additional edits and additions were obtained from Mr. Rotmil in 2024.

The Singal Family accounts are taken primarily from the interview of Judith (Singal) Catz conducted by Leonard Langer, February 12, 1991, as well as interviews and correspondence with the author by the Hon. George Singal during the summer of 2023.

Julia Skalina's account is taken from her interview by Ann Bernard of the Holocaust and Human Rights Center of Maine on July 24, 1997. Transcript provided to the author by the HHRC.

Jerry Slivka's account is taken from his interview by Dr. Konnilyn Feig on August 26, 1976:

Slivka, Jerry. "Jerry Slivka" (1977). *Portraits of the Past: The Jews of Portland*. *37*. Retrieved from [https://digitalcommons.portlandlibrary.com/jewish_oral_history/37]

Rochelle Slivka's account is taken from her interview by Gerda Schild Haas and Martin Margolis of the Holocaust and Human Rights Center of Maine, September, 1989. Revised transcription by Nicci Leamon, June 2001, for the HHRC. Transcript provided to the author by the HHRC.

Alan Wainberg's account is taken from his interview by Gerda Schild Haas of the Holocaust and Human Rights Center of Maine, November 5, 1990. Revised transcription by Nicci Leamon, December 30, 2000, for the HHRC. Transcript provided to the author by the HHRC.

Walter Ziffer's account is taken from several sources, including his interview by the Holocaust and Human Rights Center of Maine on August 26, 1993. Transcribed by Cyrille White, April 14, 1987; edited by Walter Ziffer, May 1989. Revised transcription (as originally taped) by Nicci Leamon, June 2001, for the HHRC. Transcript provided to the author by the HHRC.

Additionally, the author relied upon extensive correspondence with Mr. Ziffer who edited his chapter and generously wrote the Afterword at the author's request.

CHAPTER 25

Acknowledgements

I have been blessed with the help and support of many people over the 30-plus-year life of this project (often referred to as the *Soul Survivors* project.) In the mid-1990s, I was early in my days as a portrait photographer when I conceived the Maine Holocaust survivors series. It was my law partner, Sumner Bernstein, who quickly embraced the project and opened doors for me with the Jewish community that I would never have been able to open on my own. Once I was able to move forward, it was my secretary Diane Lankton who organized the outreach to the survivors, managed the schedule for their portrait sittings, and handled a myriad of related tasks. Sumner died in 2002, but Diane's commitment continued into the creation of this book, for which she has served as a reader and copy editor. Sharon Nichols, then Executive Director of the Holocaust and Human Rights Center of Maine, was instrumental in moving the portrait project from conception to execution. It was Sharon who allowed us to identify the survivors and who made the initial contact with them, encouraging them to participate. Additionally, Dorothy "DeeDee" Schwartz, Director of the Maine Humanities Council, embraced the project, assuring its wide audience beginning with an exhibition and series of lectures at the Portland Public Library in 1998.

In 2018 we began moving forward with the idea of creating a book based upon the portrait images I had made in the 1990s, and which were on permanent display at the Maine Jewish Museum in Portland, and the Holocaust and Human Rights Center of Maine (HHRC). David Greenham, the HHRC's Associate Director, and Gary Barron, then Director of the Maine Jewish Museum, were partners as we moved forward to explore options. COVID and other issues intervened. The project went on hold until the fall of 2022, when I met a fellow Maine photographer, Skip Kline, who stepped forward with generous funding for the creation and printing of this book. Skip's deep concern about the rise of antisemitism and his commitment to supporting photographic artists have found him quietly supporting other important publications aimed at assuring that the truthful record of the Holocaust is preserved. His generous contribution became the spark for getting the project moving forward again. I am also very grateful to my friend Justin Schair, as well as to Ruth and Bob Finegold for their contributions in support of this book.

Professor and Holocaust scholar Steve Hochstadt played a critical role in the presentation of the *Soul Survivors* images displayed at exhibitions throughout Maine, including at the Portland Public Library, the State House in Augusta, and other venues. Steve created the moving text that accompanies the photographs at the Maine Jewish Museum in Portland.

Tam Huynh, Executive Director of the Holocaust and Human Rights Center of Maine, has been a wonderful collaborator as we have moved forward to completion and publication of this book. The HHRC has been instrumental at every turn in bringing this project to fruition. HHRC Board member Joan Kidman has been an invaluable and very patient ally in keeping the project moving forward. Additionally, my friends Jody Sataloff (founding President of the Maine Jewish Museum in Portland), and the Museum's founding Executive Director, Rabbi Gary Berenson, have provided invaluable support for this project through the years, as has Steve Brinn, the past president of the Museum's Board of Directors. The assistance and support of the Maine Jewish Museum has been most helpful in the planning and execution of this book project. I am grateful that the photographs in this book are on permanent exhibition ahe Maine Jewish Museum and the Holocaust and Human Rights Center of Maine.

I am very grateful for the generous support of the Sam L. Cohen Foundation of Maine, which will allow the book to be distributed to all public schools in Maine teaching grades 6 through 12.

Caitlin Lampman, Reference and Outreach Archivist at the Edmund S. Muskie Archives and Special Collections Library at Bates College in Lewiston, Maine, was extremely helpful in assisting me in navigating the personal papers of Gerda Haas, Jutka Isaacson, and Rose Magyar that are preserved there.

I am very grateful to several of my close friends who have been invaluable guides to the worlds of publication. These include Roger Conover, a writer, editor, curator, and founding editor of the art and architecture publishing program at MIT Press, who has been generous with his advice. Also, my friend Dr. Aaron Rosen has been an enthusiastic supporter of the book and has shared countless suggestions based upon his own extensive publications on contemporary issues of religion and art.

I have been fortunate to have several highly qualified readers who have spent considerable time reviewing the text and helping to assure its historical accuracy, as well as that of the Appendix. My friend, Bowdoin College Professor of German Emeritus Steve Cerf (the son of a Holocaust survivor), has taught Holocaust studies for decades and provided me with very helpful suggestions and corrections. Robert Bernheim, a former student of Steve Cerf and now an Assistant Professor of History at the University of Maine at Augusta, has been an invaluable aid in assuring the accuracy of many matters, including the Appendix, which serves as the historical backbone for the testimonies of the survivors. His own research centers on the Nazi Holocaust and World War II in Europe. Additional readers have included Leslie Applebaum, a wonderful teacher in the public school system of Portland, Maine, who has taught Holocaust and other human rights studies in the school system for years, and who provided me with helpful insights aimed at focusing the text as a resource for other teachers. I also incorporated important additional input from readers on the educational team at the Holocaust and Human Right Center of Maine, including Erica Nadelhaft and Piper Dumont.

My thanks also to my team of loyal readers, who scoured drafts of the manuscript for spelling and formatting errors. They did a great job and completed it in very short order. These include Amy Brown, Ann Ritchie, Louise Midwood, Linda Voigt, Paula Reutershan, Ruthanne Singal, Tam Thanh Huynh, Julie Feldman-Menke, and my wife Deede (who has now read the book about 20 times). I am very grateful for their keen editing of the manuscript.

My friend, art educator and author Dr. George Smith, has been a source of sound advice, both on this book and many other matters through the years. It was through George that I met Kieran O'Hare, who is now a key editor of the book. Kieran's task has been challenging, editing excerpts from 40-year-old interviews to assure their readability, while assuring that the language remains true yet concise. His deep understanding of the history of this period was an unexpected blessing, allowing him great sensitivity to the nuance of the testimonies of the survivors.

I am deeply indebted to my friend, Bruce Kennett. He is an outstanding book designer and has provided sound advice and support in bringing this book to print.

Sara Lennon of the HHRC has been instrumental in getting the book online for review by various participants in the project. It is now also available for teachers to download by chapter without charge for distribution (but not sale) to students. My skills in web design with Squarespace are limited. Sara jumped into the project and quickly took it over the hurdles to complete the webpage version.

Of all the assistance I have had in creating this book, none has been more meaningful than that of the three living survivors, Tamara Feinberg, Charles Rotmil, and Walter Ziffer. All three have become my friends, and our interactions have given me the highest level of inspiration to see this project through. They are living examples of what it means to be a survivor – to reconstitute their lives after the most horrific experiences and terrible personal loss of family members. I am moved, both by their resilience, and also by their sadness, as they look upon a world that seems bent upon forgetting the lessons learned from the period 1930 to 1945.

And lastly, my thanks to my wife, Deede, my supporter, counselor, editor, and reader for this project over the last 30 years, without whom none of this would have come about.

Freeport, Maine, 2025

www.ingramcontent.com/pod-product-compliance
Lightning Source LLC
Chambersburg PA
CBHW060411130626
46555CB00005B/2030